INNOCENTI
LAMBRETTA
THE DEFINITIVE HISTORY

VITTORIO TESSERA

INNOCENTI
LAMBRETTA
THE DEFINITIVE HISTORY

GIORGIO NADA EDITORE

Giorgio Nada Editore s.r.l.

Editorial coordination
Antonio Maffeis

Layout
Giorgio Nada Editore

Graphic design
Sergio Nada

English translation
Eric Dregni

Photographic material
Lambretta Club Italia archive, Giorgio Nada Editore archive,
Aragozzini, Gian Colombo, Studio Crabb, Vittorio Tessera,
Roberto Zabban

Acknowledgements
The author and the publisher wish to thank all Lambrettas friends who
gave significant contribution in collecting news and photographic
material to complete Innocenti motorcycling production: Ing. Araldi,
Stefano Balboni, Stefano Barattini, Gianni Belli, Howard Chambers,
Aldo Castiglioni, Ennio Castellani, Nigel Cox, Armando Dammicco,
Franco Giudici, Mario Montorsi, Studio Navone, Riccardo Pedretti,
Carlo Pisaroni, Alfredo Ponzoni, Giuseppe Preti, Tino Sacchi, Ing.
Sartori.
A special debt of gratitude goes to the Innocenti Family for having
saved all historical documents on the very first Lambretta's projects
and drawings, donating them to the Lambretta Club Italia Museum.

This book is dedicated to my beloved parents, Gianni and Laura, who gave me all their support and help.

*The catalogue of Giorgio Nada Editore pubblications is available at the
following address:*
Giorgio Nada Editore, via Claudio Treves 15/17,
20090 Vimodrone (MI)
Tel. +39 02 27301126
Fax +39 02 27301454
E-Mail: nadamail@work-net.it

Innocenti Lambretta - The definitive history
ISBN: 88-7911-214-7

SUMMARY

FOREWORD

In the huge international field of books specializing in historical motorcycles, there has always been a glaring gap for an important vehicle from the 1950s and '60s: the Lambretta, the celebrated scooter built by Innocenti of Milan and sold in every corner of the world.

Finally this hole has been filled thanks to the patient research of a dear friend and colleague, Vittorio Tessera. Following his first work, "Scooter made in Italy," he threw himself headlong into finishing this project with his usual precision and perfection.

Two years of hard work in Tessera's freetime will surely be compensated by the success that this volume is sure to have with Lambretta aficionados in Italy and the world.

As everyone remembers, the Lambretta was one of the most popular forms of transportation of the 1950s and 1960s, was a valid surrogate to the automobile, and faithful travel companion to hundreds of thousands of Italian families that had the chance to ride one to work or for fun. Together with the Vespa, it monopolized the Italian scooter market, and knew how to set itself apart in the international market with its own original technical characteristics and particularly elegant and exceptionally modern frame.

Its commercial success had no boundaries: from the Fiji Islands to Pakistan, from Polynesia to South Africa. It was built under license in many foreign countries, and is one of the very few products from the Lombardy province of Italy to be well-known in the whole world.

Because of all this, it's impossible not to have a book dedicated to this important Italian scooter!

Thumbing through the printer's proofs for this book, I was especially impressed by the great care and scrupulous analysis given to each model, making it almost a restoration guide, which is sure to please many Lambretta aficionados. This book will certainly help to conserve the historic quality of the Lambretta, the first objective of A.S.I. and its associates, and most simply to deeply understand the technical and esthetic evolution of the Innocenti's motorscooters and other vehicles. I also was pleased to notice the thorough documentation and photographs of Innocenti's three-wheelers, once again filling a gap in the history of light transport.

Especially interesting to me was the chapter dedicated to various studies of prototypes, many, unfortunately, only on paper. Even so, it can't hide how marvelous these scooters could have been. These drawings have been closed in the cabinets of the factory's "Centro Studi" for many years and finally saw the light of day thanks to the Innocenti family, especially the engineer Luigi Innocenti who, unfortunately, recently passed away.

Benito Battilani, vice president of A.S.I.

THE HISTORY OF INNOCENTI AND ITS FACTORIES

On the first of September 1891, Ferdinando Innocenti was born in Pescia, Italy to Dante Innocenti. His father was a well-known blacksmith in this small Tuscan town. A few years after Ferdinando's birth, the Innocentis moved to Grosseto where Dante put aside his skills as a metal worker and opened a hardware store in Galilei Street. Following the success of the first shop, Dante Innocenti opened a second hardware store thereby becoming one of the wealthier families of Grosseto, Italy.

As a chip off the old block, Ferdinando Innocenti finished his technical school training and teamed up with his older brother Rosolino to help their father running the Innocenti Hardware. By eighteen years old, Ferdinando showed a remarkable aptitude at merchandising various mechanical products in the store. He took up buying and selling used metal, which he salvaged from the shipyards around the town of Maremma. He then exchanged some of the metal for lubricating oil, which could be sold in the hardware store and turn a profit for the store.

In 1920 at the age of 29, Ferdinando experimented with and probed the many different ways that iron tubing could be applied to the industrial sector. To further develop his interests in welding these iron tubes, Innocenti decided to move to Rome in 1923. With 500,000 Italian lira, he wanted to set up a business for his tubing and all the possible applications in the largest city of Italy.

Unfortunately, the bank in which Ferdinando had opened an account failed just a few months afterwards, and he was forced to suspend his plans and return home to run the company. In the meantime, however, he was able to launch a small factory specializing in the resale of metal tubing produced by Dalmine under license from Mannesmann.

Opportunity knocked in the mid-1920s and allowed Ferdinando to play with the big boys. Because of an initiative by the Fascist party which had recently taken over the government to modernize and industrialize the capital, Innocenti decided it was time to get down to business.

Ferdinando didn't miss out on the opportunity and bravely opened an important warehouse/factory catering to manufacturing building materials. The company was dubbed "Fratelli Innocenti" (The Innocenti Brothers) since even Rosolino got in at the ground level of construction of the new company.

In 1931, Fratelli Innocenti signed a lucrative new contract to design a system of rain irrigation for the papal gardens at Castelgandolfo. Using rain and water from the Albano lake the Innocenti brothers succeeded in watering the fourteen hectare garden to keep the popes happy. The success of this project opened up the road for a profitable relationship with the Vatican, which proved to be one of the most important clients for the brothers throughout the 1930s. Besides, the tight relationship with the Holy See kept Innocenti afloat during the troubled times of the war and ultimately helped establish Innocenti as an industrial giant.

One of the most important commercial contracts reached for the Fratelli Innocenti was signed by Ferdinando with the British company Scafoding in 1933. This deal allowed Innocenti to use their newly patented metal clamps for scaffolding for construction of large buildings for the first time. Soon after, all the major construction companies in Rome began using this modern and practical system of metal tubing and clamps for scaffolding rather than the traditional and unreliable wooden boards and nails. Even today, the Innocenti scaffolding is widely used in construction as well as in sporting events for short-term platforms and light-weight barriers.

In the same period, Ferdinando Innocenti decided to expand the operations with the construction of a Milan factory in the beautiful Lambrate section of town in Via Pitteri. Initially, the factory in this northern city in the wealthy Lombardy province focused on continued construction of the new scaffolding clamps. With this expansion, the Fratelli Innocenti now had a total of 5,000 shares of stock at 1,000 lira each of which Ferdinando owned 3,100 and his brother Rosolino had 1,900.

In just a few years, Ferdinando Innocenti had succeeded in placing himself among the largest industrial giants in Italy. His entrepreneurial spirit pushed him on, even so, he didn't talk much and usually spoke softly and slowly. He shunned the limelight, and orchestrated the whole operation from behind the scene while only letting a few trusted people close to him. With just a handshake or a smile he could gain the confidence of his fellow workers. But at the same time, he avoid-

The Innocenti hangars were almost completely destroyed following an enormous Allied bombing on the 30th of April 1944. Nearly every window in the entire factory was shattered following wave after wave of bombs.

ed going out to theaters or on the town since he loathed all the pretensions of high society.

He was a true industrial leader since he was ready to defend what he called his "navy" and "sailors" during the most difficult economic crises. Often he would even put his own personal savings at risk to ensure that the company would stay afloat for the good of all his employees.

His work was extremely demanding, requiring the highest level of attention to the needs of the enormous company and all his collaborators. His hard work was finally recognized on October 23rd, 1953 when the University of Politecnico of Milan named him Engineer "Honoris Causa" for "the contribution he gave to the development of Italian mechanical industry, to the practical factories he created, and to the incredible solutions he came up with in various technological fields."

By the mid-1930s, however, the Innocenti firm had two factories: one in Milan and the other in Rome. Plus, nine branch

offices were opened around Italy and the company seemed to be in continual expansion with its considerable number of products in high demand. At this point, there were four areas of production and business:

1) Production of supplies for building construction, including scaffolding, antennas, pylons, gates, fences, and light poles.

2) Production of agricultural and sporting supplies such as pipes for aqueducts, rain gutters, irrigation tubes, risers for spectators, and bars for gymnastics.

3) Industrial production for thermoelectric plants, including pipes for air and vapor, cylinders for gasoline, and bits for drilling and perforating.

4) Industrial mechanical production with tubing for truck chassis, transmission shafts, pipes for other automobile construction, gun barrels, cylinders and hydraulic pistons for presses, and cylinders and rolls for glass production.

Showing how successful the company was, in 1935 just two

Center. This photo was
taken during WWII of
the Innocenti factory
which sustained heavy
damage. Nevertheless,
the camouflaged water-
tower withstood the at-
tacks and was actually
still in use at the time of
the photograph.
Next page, above.
Having made cartridges
and fuses for the war
effort, this section of the
Innocenti avoided dam-
age and the vast array
of machines was still
usable postwar.
Below. By mid-1952, the
"Centro Studi" building
was finally finished and
became the centerpiece
of the Innocenti plant.
Inside, all Innocenti de-
signs for motorscooters
and automobiles came
to life.

years after its formation, Fratelli Innocenti doubled its stock
with another 5,000 shares at 1,000 lira each. To top off his
success, Ferdinando Innocenti sought to acquire the lion's
share of stock in Dalmine, a company which produced steel
pipe. This way, Innocenti would not have to continually give
a cut of its profits to the production of the tubing which was
their cash cow. Unfortunately, Innocenti's plans were
blocked when the IRI, or Institute for Reconstruction of
Industry refused to sell its majority stock in Dalmine and
closed every door of opportunity for Innocenti to buy them
out.

Innocenti didn't lose hope, however, and in 1936 profited
from financial concessions from the Italian government for
the opening of a small plant in Apuania, and succeeded in
opening its own steel tubing factory with the help of
Dalmine. The factory was named SAFTA, Società Anonima
Fabbricazione Tubolari Acciaio, when it was finally finished
in 1942 after many delays. Since construction was completed right in the middle of World War II, production was almost completely for the war effort. It wasn't until postwar
around 1948 that SAFTA was able to produce steel tubing.
At that point Dalmine took over production, making it their
second factory, so they weren't competing against themselves.

Helping with the war effort turned out to be quite a task for
Innocenti. Another factory was completed in Rome between
1939 and 1940 and put out 40,000 bullets a day. Two more
factories were to be added in Milan-Lambrate called "Guerra
II e III" (Second and Third War), where copper grenades
rings and steel cartridges were to be produced. The Allies
bombed the factories on April 4th, 1944, destroying almost
all of the "Guerra III" factory, so production was halted.
Also, the other factories converted their production to
wartime materiel, especially bullets. Ferdinando's ability to
produce for Italy's army earned him the Innocenti company
the dubious title of "Model Fascist Factory."

During these sad years, Innocenti tripled its factories, and the
number of employees surged from around 800 in 1938 to
3,000 in 1941 and finally to more than 7,000 in 1943. At this
point, Innocenti had become one of the most important companies in Italy.

Since Ferdinando had a great gift for working the politics of
the time to his advantage, he was able to walk the tightrope
between the occupying German army of the time and the de-
mocratic partisan forces. Innocenti even slipped money on
the sly to the partisan general Poletti, who then vouched for
Innocenti's anti-German stance once the Allies took over.
Therefore, Ferdinando Innocenti was able to avoid any
repercussions postwar of having helped with the Italian war
effort.

Once the war was over, Innocenti had to change its tune.
There were now three possibilities for use of its factories:
1) Production of a widely used and popular vehicle sold at a
low cost.
2) Construction of metal machinery and industrial installa-
tions.
3) Development of metal parts.
For the first point, General Engineer Pier Luigi Torre was
given the task to design a new form of transportation. The
second point was entrusted to SAFTA with all its experience

in producing tubing with weak weld spots. The third point consisted of new production of axle boxes and bearings for electric motors.

Unfortunately, the plan for the conversion couldn't be put into action anytime soon since the Milan-Lambrate factory had been acquired by the Allied Forces and financing for its reconstruction faced numerous delays. Finally around mid-1946, Ferdinando Innocenti could begin on his new plans to completely redo his factories and begin production.

Already by the end of 1946, important contracts were in the works to supply six special machines to Dalmine and for several rolling mills for tubing to be sent to Yugoslavia and Poland. The rebirth and new expansion of this company in the whole world was due to the work and continued persistence of one man: Ferdinando Innocenti.

Full-fledge production of the Lambretta would have to wait until the beginning of 1948, during which time Innocenti's production of bearings was deemed obsolete because of other technological breakthroughs.

Side. This aerial view shows the entire area occupied by the Innocenti factory by the end of 1940. The construction of the buildings in a cone shape was an attempt to be anti-aircraft shelters but were demolished anyway.

Below. Once the finishing touches on the Lambretta LD 125 were applied, the brand new scooters rolled out the door. Innocenti was the first Italian motorscooter or motorcycle to utilize the assembly line to speed up production.

During the 1950s, the Innocenti factories were going full force. The motorscooter section worked quickly with a daily production of 250 units. While the mechanical sector of the company had struck a deal with Australia ensuring the company of financial stability for more than two years.

In 1955, Ferdinando concluded one of the most important deals of his lifetime: the construction of a steel factory for the Venezuelan government worth a total of 350 million dollars. At first, FIAT thought it would jump into the game along with Innocenti, but the huge automobile manufacturer out of Turin preferred to let Ferdinando go it alone. Even though this joint venture fell through, Innocenti wrapped up the project in just five years thereby keeping the full sum for itself.

Towards the end of the 1950s, Innocenti couldn't help but notice the booming automobile market, even if Ferdinando didn't think that Innocenti could compete. His son, Luigi, thought otherwise. Becoming the vice president in 1958,

Side. This workshop in the "Centro Studi" building saw the construction of prototypes and race vehicles. On the two stands are mounted the two Lambretta 250 engines. The closest is the most recent version with only one magneto while the other is the older version using two magnetos. On the shelves lay the rims, tires, and different sized forks for the Lambretta 250.
Below. The Venezuelan government hired Innocenti to design and build this steel factory on the banks of the river Orinoco.

Luigi Innocenti took it upon himself to transform the company into a viable competitor to Fiat and to give the ubiquitous Fiat 500 a run for its money.

At first, the thought at Innocenti was to produce automobiles entirely in house, but it soon realized the total lack of experience. Instead, Innocenti sought to use its factory to produce other manufacturers' cars under license and slap its own tag on them.

The first car that Luigi seriously considered was the tiny German Goggo mobil produced by Isaria. About 10,000 units had been produced in Germany, but the minuscule 400cc engine caused Luigi to back off. Instead, he opted for a deal with the British company BMC to produce the brand new Austin A 40.

In little more than a year, the production line at the Milan-Lambrate factory was ready and around the end of 1960 about 100 Austin/Innocentis were produced a day. In the following years, Innocenti's automobile production steadily in-

Side. Engineer Ferdinando Innocenti (on the left) accompanies Russian engineer Tarasou, minister of the Russian automobile industry, on a tour of the factory. On the far right is the son of Ferdinando, Luigi Innocenti. This is the last official photograph of the founder of the Innocenti factory who passed away June 21st 1966 at 75 years old.

Center. The Innocenti assembly line puts the finishing touches on Mini Minor Mk2 and the Im3 S. Notice that the difference in numbers of vehicles since the Mini accounted for more than 90% of the entire Innocenti automobile construction.

Next page, above. This section of the factory produced large industrial machines.

Next page, below. This impressive photo taken in 1969 of the end of the production line features the 50 De Luxe scooter and the three-wheeled Lambro 550 V.

creased and new models were occasionally introduced under license from BMC. The notable exception, however, was the 950 Spider designed by Bertone.

1966 was the saddest year for the Innocenti factory since its founder Ferdinando Innocenti passed away at 75 years old. His son Luigi then took over as the president of the company.

Unfortunately, the new head was immediately put to the test with labor problems and union strikes that soon wore, on his honest and sensible character. Besides that, sales of Lambrettas which had become the flagship of Innocenti production slumped due to the rise in automobile sales and the lack of interest in mopeds and scooters.

During these difficult times, first Fiat then Volkswagen showed an interest in buying out part of Innocenti for production of their own vehicles. Although the deals would have been advantageous to Innocenti, Luigi held on convinced that times would get better. Rather than throw in the towel, Luigi dropped many of the original products with which has father had turned a large profit.

Following years of union battles, the factories were shut down between 1971 and 1972. The entire operation fell into the hands of Doctor Belli who was able to find a worthy buyer through shrewd diplomatic maneuvering. The automobile division was sold off to the British company Leyland that continued to produce cars at the Lambrate factory. The motorscooter sector was sold to the Indian government, and the heavy mechanical division was incorporated into Santeustachio which then became INNSE.

This is how the industrial adventure of the Innocenti family ended. It all began thanks to the ingenuity and ability of Ferdinando, who will retain an honored position in the history of 20th century Italian industry.

15

HISTORY OF THE LAMBRETTA

The idea to build a cheap form of transport immediately after the war was born in 1944 when the allied forces had liberated Rome from the Nazi scourge. American Cushman scooters had landed in Italy and Ferdinando Innocenti got a glimpse of what the future could be.

Cushmans were used by the Allies not so much for blitzkrieg raids on Nazi troops, but rather as a utilitarian vehicle to send information between divisions or merely to transport individual soldiers around the base. For Innocenti, however, it was a brainstorm. Ferdinando soon realized that he could apply most of the already existing spare parts that he had at the factory to motorscooter production.

While the war still raged in northern Italy, Innocenti straddled the fence between the two sides. He immediately hired a designer in Rome to get to work on a small, economical motorscooter roughly based on the Cushman model 32 that was now zipping around the Roman piazzas.

"Experiment O" was the name of the first prototype

Lambretta which was completed in just a few months. The Roman engineer was inspired by a torpedo for the relatively sleek lines of the "O" compared to the chunky, utilitarian design of the Cushman—which boasted welding spots as a sign of quality.

The wooden model showed how the front headlamps would be incorporated into the full-body sheath that covered everything from the motor to the gas tank. The telescopic front suspension incorporated the steering column and the

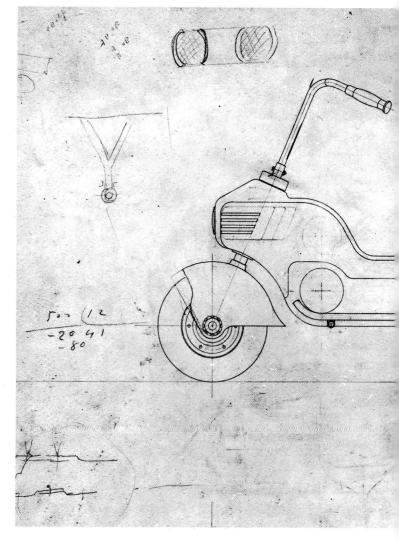

front forks and covered the works with stamped metal. The rear suspension, however, left something to be desired. Drawing from the Harley-Davidson design of the era, Innocenti simply relied on the springs under the saddle to smooth any bumps the scooter would hit.

The placement of the motor followed the motorcycle trend of the 1930s and squeezed it between the rider's legs. The chain from the motor then extended back to the rear wheel with the whole assembly covered by pressed steel.

It's unknown why the "Experiment O" never went into full production. Possibly Ferdinando Innocenti wanted to further tweak the esthetics and technical aspects of his debut scooter. Or perhaps with all the wartime chaos, the project slipped by the wayside.

Since Ferdinando couldn't slip by enemy lines in 1945 to check up on his Milan-Lambrate factory, he continued his work to mobilize the masses through motorscooters. He entrusted the project to a young aeronautic general, Pier Luigi Torre, who had proven himself before the war with his various design of mechanical parts for airplanes.

Torre started from scratch, but was nevertheless influenced by the American scooters cruising around at the beginning of the 1940s. In particular, the military Cushman Model 32 caught his fancy. While Torre's prototype, still called "Experiment O," wasn't as ground-breaking stylistically, the scooter was much more mechanically sound. His innovative design incorporated the motor and the transmission

In the center lies the photo for the unedited version of the first Innocenti motorscooter design in Autumn of 1944. On the top part of the blueprint are a few sketches of the connection of the metal covering for the scooter. Unfortunately, the designer of this very first prototype is unknown. Below. The entire engine of the mysterious sounding "Experiment O" prototype is laid bare here. The traditional design bears an uncanny resemblance to the British Villiers' engine.

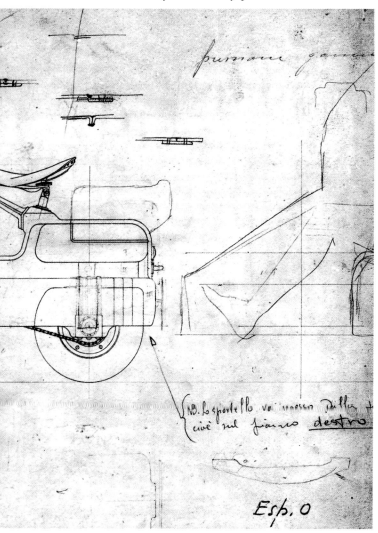

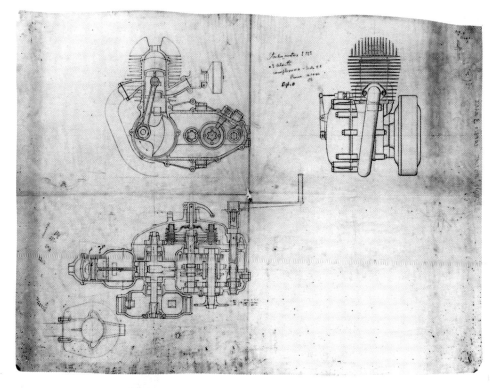

together mounted on the rear wheel. The engine size remained at 125cc but had one cylinder and two pistons with the electrical system run by a magneto. On the opposite side from where the magneto was mounted, a large fan was placed which blew fresh air on the engine to keep a constant, cool temperature.

While the gearbox just allowed for two speeds, the wheels were given more attention and Innocenti tested both six-

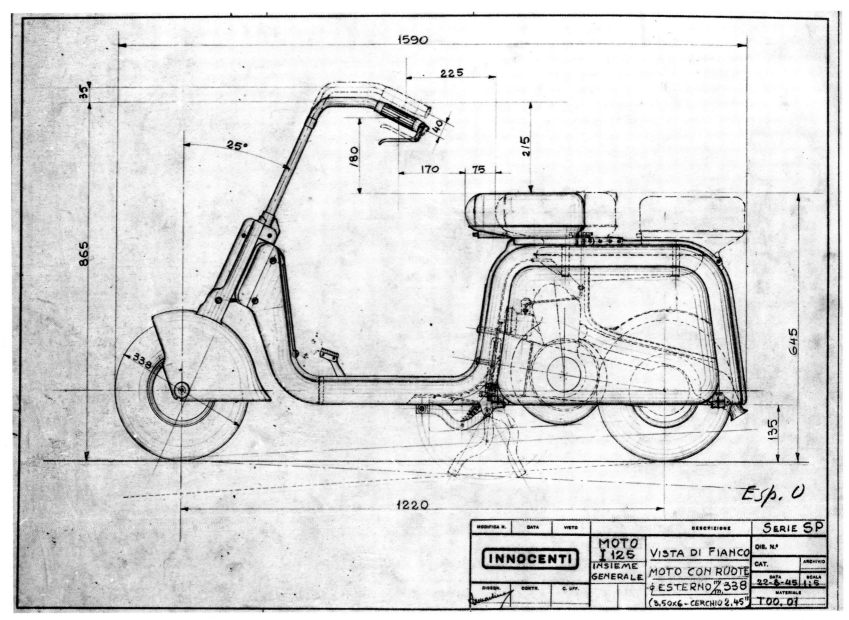

and seven-inch diameter versions. The frame consisted of one central beam of molded iron constructed in such a way to support all the weight and contortion that a scooter endures when on the road. This whole structure also formed the stylish outer body paneling, which covered the gas tank, glovebox, and motor.

Even the front fork used pressed steel electrically welded for its structure, which was exactly the same as the previous prototype. The front wheel and cover was a ringer for the wheels on light aircraft. The rear wheel, however, took basic motorcycle technology of the day, but the one innovation added was rubber torsion in place of the classic helical springs.

While the testing of the new prototype continued around the clock, Innocenti was finally able to get back to its factory in Milan to check out the state of its machines a few days before the end of the war. An ugly surprise awaited Innocenti since most of the building had been reduced to rubble following the Allied bombing of April 30th, 1944. What's more, most of the machines had been completely rusted from the rain pouring in the hole-filled roof, or damaged beyond repair from the retreating German troops.

If that wasn't enough to discourage Innocenti, the Allied troops declared that the entire factory was to be put exclusively to military use. Ferdinando Innocenti didn't lose heart even though everything seemed useless. Following a lengthy legal battle, he was able to repossess the factory and start to get it back on its feet.

Not until mid-1946, when Piaggio was already pumping out Vespas, was Innocenti finally able to completely get control of his company. Ferdinando Innocenti immediately began converting the entire factory to the continual output of the new motorscooter. Even back at the beginning stages of the scooter project, he envisioned applying the automobile assembly line to the full-scale production of motorscooters. Only through huge output of product could Innocenti hope to keep the price of the motorscooter within the reach of the general public.

While the factory was being revamped, Innocenti took the opportunity to move its temporary headquarters from Rome to Milan to a building dubbed, "Centro Studi."

Preceding page. The complete design of the new motorscooter conceived by the engineer Pier Luigi Torre. In this case, the bodywork resembles the Cushman Model 32, except for the reversed brake levers, the strange movement of the kickstand, and the placement of the exhaust behind the rear wheel. To make the motor more accessible, the two side panels hinge open.
Left. This is a nearly complete sketch of the second prototype named "Experiment O"
Below. Horizontal cutaway of the engine that was mounted on the second prototype. The primary transmission is especially interesting with large diameter gears and the magneto placed near the engine shaft.

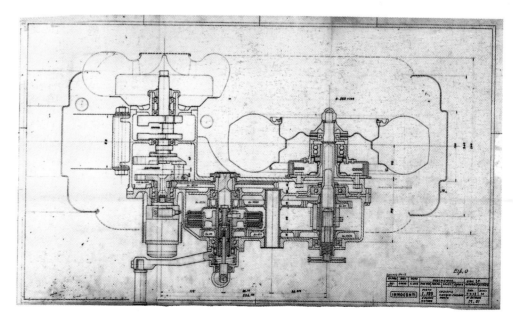

Dated January 1st 1947, this blueprint of the Lambretta tipo 2 shows how the basic design had already been established even though there are a few mechanical parts missing. Notice the strange shape of the foot gearshift, which would be totally changed by the time it went into production. The glovebox, the rear panels, the license plate holder, and the muffler would all keep this original design.

After a few months of uninterrupted experimentation, a mock-up of the "Experiment O" was prepared that was immediately brought to Ferdinando Innocenti for inspection. Finally, the new prototype was on the right path and just needed a little streamlining to make the scooter appear more aerodynamic.

Following a plethora of different ideas, the simplest was deemed the best and most original. By removing all side-panels, the beautiful engine, gas tank, and glovebox could be shown off. This idea was a break from Piaggio's Vespa which attempted to cover the entire mechanical system.

With all these modifications, the next step could be taken. "Experiment 2" soon hit the drawing boards, and was designed for almost a year until it went into production in October 1947. Ferdinando Innocenti set up a special long platform in his office to mount the new models of "Experiment 2," so he could check up on all the modifications as the process went forward.

In the meantime, the managers at the publicity area of Innocenti got busy working on a name and price in anticipation of the impending release of the new scooter. The price tag would be an affordable 135,000 Italian lira. "Experiment 2" didn't have much of a ring to sell the scooter, so the admen dubbed it "Lambretta m"—the "m" standing for motorscooter.

Why Lambretta? According to the official Innocenti newsletter Notizario Lambretta Vol. 1 No. 4, "'Lambretta' is the nickname of the small creek that runs through the Innocenti factory. The fleeting little brook flows hither and thither like a little vagabond without any myths about it or battles fought over it, which is perhaps why the Treccani completely forgot about its existence. 'Lambro' is the name of this humble river whose source is on the plain of Pian del Rancio in the valley of Val Sassina and after a capricious torrent flows into Pusiano Lake. From here, the waters of the Alserio join the Lambro and flow all the way to Monza and then widen through the Lambrate area of Milan and curiously wind by our warehouses and finally after 130 kilometers reach its destination of the famous Po river."

To promote the forthcoming Lambretta, a cute radio advertisement was prepared that was aired every day at exactly

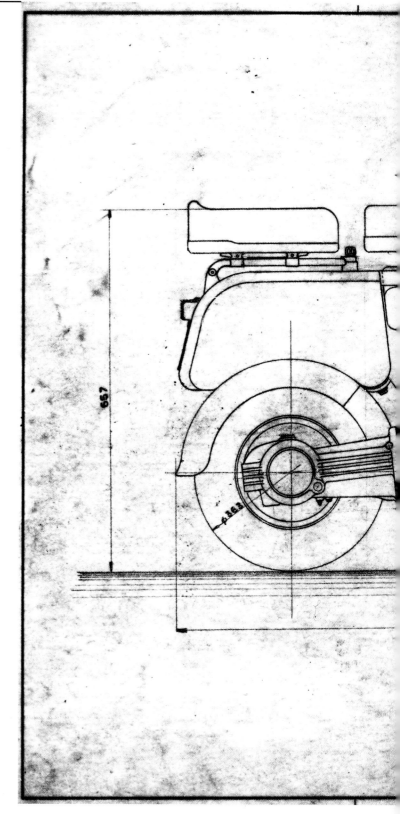

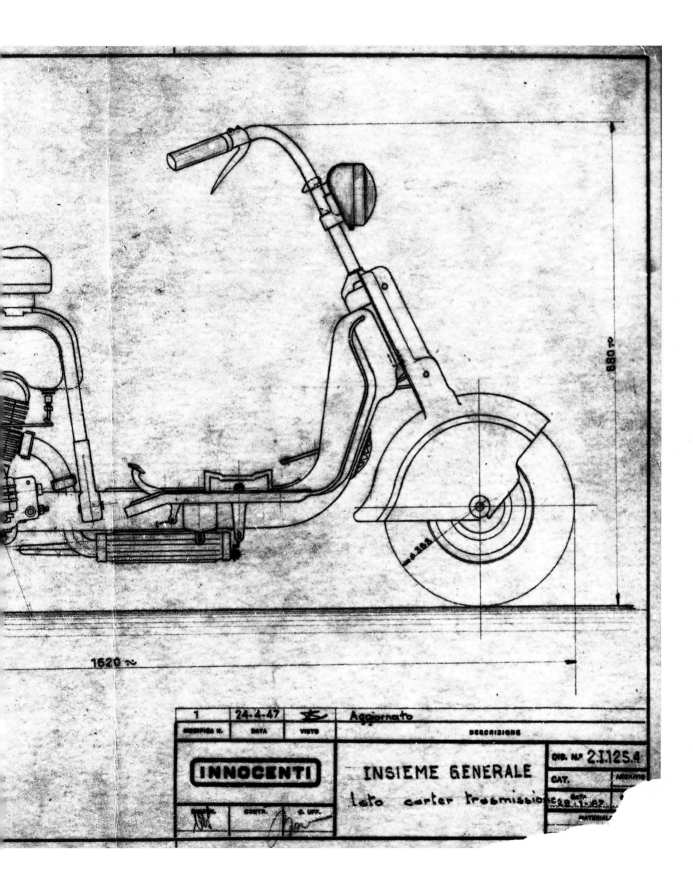

880 ~

1620 ~

1	24.4.47	⚮	Aggiornato		
MODIFICA N.	DATA	VISTO	DESCRIZIONE		

INNOCENTI

INSIEME GENERALE

lato carter trasmissione

DIS. N° 2.I.125.4

DAT.

ARCHIVIO

CONTR.

G. UFF.

MATERIALE

Side. This drawing was published by the magazine *Motociclismo* and was supposed to be the Lambretta scooter in its early phase of development.

Below. The first ever price list for Lambrettas was distributed in July 1947 to promote the new scooter and to try and garner advance sales. The large wooden box to protect the scooter is an especially strange extra offered by Innocenti.

Next page. The first brochure to hit the Italian market is printed here in its entirety with different views of the Lambretta 125 m and previews of the mini-Lambretta "truck" to try to lure customers. On the lower part of the brochure, all the different technical aspects and the accessories of the scooter are explained. The decision to use a little cowboy as the mascot is surely because of the booming popularity of the Wild West after WWII.

8:35 p.m. on all Italian RAI channels singing, "It's 8:35! It's time for the Lambretta!"

Even in its advertisements, Innocenti was revolutionary in that they were promoting a motorized vehicle that hadn't even enter production yet. No other motorcycle or motorscooter company would have jumped the gun like Innocenti was doing, betting on a scooter that no one, apart from a few designers, had even set eyes on.

After a few months of these ads, the public's curiosity was piqued. Hundreds of letters filled the mailboxes of motorcycle magazines asking precise information about this new form of transportation from Innocenti, but not one of them was able to give a satisfactory response. The exact technical and mechanical characteristics of the Lambretta were kept under wraps, and Innocenti deemed the whole project top secret to avoid copycats and also to build up expectations.

In spite of the precautions to avoid leaks of the project, an automobile magazine out of Milan published a crude sketch of what it deemed the Lambretta in February 1947. This "scoop" was picked up by the Italian motorcycle magazine *Motociclismo* that spread the design across Italy forcing Innocenti to issue and official statement denying that the drawing was in fact the new Lambretta.

This whole charade was somewhat of a publicity coup for Innocenti since the drawing actually was very similar to what the Lambretta was at that point. The sketch was probably made by an Innocenti factory worker that had seen the prototype, not by an imaginative journalist in search of publicity.

Innocenti was burning daylight, however, since Piaggio's Vespa was already on display in storefronts across Italy. The public was getting tired of hearing these advertisements for a scooter that at that point they doubted even existed. Unfortunately for Innocenti, they couldn't quite release the Lambretta yet considering that they still needed a few more months to perfect the factory assembly line. To satisfy the public and the magazines that wanted a good headline or at least a photo, Innocenti decided to show a wooden prototype of the new Lambretta. At the same time, a wooden prototype of the three-wheeled mini pick-up truck was displayed, which came in four different versions.

Finally the Lambretta came out, but the public didn't express too much enthusiasm. After all the hype, everyone expected a fancy luxury mobile, not a mini scooter that looked more like a child's toy than a serious urban vehicle

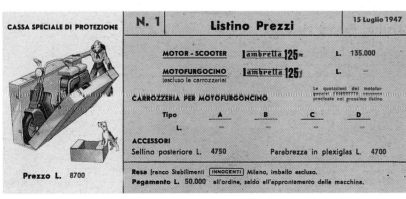

Lambretta 125f

I motofurgoncini sono dotati di un motore analogo a quello applicato sul Motor-scooter; l'impianto dei freni funzionante sulle tre ruote, la trasmissione rigida alla ruota motrice, il telaio centrale con piano di carico solidale all'intelaiatura, permettono l'agevole e facile trasporto di un carico di 200 kg.

Ruote anteriori a sospensione indipendente, piano di carico situato in basso, molleggio ottenuto mediante balestra trasversale, possibilità di applicare intercambiabilmente i vari tipi di carrozzeria, sono caratteristiche intese a rendere i motofurgoncini Lambretta mezzi organici di sicuro e pratico funzionamento.

Lambretta 125f/a

Lambretta 125f/b

Lambretta 125f/c

Lambretta 125 ..un prodotto degli stabilimenti INNOCENTI

Lambretta 125m gioiello della meccanica moderna, il più pratico ed economico mezzo di trasporto

Telaio in acciaio, cambio di velocità con preselettore, trasmissione rigide con giunto elastico, sono garanzie della grande robustezza, del perfetto funzionamento, dell'integrità e della lunga durata del Motor-scooter Lambretta

Sedile in gomma piuma su molle, forcella elastica su supporto antivibrante, pneumatici Pirelli a larga sezione, rendono estremamente confortevole viaggiare su Lambretta

Rapida chiusura del portabagaglio, sistema di scappamento reso assai silenzioso, impianto di illuminazione di sicura efficacia, concorrono a completare l'organica praticità del Motor-scooter Lambretta

SU LAMBRETTA UN SECONDO PASSEGGERO PUÒ TROVARE POSTO SU UN SEDILE POSTERIORE E UN BAMBINO SOPRA UNO ANTERIORE

IL RIGORE DEL FREDDO E LE AVVERSITÀ ATMOSFERICHE, SONO ATTENUATE SU LAMBRETTA DA UN PARABREZZA IN PLEXIGLAS

UN PICCOLO BAULE PUÒ CONTENERE COMODAMENTE IN LAMBRETTA IL BAGAGLIO DEL VIAGGIATORE

SU LAMBRETTA TUTTO È STUDIATO, PERCHÉ SIA RESA RAPIDA E FACILE L'ISPEZIONE AGLI ORGANI PRINCIPALI DELLA MACCHINA

SU LAMBRETTA IL CAMBIO DEL PNEUMATICO È FACILITATO DALLA POSSIBILITÀ DI SMONTAGGIO LATERALE DELLA RUOTA

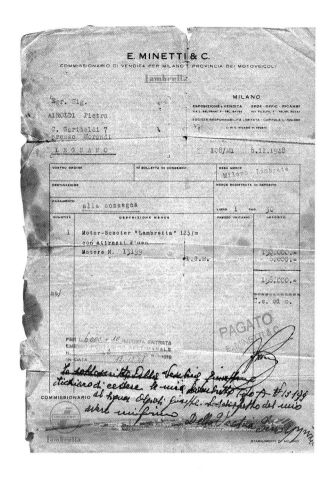

This contract between the Minetti company of Milan for a Lambretta 125 m, which was for one of the last built and was sold after production of that model had ceased.

In October 1947, Innocenti succeeded in producing a small number of Lambrettas to whet the appetite of the impatient dealers, so they could at least have something to show their customers. Many dealers, however, couldn't wait to see the Lambretta in the flesh and demanded a refund from Innocenti. Instead they turned to Innocenti's tenacious competitors.

Finally by the beginning of 1948, the production line went into full swing and put out a total of 50 units daily, which was able to fill the huge quantity of orders that had come pouring into the factory.

How was the final product finally reached? As we saw earlier, the ideas from the "Experiment O" were elaborated with significant mechanical improvements that ended up being "Experiment 2." The rear paneling was removed exposing the tube structure that made up the frame rather than the stamped steel which was originally proposed. This tubing held up the gas tank and the glove box in the rear of the scooter under the saddle. In the front, a small legshield offered ample space for the driver's feet and also provided protection from the elements.

The motor was completely redesigned with the complicated two piston version thrown out in favor of the more reliable single cylinder. The electrical system was simplified as well with a flywheel magneto with 6 points that provided the electricity to start the scooter as well as for the lights and horn. The transmission was a complex system of dual cones, a torsion shaft and a three-speed gearbox with a smooth shifter controlled by a foot lever mounted on the foot rest.

The muffler, that was originally mounted on the rear part of the frame on the preceding prototype, now followed the frame near the front part of the floorboards then turned and the exhaust was let out under the motor crankcase. Much attention was paid to the style of the mechanical aspects and the frame of the scooter before it went into full-scale production. All the cables and electrical wires went through the tubing giving the Lambretta sleek and elegant lines. To help ease the shifting of the scooter, a speedometer was placed on the right side of the legshield while an internal gear regulator inside the motor prevented the driver

for adults. Even so, all great leaps forward are met with doubt and detractors, and the little Lambretta was no exception.

Innocenti was convinced that it was headed down the right path. Before the Lambretta even went into production, dealers across Italy had placed orders and reserved many of the new motorscooters to be shipped for their storefronts. Once again, Innocenti was right on target, and in just a short while, thousands of orders flooded in with a 5,000 lira deposit on each scooter.

When everything seemed ready for the official release of the Lambretta, the factory line was still held up by little problems. Production would have to wait until all the quirks were worked out during test runs of the line.

Acquista una **Lambretta**

e spendi la differenza

Left. The first design for authorized Lambretta service stations was later replaced in the early 1950s with round signs and a red background. Side. To promote the launch of the new Lambretta 125 B, Innocenti used this now very famous drawing. On the inside of the brochure is a description of all the new technical aspects of the model with cute drawings on how to use a Lambretta. On the back of the brochure is the convincing slogan that a scooter costs less than the tram and gives you as much independence as an automobile.

from shifting without disengaging the clutch.

To save a little cash in production costs, the rear suspension was essentially nonexistent and relied only on a couple of helical springs under the saddle. No expense was spared for the other accessories: a large glovebox that could be locked with a key was placed under the seat, a button for the headlamp, chrome trim, and a little measuring cup to get the right amount of oil to mix with the gas. For just a little bit more, customers could purchase a second seat to go on back, or a pillion pad for junior, a plexiglass windscreen, and a special wooden box that the whole scooter could be put in for when it had to be moved.

The strangest accessory choice was to not put a modern electric horn, but instead a mechanical clacson triggered by a pedal, technology that hadn't been used for almost twenty years. In spite of youthful indiscretions such as these, up to that point in time, the Lambretta was the best example of postwar Italian motorized vehicles. Compared to other motorcycles of the era, the Lambretta's attention to detail and extremely modern esthetics made it beyond compare. Every aspect of the Lambretta—from the frame to the motor to the mechanical system—were esthetically integrated to form graceful lines unseen in Italian design.

To further enhance the beauty of the Lambretta, Innocenti offered the little scooter in six "pastel" colors: gray, ivory, azure, red and amaranth. Even in this case, Innocenti was ahead of the other Italian motorcycle companies since it knew that their market wanted a variety of colors.

Around the summer of 1948, Innocenti realized that it had overproduced the little Lambretta and couldn't sell all of them into the Italian market. In spite of the expectation that the scooters would immediately sell out, Innocenti made the best of the situation and instead made history. Rather than lowering the prices of the scooter and having a firesale just to cut its losses, Innocenti decided to start exporting the extra few hundred scooters.

Rather than just sending a few here and there, the company prudently chose a country that already had a tight bond with Italy: Argentina. Thousands of fortune-seeking Italian immigrants in Argentina were eager to get their hands on anything from the Old Country. In that faraway land, the peppy 125cc motor and the easy handling of the Lambretta succeeded in winning the hearts of its riders.

In October of 1948, Innocenti half-heartedly decided to suspend production of this first model of Lambretta since the warehouses were still full of unsold stock. Instead, engineers began designing a new model to improve on the old one and hopefully increase sales at the same time.

This new model had already been on the drawing board for a few months and was finally presented to the general public in December of 1948. At this point, production was already underway with 100 units being produced daily. The name of the new motorscooter was simply "Lambretta B," at which time the original model was dubbed the "A" version.

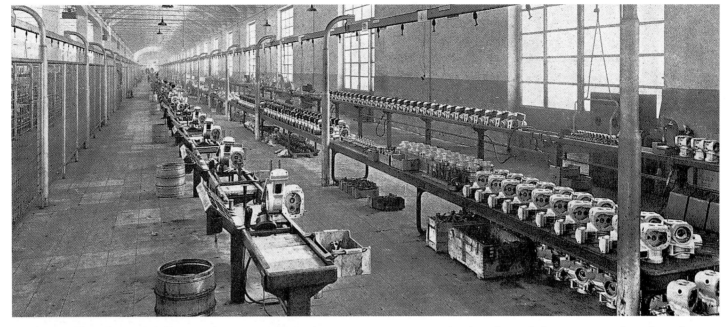

Side. The assembly line for the motor of the Lambretta 125 B worked practically non-stop as shown in this impressive view. The last part of the line would test the engines without compression for a few hours to see if the motor was up to par.
Below. At the Milan Fair in 1949, Innocenti posted a huge sign declaring all the improvements of the new model Lambretta, but at the same time showed all the defects of the older version. In the front row of the photo, the Lambretta f three-wheeler is featured with a wooden side panels.

Among the innumerable improvements to the new Lambretta, the most important were the rear suspension, the hand-shifter for the gears (rather than the motorcycle-like foot-shifter), and the larger eight-inch wheels.

With its commercial success, Innocenti could now be counted as one of the new industrial giants of postwar Italy. Its continual rise of production soon made Innocenti the second most important producer of motor vehicles in Italy. From this moment on, the Italian scooter phenomenon became legend. The two large scooter manufacturers, Piaggio and Innocenti, were the players that clogged the Italian streets with their little two-strokes and mobilized Italians. In the 1950s, not a town in Italy didn't have the little mo-

torscooters zipping through its center, and each and every burg had a special service station designed specifically to keep this new form of transport on the road.

Looking ahead to the future, both Innocenti and Piaggio wanted to keep the scooter a viable form of transport for years to come, not just a passing fad. To maintain their market share and to keep customers loyal to their brand, the two companies gave birth to scooter clubs. These new groups promoted Sunday drives in the countryside, but of course these rides started in the town center so scooterists could be seen by walkers out for their weekend stroll. The clubs would help each other with the bureaucratic and technical necessities in having a scooter, and would even offer a sort of driver's education to inexperienced scooterists. These clubs were able to transform this humble form of transportation into a new form of leisure that swept the country.

To spread the word across Italy about this new lifestyle dubbed "Lambrettismo," Innocenti began publishing a newsletter in the spring of 1949. The *Notiziario Lambretta* helped unite all the Lambretta clubs around the country and made them feel part of the larger movement. The magazine informed all its members about scooter rallies, new technical information, and responded directly to queries from loyal Lambretta riders.

At first, the *Notiziario Lambretta* was only published in Italian in black and white and distributed every other month. Because of the large number of exported Lambrettas, the newsletter was soon translated into many different languages.

Special color sections were added, and the magazine hit the stands every month.

The first Lambrettas to use the pages of the *Notiziario Lambretta* to announce its debut were the C and the LC. In 1950, this new design—featuring strong sectional tubing for the frame—was inaugurated. With the LC, Innocenti offered for the first time a scooter with an integrated legshield and body paneling. This elegant new design covered the motor from view and protected the rider from the elements. This new "Lusso" Lambretta was aimed towards a different clientele: one that still needed the re-

Above. Doctor Diego Scotti headed up the *Notiziario Lambretta* newsletter that was aimed towards Lambretta clubs in Italy and abroad. Articles included features on relations between Lambretta clubs, technical advice, road tests of new models, and other interesting tidbits on scooters. Side. Masses of Lambrettisti were a common sight at the beginning of 1950 as they turned heads of passerbys when they swarmed through cities. Lambrettas became a means of transportation that crossed all class and social levels.

liability and economy of the Lambretta, but wanted the high-class luxury version.

The Lambretta C, on the other hand, offered a refined version of the first two models but now the price was so economical that many Italians could afford a scooter for the very first time.

In 1951, a deal was struck for the first time with a foreign company to begin production of Lambrettas under license. The honor was bestowed on the German company NSU that was known for its efficient production of motorcycles. The German factory would soon be set up with an Innocenti-style production line to produce large quantities of Lambrettas.

The creation of foreign licensing and the production of Lambrettas abroad came about because of the idea at the Innocenti base in Italy that it wanted to spread the word (and sales) of this marvelous new scooter across the world. Innocenti focused especially on the South American and the Asian continent to increase sales. In the 1950s and '60s, it gave the rights to many countries to set up innumerable factories in India, Argentina, Brazil, Congo, Spain, Columbia, Indonesia, Sri Lanka, Formosa, Pakistan, Turkey, and France. If Ferdinando Innocenti had his way, he would have had a Lambretta factory set up in every somewhat-industrialized country in the world, which would create a standardized mode of production for their assembly lines. This way, Innocenti could simply propose to any country a complete system—already tested in Italy and other countries—to mobilize their people on motorscooters. Apart from standardized blueprints to set up the new factories, specialized engineers and technical assistance would be available from the Milan headquarters to help out in case of an emergency.

Unfortunately, this bold beginning got a dose of reality within a couple of years for two reasons: The first was the notable lack of competent workers in the lesser-developed countries. This caused enormous damage to the machines and made the entire production line ineffective, and therefore the scooters ended up not being at all economical to sell. The second reason was the automobile boom of the 1960s that allowed even the lower middle class to afford a car, which up until that point was the main market for motorscooters.

The only two countries that were able to maintain production in spite of these facts were India and Spain. Even after

basta una leggera pressione
a questa levetta
e il motore è avviato

costa L. **153.000**

Lambretta

PRODUZIONE 1953
CONCORSO TURISTICO

N. 1 · GENNAIO-FEBBRAIO 1953 · SPEDIZIONE IN ABBONAMENTO POSTALE · GRUPPO IV

Near left. On the cover of this *Notiziario Lambretta* newsletter number one from 1953, Innocenti displays the three new models for that year: the super-economic Lambretta 125 E, the updated LD model 1953, and the three-wheeled FD pickup with rear carrier.
Above left. This Lambretta 125 D was shown at the 1952 motorcycle show in Milan and was placed in an enormous wheel, which allowed spectators to inspect the movement of the suspension and the engine.
Below. The first version of the luxury Lambretta LD in 1954 boasted six-volt electrical system with a single battery to help start the engine.

Innocenti shut its doors in Italy, these two countries were able to continually update models mechanically and esthetically and even to export Lambrettas abroad.

Going back to Lambretta production during the 1950s, an important step forward for Innocenti happened towards the end of 1951 when the new 125cc D and LD models were presented. While keeping similar lines as the previous Lambrettas, the numerous technical advancements made this new series the warhorse of the Innocenti line.

The new rear suspension, the shaft-driven motor, and the front forks and hermetically-sealed suspension were all part of the new package that would remain in production for more than six years, which just showed how farsighted the initial project was.

With the economical model D, Innocenti had reached the apex of its initial idea for a motorscooter. The D could be summed up in three words: simplicity, economy, and sturdiness.

TUTTO IL MONDO IN LAMBRETTA

It's interesting to note that when these two models were initially released, the D was by far the most popular. Within a few years, however, the luxury LD became the favorite even thought it had a higher price tag. The LD can be proud that it was the first Italian scooter put into full-scale production that had the advantage of 6-volt electrical system.

Because of the huge commercial success of the D model, Innocenti decided to propose an even more economical model in 1953 to put people even with an extremely modest income on the road. In spite of these intentions, the new "E" model was a notable failure for Innocenti. With an alluring price of a mere 108,000 Italian lira, the Lambretta 125 E had numerous mechanical defects, which therefore caused Innocenti to suspend production after only one year of life. The starter for the Lambretta E was a pull-string, just like on outboard motors for boats. The interesting monobloc, horizontal motor succeeded in simplifying the mechanical system and the transmission.

With the essential technical improvements and the return of the kickstarter, the Lambretta 125 F was introduced coming from the ashes of the unfortunate Lambretta E in 1954. Even though the F model was one of the most reliable Lambrettas thus far, it couldn't conquer the loyalty of the public after the bad experience with the previous model.

In its place, the renewed D and LD models boomed with a bigger 150cc engine that satisfied the scootering public and finally showed what a scooter could do with an enlarged motor. To assure the cooling of the engine even under the most difficult circumstances, an airscoop and fan wheel were mounted on the Lambretta 150 D and the chain-driven Lambretta LD.

With the introduction of the D and LD models, Innocenti abandoned the hand-shifter that used the Teleflex cable for the more simple double bowden cables. This new system was both more economical and made the hand-shifter infinitely more simple.

During this period, international scooter rallies and individual scooter raids were booming. Innocenti began to see how this new trend could be used to show the Lambretta's absolute reliability could be demonstrated in lengthy voyages.

Near right. Edoardo Mari was a famous Lambretta "raidman" in the 1950s who traversed Africa, traveling 17,000 kilometers on his Lambretta 125 D.
Above left. This Lambretta 150 D was specially prepared by the Innocenti experimental unit for Cesare Battaglini for long voyages. The scooter was equipped with an extra gas tank on the sides of the rear trunk and a huge air filter designed for the desert.
Lower left. Battaglini hooked up with Doctor Ferrante while they traversed South and Central America. Here they can be seen arriving in Caracas, Venezuela.
Lower right. Following in the footsteps of Giancarlo Tironi, who first conquered the north in 1949 on a 125 B, Aldo Zidaric made it to the Arctic Circle in 1951. Zidaric won the raid contest of that year when he went from Trieste, Italy to Casablanca, Morocco via the Arctic Circle.

To promote long distance trips, Innocenti began an ad campaign called "More than 100,000 kilometers by Lambretta" in 1950. Large amounts of money and many premiums from sponsors were held as the carrot for the best trips completed. This promotion caused hundreds of loyal Lambretta riders from around the world to give it a shot. So much publicity was garnered that Innocenti kept the campaign going with the same formula for the next few years and upped the prize money.

The most impressive performance of any scooterist was probably Doctor Cesare Battaglini who circled the globe from 1956 to 1959. He covered every continent including Australia on his Lambretta and totaled 160,000 kilometers, a new record.

For his long trip, Dr. Battaglini used a Lambretta 150 D that was specially prepared by the experimental laboratory of Innocenti in Milan. Two gas tanks were placed on the rear of the scooter to allow longer trips between towns. A spare

tire was added and the air filter was enlarged and equipped with a special filter, while the motor had an extremely careful check-up before hitting the open road. Among the other fearless and foolhardy vagabonds that impressed the world on their Lambretta saddles was the Innocenti prize winner of 1952, Mr. Aldo Zidaric who went to the Arctic

Side. The new two-speed Lambretta 48 moped scored the cover shot for the October 1955 *Notiziario Lambretta* newsletter. The new little moped set itself apart from the competition because of its low price, easy shifting, and two colors of red and gray.

Below. With 53 Lambrettas making the trip, the Innocenti club won the international rally of 1958 in Monaco. In the front row is a FD/C three-wheeler as the leader of the pack.

Circle and the Sahara Desert on his Lambretta 125 C. Another brave soul was Mr. Edoardo Mari who traversed the African continent—from Algeria to Nairobi to Capetown—completing 17,000 km on his Lambretta 125 D.

Between 1950 and 1960, Innocenti organized huge international raids in all the most important European capitals. Perhaps one of the most memorable was the 1962 rally in Istanbul, to which 176 *Lambrettisti* came from all over Italy. All these scooterists traveled 2,700 km for 13 days without any major breakdowns. The return trip, however, was by ship. The official representative of Innocenti was the head of the Lambretta Club Gigi Villoresi, a famous race car driver from the 1930s to the 1950s.

In the mid-1960s, the activities of the Lambretta Club lost interest to scooterists who became more fascinated with automobiles instead. The Sunday trips to the countryside with a picnic lunch were all but forgotten. Times were changing, and the scooter that was once king of the road in the 1950s became a mere tool to get to work and back. The Innocenti newsletter *Notiziario Lambretta* ceased publication, and Lambretta clubs, flagbearers of the "Lambrettismo," were soon dissolved or became part of other motorcycle clubs.

Going back to the 1950s heyday of the scooter, or more precisely to 1954, Innocenti decided to place on the motoring market a sort of bicycle moped with large wheels at the extremely affordable price of 78,000 Italian lira. With the slogan, "Motorize your legs," the Lambretta 48 hit the Italian market with an enormous ad campaign that dusted off the cute cowboy and his puppy, which was originally used to launch the Lambretta A.

The Lambretta 48 had a frame of stamped steel, a gas tank positioned under the seat, and an extremely quiet two-stroke, two-gear motor.

The new moped had tough competition with the other Italian makes, especially Motom and Garelli, and never quite succeeded in conquering, or at least having a good position on the Italian market.

In 1955, Piaggio shook the staid scooter world with the arrival of the Vespa 150 GS that could easily reach 100 km/h with its quick acceleration that could even pass up many of

Bicyclist Fausto Coppi keeps up with his time keeper/"mechanical coach" Rizzi as he sets the pace on his first series Lambretta 175 at the Vigorelli velodrome. Just for pacesetting, the carburetor on this particular model was shifted to the right side to balance the scooter on the steep banks of the velodrome.

Coppi a Telematch dietro **Lambretta TV175**

the light motorcycles of the era. With this new model, Piaggio opened up a whole new "sporting" market that demanded the fastest scooters possible. Innocenti was completely unprepared for this gauntlet thrown down by Piaggio, but nevertheless set its engineers to work on the grave lack of speed of Lambrettas.

The design of the new Lambretta was entrusted to the engineer Torre who steered clear of tradition and instead envisioned a scooter with a frame and mechanical system that had never before been seen. The cylinder head was horizontal to lower the barycenter, while the transmission used a duplex-covered chain. Ten-inch wheels, four-speed gearbox, and a bench seat were placed on a Lambretta for the first time that went into full-scale production. The frame was well-proportioned with the fixed front fender and the aluminum alloy headstock that incorporated all the cables. The relatively large 175cc engine mounted on the new Lambretta TV (*Turismo Veloce*) put the new scooter at the top of its class in performance and power. Unfortunately, the mechanical system of the scooter was far too delicate

Near right. San Babila square in the heart of Milan was home to this beautiful exposition storefront, which was inaugurated April 10th, 1957.

Above right. On the far right, Mr. Cassola helps test the new series of motors designed especially for the forthcoming 125 and 150 LI model.

Below. This photo shows the group of workers that experimented on new versions of Lambretta scooters. The frame in the front row belongs to a 1959 Lambretta TV series II.

and caused this model to be suspended by 1958. In its place, the Lambretta TV Series II took over with a new motor derived from the newborn series LI 125 and 150cc. Even so, the 175 TV was extremely important for Innocenti since it inaugurated a new philosophy for the company, that of high performance and constant improvements of each new model.

At the same time the 175 TV was presented, a modern exposition center to show off Innocenti scooter production was opened in the busy San Babila Square in Milan. This huge showroom offered two-story windows that circled the entire building. This Mecca for loyal Lambretta riders kept them abreast of the latest improvements in scooter technology and was a favorite meeting place to discuss the new models.

So in 1958, the first part of the history of the Lambretta came to a close with the end of production of the glorious LD that was directly descended from the Model A. The LD

Lambretta li 2ª serie

INNOCENTI DIVISIONE MOTORI

Innocenti used a variety of advertising themes in the 1950s to promote the first and second series LI and TV Lambrettas, as seen in these publicity photos.
Above left. Comic actor Macario sits proudly on a 150 LI series one with the classic paint scheme of gray and red.
Above right. This interesting cutaway featuring a series two LI was drawn by Loiacono.
Center. This cutaway 175 TV Series II allowed the public to ogle while they passed by the Innocenti showroom in Piazza San Babila in Milan.
Below. These four Lambretta 150 LI Series II scooters were ready to serve the press for the 1960 Olympic Games in Rome.

Macario e due soubrettine della sua rivista 1958/59 « Chiamate Arturo 777 ».

The famous Italian comedian Macario with two girls from his 1958-59 show « Call Arturo 777 ».

Le fameaux comique italien Macario et deux girls de sa revue 1958-59 « Appelez Arturo 777 ».

Der bekannte italienische Komiker Macario und zwei Soubretten seiner Revue 1958-59 « Ruft Arturo 777 an ».

was the pinnacle of Innocenti's early years having been in production for more than six years with great commercial success in all the countries of the world.

The LI 125 and 150 took the LD's place and at the same time was based on the body of the TV from 1957. While the LI's mechanical system was similar to the TV's, the motor was completely redesigned with a simplified transmission and gearbox, and the clutch was significantly improved.

After little more than a year from its birth, the Lambretta LI became the Lambretta LI Series II. Just like the TV Series II which had gone into production a few months prior, the headlamp of the new LI was incorporated with the handle-

Near right. Looking closely at this view of the Lambretta production line, a group of LD motors is displayed with electric start and the modified glovebox (to make room for the key starter).

Above right. This dubious feat was performed by 26 Spaniards from Burgos who succeeded in going a few hundred yards on an unmodified Lambretta LI.

Below. The Lambretta showroom on wheels would always show up at the most important scooter rallies thereby making it an official Innocenti event.

bars, so it could now turn with the wheel.

During this period, the production of Lambrettas reached its zenith. The assembly line pumped out a Lambretta every fifty seconds and reached a monthly production of 15,000 units. By now, not a country in the world didn't have at least one Innocenti vendor. Both the Lambretta and the Vespa became the best-known national products of Italy around the world, representing the most advanced Italian motorized technology.

Between the two big scooter manufacturers in Italy, Piaggio and Innocenti, they produced a good 436,000 units in 1960 alone. More than half of these were exported around the world. Keep in mind that this was only the production within Italy and doesn't include all the licensed manufacturers scattered around the world.

Even though the Lambretta LI and TV were enormously successful, Innocenti didn't rest on its laurels but continued to research and experiment on new models. One interesting design was proposed by Ghia that prepared two different wooden models to be built.

Ghia preferred to avoid distorting the lines of the Lambretta and thereby limiting itself to a slight redesign of the original. The final product was too shoddy to be considered further and was soon abandoned.

Innocenti preferred to continue working on its two new models and create a new body that would be molded

Above left. The design center of "Centro Studi di Ghia" built this wooden prototype in 1959 in an attempt to replace the body of the second series of LI and TV Lambrettas.

Above right. This prototype for the Lambretta LI Series III was almost identical to the final version, except for certain characteristics held over from the second series, including the handlebars, the crankcase, the muffler, and the rear grille.

Near left. Even this early photo of the third series of the TV 175 wasn't quite the finished version. Strangely, even the chrome flame piece on the rear of the sidepanels is missing.

Below left. Jayne Mansfield was called up by Innocenti to plug the new line of Series III Lambrettas.

around the motor already in production.

At the end of 1961, the new Lambretta was ready to be put on the market in place of the LI Series II, and this third series became known as the "Scooter-linea" (Scooter Line). The Series III was only available in the 125 and 150cc versions; the 175cc model wouldn't be out for several months. The very modern streamlining of the Series III made it tops in the scooter category, once again showing the high level of design and production of the Innocenti name.

The 175 TV Series III followed a few months later with the distinguished honor of being the first motorscooter or motorcycle in full-scale production to have a disc brake mounted on the front wheel. Up until this point, disc brakes were only used on the fanciest racing vehicles.

Above. At the 1961 Salone di Milano motorshow, Innocenti debuted its Lambretta 50 aimed towards the fourteen-year-old market. Unfortunately, the little Lambretta wasn't well-received, so Innocenti couldn't afford to risk full production of the 50cc scooter.
Below. Dated March 3rd, 1963, this micro-Lambretta shows the evolution of the 1961 Lambretta 50. Although the two versions are similar, the body was significantly redesigned and enlarged as well as improved brakes, new wheel rims, and headlamp.

In the meantime, production of the Lambretta 48 was suspended since it never reached the level of success that Innocenti had hoped for. In its place, engineers began work on a 50cc scooter to meet the demands of a new market that searched for small engine scooters and mopeds that could be driven without a license in Italy.

The first prototypes were presented at the Salone di Milano in 1961 mostly to test the waters to see if the public would actually be interested in purchasing the little scooters.

To produce the new prototypes, Innocenti stepped out of their usual ideas and instead adopted the monocoque frame used on the Vespa. This one-piece frame allowed for more durability as well as being much easier to construct. The motor was essentially the same as the LI except that the cylinder was vertical and the induction was regulated by a rotating distributor.

This new line of scooters introduced several new styling cues that would be adopted for the design of the Lambretta Series III. The size of the scooter, however, was so small that only people of medium build or smaller could ride it.

The first contact of the little scooter with the public was met with a lukewarm reception at the Salone di Milano, so

Center. England was the land of scooter racing, and this line of Lambretta 200 TVs was no exception.

Above. One of the highlights of the Innocenti stand at the 1965 Salone del Ciclo e Motociclo di Milano was the blow-up elephant propped up on the trunk of the three-wheel Lambro to show how strong the little pickup was.

Below. This hefty load of 150 Specials and 125 LIs leaving from the factory was destined to make 52 Lambrettisti happy!

the project was temporarily put on hold.

Seeing the initiative taken by its nemesis, Piaggio took the bull by the horns and immediately developed a mini version of the Vespa to sell to the underage market that wasn't old enough to get their driver's license. In the shortest possible amount of time, the new "Vespino" was marketed across Italy, taking Innocenti completely by surprise.

Dusting off the prototype that was put on the shelf, Innocenti enlarged the little scooter slightly, making it possible to drop in a more powerful engine.

The new model was finally completed in 1964, but for some reason only appeared in a 98cc version especially for the foreign market. Not until the end of 1964 did the

50cc version appear for the Italian public.

Strangely, the new Lambretta wasn't equipped with the interesting rotating valve air intake that was presented on the prototype. Also on the 50cc version, Innocenti opted to mount 9-inch wheels in place of the 10-inch ones in the original design.

In the same year, the TV Series III-with an extremely potent 200cc engine-saw the light of day. This new model was designed to appease the English market that was clamoring for a super Lambretta that could easily reach 110 km/h.

On the Italian market, two different models of the 150 Special were offered the year before, which were nicknamed Silver and Golden, depending on the paint job.

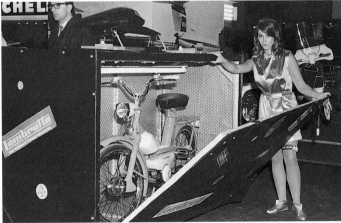

Above. The Lambretta TV 200 was identical to the Lambretta GT 200, as pictured in this original Lambretta advertisement.
Below. At the 1966 London motorshow, the little Lambrettino 39 was previewed.
Facing page, above left. The spartan lines of the first Lui prototype shown in this factory photograph made it necessary for a redesign.
Above right. Bertone put together this wooden prototype using parts from the Lambretta Junior 50 and the Lambrettino 39. In spite of this model's rough lines, the lines of the two-cylinder Lui could already be seen.
Below. Finally the lines of the Lui were taking shape, but still the wheels, crankcase, and taillights would be modified.

since it was dubbed the fastest scooter in the world and inaugurated a whole new class of 200cc scooters on the Italian market.

Also in 1966, a deal was struck with Italian Motom to produce 39cc motors under license that would be mounted on the successful moped Daina. Using this interesting little motor, Innocenti began producing its own moped with pedals that was simply called the "Lambrettino" and sold for a very reasonable 59,000 Italian lira.

With a mediocre design and modest performance, the Lambrettino had a hard time finding its niche in the competitive youth market and was replaced within a year by a new version with a 49cc engine and automatic shifter. The new model was called the SX Automatic and performed well especially in acceleration from a stop and didn't seem to consume much more gas when going all out. Throughout the history of the Lambretta, this was the first and only time that Innocenti let an outside company design its engine rather than trust its own engineers.

In the meantime, the marketing department at Innocenti took a new tactic to try and draw in customers since the sales had began to slump. In a break from the initial sales strategy of selling one model to everyone, a whole line of models was produced to meet every possible market niche. In 1967, the marketing department decided to focus on the one area of customers that kept Innocenti optimistic about the future: fourteen year olds. Just for that small age bracket, a little "scooterino" was designed that would be economical and modern looking.

To save on production costs, the Lambretta J 50's motor was used in this new scooter, and the design of the body was entrusted to the pen of the famous Nuccio Bertone who had already collaborated with Innocenti on their 950 Spiderina.

In spite of not being overly familiar with the technical aspects of scooters, Bertone was still able to invent an original and modern-looking design for the newborn Lambretta. This new Lambretta 50, lovingly called "Lui," can easily be called one of the best examples of collaboration between a studio designer and a huge motor vehicle company.

Unfortunately, the decline of the motorcycle market was beginning and hit every Italian motor vehicle company. In an attempt to stave off the inevitable crash, Innocenti took the initiative to continually renew each model with sometimes slight but visible changes. Between 1965 and 1966, the 125 Special, the 125 Junior with three or four gears, the 150 X Special, and the 200 X Special were all put on the market. The new Lambretta 200 X Special was groundbreaking

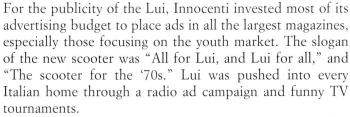

For the publicity of the Lui, Innocenti invested most of its advertising budget to place ads in all the largest magazines, especially those focusing on the youth market. The slogan of the new scooter was "All for Lui, and Lui for all," and "The scooter for the '70s." Lui was pushed into every Italian home through a radio ad campaign and funny TV tournaments.

Innocenti placed all its hope for a miracle on the Lui, but the economic crisis hit the whole Italian motorcycle sector hard. Many companies went out of business or were bought out for firesale prices by competitors. Moto Guzzi was taken over by the Italian government; Moto Gilera was taken over by Piaggio; and Bianchi, Parilla, Mival, and Sterzi simply closed their doors.

To try to pump life back into Innocenti, the Lui was offered in two different 75cc versions, the 75 S and the 75 SL. For the first time on any Italian scooter, an automatic gas-oil mixer was offered on the 75 SL. This new system was called "lubematic" required a supplemental device that sent the correct quantity of oil into the induction to lubricate the crankcase and the piston, varying amount according to the rpms of the engine.

In spite of the critical acclaim that this new invention received in the press, the general public didn't trust the new gadget and preferred the 75 S version, so they could mix

their own oil or use the premixed gas-oil combination from the gas station.

Sometimes it's difficult to explain the reason of some commercial flops and other successes. Many factors play a part: marketing expertise, the psychology of the customers, etc. Even the Lui should be analyzed as to why a modern scooter,

125 dl
150 dl
200 dl

Lambretta
INNOCENTI

Side. "A three-cylinder line" of Lambrettas declared this advertising brochure. The DL was one of the most successful Lambretta scooters—especially the 150cc version—but the difficult financial situation at Innocenti caused them to take it off the market.

Below. Ric and Gian, two popular Italian comic actors, posed for a photo op on the Lambretta 50 De Luxe.

Facing page. This proud model sits atop a Lambretta 200 GP built in the Far East after Innocenti sold all its machinery to the Indian government.

sold at a competitive price from a trusted brand, could miss out on the success it deserved.

Already by the end of 1969, just a little more than a year after it was introduced, the Lui was pulled from the production line, so Innocenti could sell off the considerable stock lying in the warehouse.

After having a good working relationship with Bertone, Innocenti decided to choose him again in 1968 to work on the restyling of the LI and SX line of Lambrettas. The goal was to focus mostly on the outer body paneling redesign and less on the mechanical alterations. In spite of rigid mechanical and frame limitations to work with, the designer from Turin once again showed his stuff and transformed the old

Lambretta LI into a modern-day, elegant riding machine. The name given to the new series with three different-sized engines was DL for De Luxe, and was offered in various color schemes according to the size motor. To add a touch of personality to the newborn DL, the right side of the front legshield was adorned with a sticker meant to look like an ink spill. Because of this strange finishing touch, the DL became known by the public as "the black stain."

As the flagship of the fleet, the new and improved 200 DL kept the title for Innocenti of the fastest scooter in the world due to its outstanding performance. In 1969, it was further equipped with an electric starter; once again, Innocenti was the first to add this feature to any scooter.

In step with its big brothers, even the little Lambretta Junior 50 was equipped with constant esthetic improvements to keep it in tune with the times. In 1968, the DL model was introduced, then in 1969 a "Special" version was put on the market with a long, two-color bench seat and black rubber floormat.

In spite of all these improvements to the models, the scooter economic crisis had reached its height. Luigi Innocenti was tired of the fight and preferred to just sell the industrial complex and get out of the business.

The production line was officially halted in April 1971, while a batch of 600 V three-wheelers weren't finished until the first days of 1972. Unfortunately, it was difficult to find anyone who wanted to take over or buy all the machines and the production line of the Lambretta and the Lambro. The Indian government surprised Innocenti when they offered 3,000,000,000 Italian lire (about 2 million dollars) for all the machines. Perhaps the Indian government stepped in because by this time Lambrettas were everywhere in India and quite popular for their style and reliability.

Finally, the negotiations were closed after heated discussions. This is how our dear Lambretta, born on the banks of the Lambro river, will continue its long existence in the Far East on the banks of the Ganges, and will forever give satisfaction to its future owners. Even today, the Lambretta is produced by the Indian government and is exported in various European countries. This is how the great spirit of the

LAMBRETTAS AND THE COMPETITIONS

Below left. Rizzi (number 96) and Cassola (number 97) pose with their stock Lambrettas instants before the Milano to Sanremo time trial.
Below right. The first racing Lambretta was based on the Model A with a huge gas tank and a little cushion on top for when the rider assumed a more aerodynamic position.

The scooter is a means of transportation destined to a market that needs an economic substitute for the invincible automobile, an efficient commuter vehicle, and a way to take a pleasant Sunday ride in the countryside.

It's hard to imagine that this practical little two-wheeler could be transformed into a mean, racing machine that showed its stuff against the small-cylinder motorcycles. Anything was possible right after the war, however, and even the smallest town could easily be turned into a racetrack. All you needed was a few bales of hay, a few cones to make any town a mini version of the famous racetracks in Monza and Imola.

Innocenti saw that these local races were the perfect means to publicize its scooters across Italy. Just a few months after the first Lambretta debuted, it had already lured two famous racers to its team: Cassola and Rizzi. The Lambretta's launch into the world of racing began when these two drivers ran a time trial from Milan to Sanremo. This would be just the beginning of Innocenti's long and emotional career in the high-speed world of racing.

Not a Sunday passed that the Lambretta didn't triumph in at least a race, gymkhana, or a time trial. Following all these victories, interest was growing at Innocenti to have a real racing division and team made up of such legendary riders as Masserini, Masetti, Ambrosini, and Ferri.

This new area of development fell under the scrutiny of the engineer Torre who souped up four to six Lambrettas to be brought to dealers around Italy and abroad to be driven in local races, especially in the areas where Piaggio's Vespa was considered the fastest scooter.

The racing scooters were based on the Lambretta 125 B, with a special muffler and an enlarged gas tank to ensure enough fuel for the enlarged carburetor. A few of these hot-rodded scooters were shipped off to official Innocenti racers to compete in regular races. Besides modifying the engine, these last scooters also had a lighter frame and had aluminum streamlining over the front wheel.

Because of the success of these scooter races, Innocenti organized an Innocenti-only race in 1949, dubbed the "Lambretta d'Oro" (Golden Lambretta) for people from all over Italy. Anyone from anywhere in Italy could participate as long as they were at least 18 years of age and their Lambretta was stock. No extras or special parts could be substituted, and a trained Innocenti team went around to each scooter to check that every scooterist had obeyed the strict rules.

Above. On your mark, get set, go! Just a few Lambrettas are needed to organize a heated race, with the fans all around the track. There's even a Vespa right behind number 9, but who knows if it could keep up with all those speedy Innocenti rockets.
Center. On the Monza racetrack in northern Italy, these four scooterists in rectangular formation are competing in the "Lambretta d'Oro" (The Golden Lambretta) Race. Notice the different aerodynamic positions that the drivers assume to try and cut wind resistance.
Below left. Once again the two endurance race drivers Rizzi and Cassola stop for a photograph with the young driver Masetti during the Six-Day Time Trial to Sanremo in 1949. The Lambretta number 25 was equipped with a front brake with a cooling airduct, which would later be standard on the 125 Lambretta C and LC models.
Below right. Masetti takes a breather surrounded by seasoned Lambretta mechanics.

The race was run in two distinct phases. The first was called the "Lambretta d'Argento" (the silver Lambretta) and the two scooterists in each group that won went on to the "Lambretta d'Oro."

In September 1949, the finals were held at the racetrack of the Autodromo di Monza with 17 competing drivers from all over Italy and from all walks of life—from mechanics to journalists, from blue collar workers to white collar professionals. Victory was bestowed on Franco Massironi from Milan who beat Elfo Frignani by a hair with an average speed of 83.23 km/h. The grand prize was a "Fido" radio donated by the Italian company Marelli.

Strangely, the Lambretta d'Oro race was never run again in

ond respectively in the difficult Milan-Taranto race. The C even received an honorable mention in the English International Six-Day Race when put up against high-speed motorcycles.

Even on French soil, the Lambretta had no rivals. At the famous "Rallye des Alpes Françaises," it ranked first without any penalties. One of the stranger events of the race happened during the Aix-Barcelonnette stage when the Lambretta was supposed to arrive at 5:30 p.m. Since the driver kept an average speed of 51 km/h in spite of the difficult terrain, he arrived at 2:27 p.m. and couldn't find the timekeeper!

1950 ended on a high note with an important victory for Innocenti when the two scooter racers Carancini and Bruzzone drove their Lambrettas in the Rome-Nice-Paris time trial and ranked first along with eight other French racers.

All the great racing results seized by the Lambretta during the 1950s pushed Innocenti in the direction of funding new competition projects to attempt to improve the award-winning scooter even further.

This was how a new competition model was born in the early months of 1951 that would be used exclusively on closed racetracks and for the Milan-Taranto race. The strong point of this "super" Lambretta was the motor with an as yet unseen four-speed gearbox with a foot shifter, two backwards facing batteries, and a carburetor placed in the front for better air flow through the conical intake. The increased air created slightly higher pressure to the cylinder via the carburetor and in turn made for a much higher velocity of 100 km/h. The mechanics and drivers had to pay close attention when the motor was run, however, because if they were distracted for just a moment, the engine could get fouled.

As far as the frame is concerned, a large gas tank was mounted with a design that was obviously based on motorcycle styling. The frame was simplified, especially the rear suspension which became a simple torsion bar, a design that would be taken up by the new 125 D. The wheels, on the other hand, were aluminum rims measuring 12 or 14 inches.

With this new design and the Lambretta C (which was well tested in numerous time trials), Innocenti looked like the fa-

Above. The victorious arrival of the Innocenti team to Taranto featured the driver of the truck Mister Mainotti (far left) and Count Carancini (number 45) as the winner in the scooter category with the average speed of 62 km/h.

spite of a huge national following of the event. All the possible dangers of the race, especially by people not accustomed to high speeds, probably caused Innocenti to wisely put this particular race on the back burner.

Going back to true scooter racing, Innocenti was preparing a modified version of the newborn Lambretta 125 C to be used mostly in time trials and long distance racing. For closed racetracks, Innocenti preferred to continue using the tried-and-true scooters it had been racing with minor updates.

As soon as the C left the starting line, it was obviously unbeatable whether in uneven terrain or the straight away. Driven by Carancini and Fumagalli, it placed first and sec-

vorite at the beginning of the 1951 racing season. The two big competitors, that needed to be shown the power of Innocenti in time trials and speed were Piaggio and MV Agusta. As though these two competitors had struck a secret deal, Piaggio focused all its efforts on time trials, and MV Agusta went for pure speed.

From the starting line, Innocenti found itself against two extremely well-prepared opponents who had no intention of letting Lambretta drivers pass them up. MV was out to win at any cost. It participated in the "Trofeo Italiano" (the Italian Trophy) with a mini motorcycle dressed to look like a scooter with the bialbero, four-speed motor that had been used in grand prix racing already. This is an example of how elastic the interpretations of the F.M.I. regulations were at the time.

In reality, it was prohibited to use any equipment that was in regular use on grand prix motorcycles in motorscooter racing. Even so, MV was able to skirt the rules, so it could still compete. To remain competitive, Innocenti asked if it could use a special fuel mix of alcohol, castor oil, and other substitutes to increase combustion and to keep the engine cool. In this case, the F.M.I. wouldn't let Innocenti use this new fuel, so by the end of the year, Innocenti protested by taking itself out of the running.

One of the last official showings of the Lambretta with dual exhaust happened during the Milan-Taranto race. The scooterist Romolo Ferri was forced to withdraw, however, after he fell near Florence. He had already set a record on the Milan-Florence stretch, even beating light 125cc motorcycles.

The "dual exhaust" eventually was transformed to just one cylinder and only a single front exhaust pipe (and rear carburetor) with the idea of primarily running it in acceleration races. Two examples of this bike were sent away to Australia, where they even competed against light motorcycles. Also Germany saw the dual-exhaust Lambretta conquer the German public's heart when it was raced by the popular Otto Draiken against light motorcycles.

Piaggio was Innocenti's arch-rival during time trials with its speedy Vespa Sport.

The two makes would alternate victories, always trying to

Above. Ernesto Longoni leaned hard on a time-trial version of the Lambretta 125 C (1st version) during the "Southern Gold" race where he would tie for twelfth with another competitor.

Below. The speedy driver Copeta blasted along on this dual-exhaust Lambretta for the second trial for the motorscooter trophy in Bologna. Unfortunately, he placed only second behind an unbeatable MV bialbero driven by Bertoni.

outdo the other through minor modifications.

One of the most important triumphs that can't be forgotten was during the extremely difficult 1951 Milan-Taranto race won by Longoni Ernesto on a Lambretta C decked out for the long marathon. In just seventeen hours and 26 minutes, he went the entire 1,340 kilometers with an average speed of 75.9 km/h. Another Innocenti scooterist ranked third, Domenico Carancini, who had come in first the preceding year.

Another important feat, this time on an international level, was achieved by team of Longoni and Carancini, who won the time trial race from Liege to Milan and back. They ran the entire race in one fell swoop without stopping—2000 kilometers over a day and a half.

On the other hand, Innocenti made one of its worst showings since it had begun racing in 1948 during the International Six-Day Time Trial of Varese. The probable culprit was the dual cones of the second transmission that likely caused an electrical malfunction.

At the end of the year, the racing Lambretta C was replaced after two years by a new model, which was a direct descendent of the 125 D. For the most part, the racing D was the same as preceding model except for the suspension, twelve-inch wheels, and a four-speed gearbox controlled by a foot-shifter that had already been used on the "dual exhaust" scooter. This would be the last official racing Lambretta used in time trials on Italian soil for 1952.

Even so, some of the racing 125 D versions were sold to Innocenti's favorite racing scooterists who continued to use the Lambretta in races around Italy. One of these racers, Luigi Fumagalli, was a long-time activist in the Lambretta club and an Innocenti mechanic. He took his D on the 1953 Milan-Taranto race, winning his class and showing once again the reliability of Lambretta's engine. This last exploit closed the chapter on Innocenti's brief but successful racing career. This adventure into speed is more of a sidebar for the Lambretta, and is in extreme contrast with the philosophy of Innocenti and the dispersion of scooters across Italy and the world.

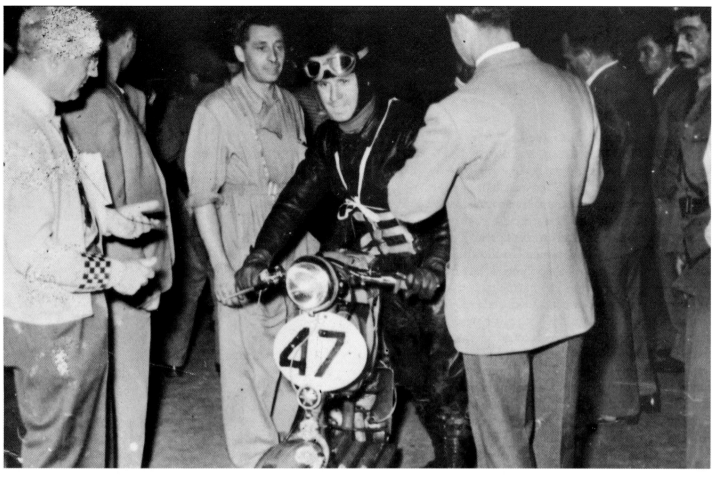

Above. Ernesto Longoni gets ready to start the 1951 Milan-Taranto race, in which he would easily win, establishing a new record in the process. Notice the extra large front headlamp for night driving.

Below right. Innocenti technician Luigi Fumagalli gets ready to leave on his four-speed Lambretta 125 D to compete in the 1953 Milan-Taranto race. His average speed in the race was nearly 70 km/h.

Below left. After almost two days of nonstop driving in the Liege-Milan-Liege race, Longoni finishes the grueling drive in first place.

RECORDS

Below. The first version of the record-breaking Lambretta was based on the construction of the A model. A few things, like the wheel rims and the hand shifter, came from the 125 B. The duct attached to the center of the frame was used to scoop air to cool the engine, which was enclosed in an aluminum shell. Notice also the extremely reduced size of the handlebars and the foot rests that have been shifted towards the rear of the scooter. Center. The invincible driver Rizzi gets ready to set his first record on the road from Rome to Ostia. On the right in white is Innocenti mechanic Giuliani, with the dark coat is Mr. Colucci, and the man pointing to his watch with the beret is the engineer Nacci.

Just one year after its birth, the Lambretta was already mature enough to start setting world records. These Italian scooters challenged the French light motorcycles that had previously dominated the 125cc class four category.

The first Innocenti experiment transformed two Lambretta As into racing machines. The structure of the frame was reduced to the bare essentials with the rear section being replaced by sections of light tubing. To allow the scooter to go on long stretches without stopping, a large gas tank was placed between the rider's legs in true motorcycle fashion.

As far as the motor was concerned, the carburetor was enlarged, the muffler was pulled with just a straight tube, and a higher compression ratio was reached. A dynamic conveyer made of aluminum was placed to help improve the engine cooling. The motor reached a maximum of only 5300 rpm, which was relatively low for a racing motorcycle. To organize the first trial of the racing bike, the engineer Luigino Innocenti, son of the great founder, was entrusted with the task. On the morning of February 11, 1949 on the road from Rome to Ostia, this Lambretta was about to reach a world record. During nine hours of uninterrupted riding, it conquered thirteen world records: nine of them in the 125cc class for four-speed gearboxes, and four for the class up to 175cc. In spite of this notable success, the engineer Torre was not sat-

isfied and attempted some modifications to shave off precious seconds. Records are like cherries, as soon as you pull one off, the second comes with it. Therefore, just two months after these first victories, Innocenti packed the Lambretta's bags and shipped it to the famous Montlhéry racetrack in France to attempt to break the records that it had just set in Italy.

This time, the objective was to break the 24 Consecutive Hour Marathon race as well. To make the scooter ready, the body underwent some alterations. An aerodynamic box was placed on the front for the headlamp, and a new carburetor with an adjustable mix to compensate for the difference between night and day temperatures.

For this race, many riders were called up: Masetti, Brunori and Rizzi, while Angonoa was replaced by the rising star Masserini, and Doctor Scotti (the very active manager at Innocenti).

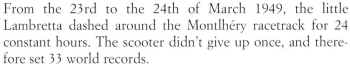

From the 23rd to the 24th of March 1949, the little Lambretta dashed around the Montlhéry racetrack for 24 constant hours. The scooter didn't give up once, and therefore set 33 world records.

An interesting note is that the French timekeepers were all but certain that the scooter wouldn't make it. They hadn't planned on having timekeepers at night, so they had to call in reinforcements from Paris. The one problem that plagued the scooter, however, was the continual burnouts of the front headlamp which forced the driver to stop innumerable times. As we said earlier, one record calls for a second, and the Lambretta, greedy for international success, showed up at Montlhéry again on the 17th of April 1949, less than one month after its debut on foreign soil. The goal this time was the 48-hour record. The same drivers and the same Lambretta were called up to challenge the world record.

Above. All hands on deck make final preparations for the high speed race at MontlhÈry, in which the Lambretta would attack the 24-hour world record for light motorcycles up to 125cc.
Center. Family photo of the Innocenti team after their heroic voyage onto French soil, conquering 33 world records. In the center, the engineer Luigi Innocenti is squeezed between the engineer Lauro and the engineer Torre (with the hat). On the sides are the four motorcyclists that switched off on the little Lambretta for 24 consecutive hours. From the left is Masserini, Brunori, Masetti, and Rizzi.
Below. This night-time snapshot was taken during an evening pause to refuel the little machine. The elegant man dressed in a suit and tie is the father of the Lambretta, engineer Torre. On the far right stands Mr. Maiotti, the driver of the Innocenti truck and the right-hand man of the entire team. Notice the homespun method to refuel the gas tank in the least amount of time possible (!).

Above. Another nighttime photograph at the racetrack of Montlhéry, this time, however, the goal was to break the 48-hour record. Comparing the photo with the one on the previous page, the differences were the front fairing with a more streamlined space for the hands and an extension of the plexiglass on the lower front section.
Above right. The signal box didn't live up to the importance of this splendid occasion, but WWII had just finished and the racetrack couldn't come up with much better.

Just a short time before, this scooter was considered just a toy to get around the city; now, it would challenge the world.

A dozen of the most internationally-accredited motorcycle journalists and a huge group of the most important technicians and engineers were on hand to witness the event. The Lambretta zipped in front of their incredulous eyes, lap after lap, for 48 hours straight without showing any signs of losing power or slowing down. At the end of the extremely tiring test, the young Masserini showed off how the Lambretta was still in optimal shape and took it for another ten laps at its maximum speed of 110 to 113 km/h. The public was awed. With these results, the Lambretta showed even the most skeptical critics the power of Innocenti. The motor was indestructible with a high-level of construction, and the stamped metal frame wouldn't budge an inch.

At the end of such a successful run, the Lambretta earned a much-needed vacation, and for the rest of 1949 remained behind the walls of the Innocenti factory to be further improved for even more races. When the new year dawned, Innocenti showed up at the track with a scooter that was completely streamlined, but still let the driver maneuver. The goal was to speed up the scooter even further and hopefully knock down some world records, set by the French rider Jonghi, that the Lambretta didn't get the year before.

During the trial runs with the new fairing, a violent crosswind on the elevated bank turns made it difficult for the three drivers, Masserini, Masetti, and Ambrosini, to hold to the track. With just two hours to go until the start, the trial was interrupted due to weather conditions. The Lambretta had to be content with just setting six world records. The Innocenti technicians were happy with the amount of work they were able to achieve in just a few months.

At the same time, the Vespa didn't fail to notice the outstanding results by its implacable enemy. In March of 1950, Piaggio debuted its covered Vespa driven by Castiglioni and Spadoni also on the racetrack of Montlhéry. Even the vespisti had to delay their time trials until April due to poor weather

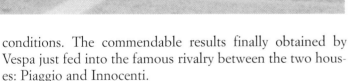

Above left. In the autumn of 1951, the first fully-covered Lambretta was ready to hit the Montlhéry where the drivers Ferri, Ambrosini, and Masetti would win 22 titles. On the left side of the photo was the able mechanic Mr. Cassola, who would afterwards be promoted to be in charge of the experimental division. Below. The "backwards raindrop" fairing was put to the test to see if the aerodynamic covering would actually cut the time of this racing Lambretta. Along the road to Terracina, Innocenti's superiority was once again proved to the world as the scooter hit 190 km/h. Romolo Ferri was the driver inside who knew how to squeeze every amount of power from this little torpedo.

conditions. The commendable results finally obtained by Vespa just fed into the famous rivalry between the two houses: Piaggio and Innocenti.

For this speed challenge, Innocenti tried its best to put together a new Lambretta that was completely engulfed in a protective fairing. The profile of the aerodynamic scooter was oval and flattened on the sides, with an ample front windscreen and with an extended rear tail to help steer. Even if the beauty of the design was somewhat questionable, the new fairing proved that it was worthwhile in numerous time trials. Between the 27th of September and the 5th of October 1950, this Lambretta driven by Ambrosini, Ferri, and Masetti conquered the racetrack at Montlhéry breaking 22 world records, and thereby annulling any progress made by the Vespa.

Having already showed the world the robust mechanical system of the Lambretta in endurance races, Innocenti then fo-

cused on speed in the 125cc category since the Vespa had already set a few records with Mazzoncini reaching the incredible speed of 171 km/h.

The engineer Torre got to work designing an extremely streamlined fairing based on the lines of a fish since it had a rear tail and air ducts in the front (which looked like gills). The motor was further supercharged with a volumetric compressor that raised the power to a good 16 hp at 9000 rpms.

Side. Poggi poses next to the record-breaking Lambretta on the race-track of Montlhéry. Compared to the racing version of the scooter from a few months before, this new model had improved fairing with more plexiglass in the front to improve visibility and redesigned front to facilitate access to the wheel. Notice that the exhaust had been shifted from the left of the scooter to the right. Below. With this photo, we can see how the rider is entirely covered by the fairing (except for a small portion of his helmet sticking out the top) to improve the aerodynamics of the ride.

With this new and improved racing machine, Romolo Ferri hit the road near Terracina on the 14th of April reaching the fantastic speed of 190 km/h, beating the Vespa by a good 20 km/h. Even during this last trial, the bad weather conditions influenced the final results. The technicians had originally predicted that the scooter could easily reach the goal of 200 km/h. At the end of May 1951, the Lambretta went to Montlhéry for the last time in an attempt to improve its speed record for one hour. In this trial, the scooter used was the same that had been used in Terracina but without the special volumetric compressor.

The two drivers entrusted with the task were Ferri and Poggi, who with their incredible skill took advantage of the power of the little motor to reach the new record of 158 km/h for one hour. With these exceptional results, any other motorcycle company would be satisfied, but not Innocenti who preferred to build on these triumphs. Just two months after this victory

Side. The four mechanics responsible for the development of this Lambretta pose next to the two drivers, Ferri and Poggi, during the preparation test to try and break the record for one hour. Notice the coveralls of Romolo Ferri and the elastic band around his abdomen to help relieve the stress caused to his body from all the vibrations of the scooter because of the rigidity of the vibrations of the suspension.
Below. These two drawings show the ideas that the designers brainstormed on to maximize the aerodynamic lines of the Lambretta to break world records. Notice the different positions of the driver of the two prototypes: in the first, he's almost lying down with all the pressure on his knees, while in the second, he assumes almost a motorcycle crouch position with a traditional seat (which can't be seen in the drawing). The number above the drawing indicates the total area of the front section of the fairing.

on French soil, all the Innocenti staff was sent to Monaco to attempt to set another record and especially to try and break the wall of 200 km/h.

For this trial, the Lambretta was further modified with a new volumetric compressor, and a redesigned frame for the fairing which made for a drag coefficient of a little more than .09.

After a few runs to get used to the new version, Romolo Ferri gave it a test drive on the highway between Monaco and Inglostadt on August 8th.

After a few warm-up runs, the Lambretta was ready to scale the steep 200 km/h wall. This first goal was easily reached both for the fastest kilometer and mile.

Besides this feat, Ferri clenched six other world records showing once again—as if there was any need at this point—the high technical level that the Innocenti *Centro Studi* had reached in the motorcycling realm in just four years since its debut. With these formidable results, Innocenti decided to cease indefinitely its plunge into the racing field. No other motorcycling company, especially Piaggio, dared to challenge the speed record set by the super fast Lambretta. Even today, the speed records for the 125 class bear the name Lambretta, usually having been knocked down to second place, but still valid records.

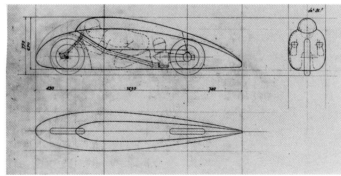

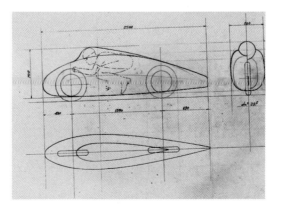

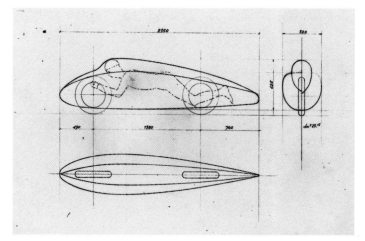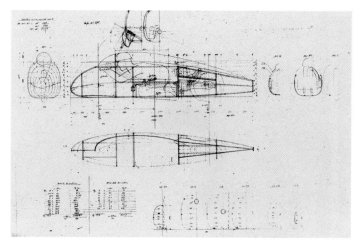

Left. With the driver completely lying down inside the fairing of the Lambretta in this drawing, it would be interesting to see what the designer had in mind for the placement of the engine!

The second design is already at a much more advanced stage with all the construction dimensions and the shape of the fairing laid out. On the top part of the drawing, one of the side flaps was shown which would help stabilize the machine at low speeds.

CHART OF RECORD LAMBRETTAS

Number	Record		Speed in km/h
	125cc Class		
1	1	km. at full speed	201
2	1	km. from a full stop	105
3	5	km.	183
4	1	mi. at full speed	200
5	1	mi. from a full stop	123
6	10	km.	150.5
7	50	km.	162.4
8	100	km.	160.4
9	500	km.	137.3
10	1000	km.	132.6
11	2000	km.	103.5
12	3000	km.	98.2
13	4000	km.	97.3
14	5000	km.	97.8
15	10	mi.	155.8
17	100	mi.	158.6
18	500	mi.	133.2
19	1000	mi.	132.7
20	2000	mi.	97.5
21	3000	mi.	97.8
22	1	hour	158.6
23	2	hours	142
24	4	hours	139
25	4	hours	137.6
26	5	hours	133.7
27	6	hours	133.1
28	7	hours	132.4
29	8	hours	132.8
30	99	hours	132.4
31	10	hours	132.6
32	11	hours	132.3
33	12	hours	132.6
34	24	hours	102.1
35	48	hours	97.6

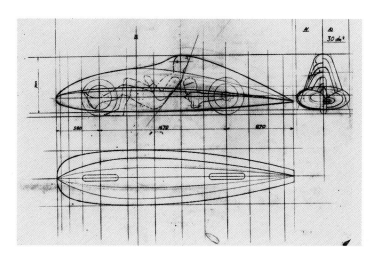 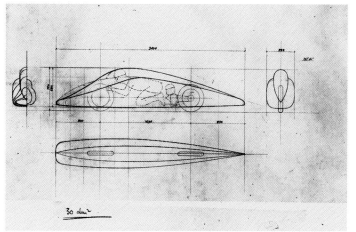

The streamlining of the fairing brought about many different ideas on how to position the driver. In the left drawing, he was completely laying down but in such a way that he could place his feet on the ground at slow speeds. This position would be adopted by the German company NSU for their record-breaking vehicles driven by Gustaf Baum.

Number	Record		Speed in km/h
	175cc Class		
36	1	km. at full speed	201
37	1	mi. at full speed	200
38	5	km.	183
39	50	km.	162.4
40	100	km.	160.4
41	1000	km.	132.6
42	2000 k	m.	130.5
43	10	mi.	155.8
44	50	mi.	160.9
45	100	mi.	158.6
46	500	mi.	133.2
47	1000	mi.	132.7
48	1	hour	158.6
49	6	hours	133.1
50	7	hours	132.4
51	8	hours	132.8
52	9	hours	132.4
53	10	hours	132.6
54	11	hours	132.3
55	12	hours	132.6
56	24	hours	102.1

Lambretta Motorscooters hold 56 world records

SPEED RECORDS

1	2/11/49	Rome to Ostia	13	records	
2	3/23-24/49	Monthléry	33	records	with dome windscreen
3	4/17-19/49	Monthléry	11	records	with dome windscreen
4	2/21-22/50	Monthléry	6	records	with fairing
5	10/27/50	Monthléry	22	records	with new, complete fairing
6	4/14/51	Appian Way, Rome	190	km.	torpedo design
7	5/19-25/51	Monthléry	7	records	torpedo design
8	8/8/51	Munich to Ingolstadt	201	km/h	torpedo design

PRODUCTION OF LAMBRETTA VEHICLES

Model		Beginning of Production		End of Production			Number
125	A	Oct.	1947	Oct.	1948		9,669
125	B	Nov.	1948	Jan.	1950		35,014
125	C	Feb.	1950	Nov.	1951		87,500
125	LC	Apr.	1950	Nov.	1951		42,500
125	D	Dec.	1951	Nov.	1956		123,141
125	LD	Dec.	1951	Nov.	1956		131,615
125	E	Apr.	1953	Feb.	1954		42,352
125	F	Mar.	1954	Apr.	1955		32,701
125	LD Electric Start	Feb.	1954	Dec.	1954		8,694
150	D	Oct.	1954	Dec.	1956		54,593
150	LD	Nov.	1954	Jan.	1957		109,344
150	LD Electric Start	Sept.	1955	Nov.	1956		2,020
48		Aug.	1955	Mar.	1961		63,223
125	LD/57	Dec.	1956	July	1958		44,665
125	LD/57 Electric Start	Mar.	1957	June	1957		52
150	LD/57	Jan.	1957	July	1958		113,853
150	LD/57 Electric Start	Apr.	1957	Dec.	1957		4,076
175	TV	Sept.	1957	Dec.	1958		10,089
125	LI	June	1958	Oct.	1959		47,747
150	LI	Apr.	1958	Oct.	1959	∗	108,984
175	TV Series II	Jan.	1959	Nov.	1961		43,700
125	LI Series II	Oct.	1959	Nov.	1961		111,087
150	LI Series II	Oct.	1959	Nov.	1961	△	162,040
125	LI Series III	Dec.	1961	Nov.	1967		146,734
150	LI Series III	Jan.	1962	May	1967		142,982
175	TV Series III	Mar.	1962	Oct.	1965		37,794
200	TV	Apr.	1963	Oct.	1965		14,982
98	J	Mar.	1964	Nov.	1965		17,642
125	J 3-Speed	Sept.	1964	Sept.	1966		21,651
50	J 20/1	Oct.	1964	Jan.	1968		69,988
150	Special	Sept.	1963	Oct.	1966		69,529
125	Special	Oct.	1965	Jan.	1969		29,841
150	X Special	Oct.	1966	Jan.	1969		31,238
125	J 4-Speed	May	1966	Apr.	1969		16,052
200	X Special	Jan.	1966	Jan.	1969		20,783
50	De Luxe	Jan.	1968	Oct.	1970		28,852
50	Lui	Mar.	1968	June	1969		27,812
75	Lui	Aug.	1968	Dec.	1970	(2,067 DL)	9,402
125	DL	Jan.	1969	Apr.	1971		15,300
150	DL	Jan.	1969	Apr.	1971		20,048
200	DL	Jan.	1969	Apr.	1971		9,350
50	Special	Apr.	1970	Apr.	1971		13,599
39	Moped	Nov.	1966	Dec.	1967		15,676
48	Automatic	Oct.	1967	Nov.	1968		8,922

△ plus 43,980 built in India, Brazil, Chile, and Argentina   ∗ plus 1,960 built in India

All the
LAMBRETTAS

LAMBRETTA 125 m (A)

The first series of Lambretta 125 m, where "m" stood for motorscooter, left the Lambrate factory in October of 1947 and blazed the trail for one of the most important commercial successes of Italian motorcycles and scooters of the postwar era.

The Lambretta m was presented to the public as a popular means of transport that was to be affordable to everyone no matter what their age. Originally offered for an extremely low price, only 135,000 Italian lira, the Lambretta m soon became an economic scooter known for excellence. Every socio-economic class of the population could afford a Lambretta, thanks to the easy, delayed payment plans offered by Innocenti.

Apart from being just a cheap form of transportation, the Lambretta was a mechanical jewel with especially refined styling cues and many accessories offered by Innocenti to further enhance its beauty. The frame structure was composed of squared, pressed metal that held the motor in place, while the gas tank, seat, and glovebox were supported by a pair of chrome tubes that kept the same style as the front handlebars.

The cables and the electrical system were completely closed within the two tubes of the handlebars, giving the front of the scooter clean and elegant lines. The front sus-

pension used a squared metal fork that was attached with a system of parallelogram connecting rods and a rubber shock absorber. The rear, however, lacked any sort of suspension whatsoever.

The wheels were especially small, with a diameter of 7 inch-

Side, above and below. These two views of the first version of the Lambretta m came from the maintenance manual and showed the optional, avant-garde windscreen made of plexiglass, which completed the sleek lines of the front of the scooter and made it extremely elegant and protective. On this very first model, the windshield was attached to the far sides of the exterior, while later versions clamped it in the center with an elastic fastener to avoid unwanted cracks or holes. Below left. The user's manual shows one of the last of the second version of the Lambretta m, recognizable because of the triangular seat and the brake pedal on the opposite side of the shifter. Strangely, the windshield is absent even though it was kept on the Innocenti price list for all of 1949.

Facing page and side. These two photos of the first version of the Lambretta m show the rear brake and the shifter arm, while sticking out right above is the chrome pedal that activates the mechanical horn. The control cables covered in rubber housing, that are the same color as the body, run along the front part of the legshield and are attached to the frame by two nickel-plated flaps. Below. This third version Lambretta m was recently restored with original light-blue paint scheme and the rubber parts tinted light gray.

es that lowered the balance level of the scooter and made it exceptionally maneuverable and easy to handle.

The motor block was innovative on every level. Positioned in the center of the frame, the transmission shafts and dual cones transferred the power to the wheel. To avoid slipping into the next gear, a regulator made the driver clutch before shifting into one of the three gears.

When the first Lambrettas hit the street in 1947, already many technical and mechanical changes had taken place since the preview models.

For Innocenti, this Lambretta was its first delve into the motorcycling world, and therefore it was only natural that it would continually test and tweak the scooter, fixing the most banal errors of the original design. The first change was on the brakes, from the traditional design on the very first examples. The brake pads on the drum brake shoes were inverted, so now it was more typical of American scooters. Cast iron brake shoes and rubber riveted to drums were used for the automatic clutch.

During the twelve months that the Lambretta 125 m was being constructed, myriad modifications and updates were added. Practically every week some mechanical aspect was changed, making it nearly impossible for collectors to make a perfect restoration of the exact original scooter.

To more easily recognize the different modifications, three basic divisions can be made, but it's important to keep in mind that there was a constant evolution and no cut-and-dry version. Innocenti never specified different models of the first and second series of the Lambretta m.

The first version of the m was built up to around serial number 6900, and can be distinguished primarily because of the rear, square pillion pad, the mechanical horn, and the chrome wheel rims. The second version was the most common and was built until around the serial number 11,000. This time the seat was triangular and the horn was electric. This model lost some of the class of the earlier model since it lacked the headlamp switch, the key lock for the glovebox, the starter, and the block on the gears to avoid switching without engaging the clutch.

The third and last version ended with about number 14,700 and introduced a few modifications that would be adopted for the new Lambretta 125 B. The seat was enlarged and redesigned with a single, horizontal spring to soften the ride. The kickstand was changed to a single piece of cast iron, so its aluminum color and that of the wheel rims now matched. The brake pedal was shifted to the opposite side of the shifter, a modification which had already been done on the last (approximately) 1000 of the second version.

With the Lambretta m, Innocenti introduced a new concept to the field of motorscooters, a wide range of six different colors for the body and the rubber pieces from which the customer could choose.

It was very uncommon for any of the competing motorcycle companies to offer a choice of paint schemes on their vehicles since each one became identified for their particular color: Moto Guzzi was red, Bianchi was blue, Gilera was red and black, etc.

Another interesting innovation that was offered as an option was the possibility to mount a plexiglass windscreen. This practical and modern accessory foreshadowed future mod-

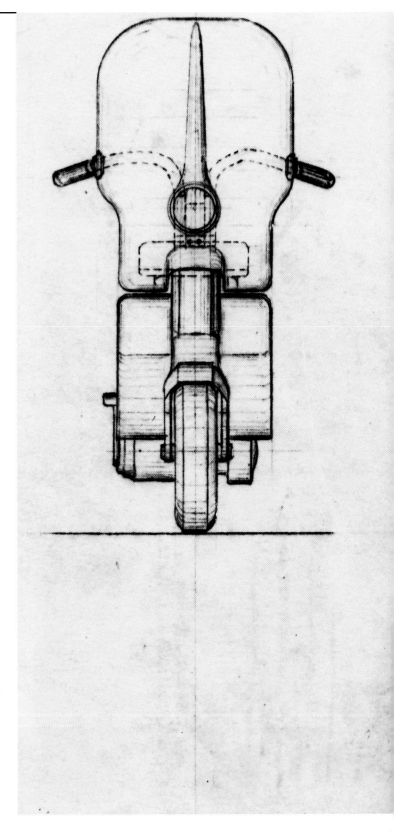

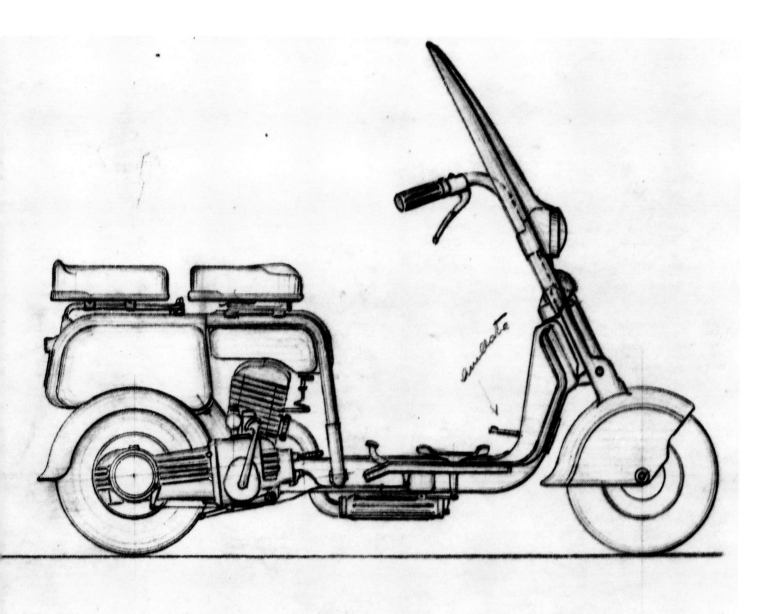

Dated September 1st 1947, this drawing was nearly the definitive version of the Lambretta 125 m. The sketch shows off the plexiglass windscreen and the positions of the controls. Even though it is written "annullato" (canceled) above the horn pedal, it was later added for a second drawing.

els with built-in windshields to protect the driver from the elements.

In October 1948, Innocenti ceased production of the Lambretta m, making room for a new model based on the old version that would be more reliable, comfortable, and was called the 125 B. With the introduction of this new series, the "old" Lambretta became known for the first time as the 125 A.

These two tidy photos portray a second version of a completely restored Lambretta m. On the large photo, the aluminum little box of the preselector of the gear shifter is under the floorboard. The small lever outside of the box conveys the movement of the shifter via a rigid rod and activates the connecting gear with a flexible "bowden" cable. Behind the preselector box is the muffler, which has been nickel-plated on the stamped metal. Contained inside the muffler are dual tubes that are partially hollow and covered with sound-absorbent material.

LAMBRETTA 125 B

Center. This second version of the Lambretta B is noticeable because of the pointed rear brake pedal and the light switch mounted on the handlebars. The evolution of this second electrical switch is especially interesting. At first, Innocenti preferred to keep the control mounted on the side of the frame, at which time the switch didn't have an off position. Then the oval-shaped control had a fixed chrome cover held on by three screws. Finally, Innocenti adopted an entirely egg-shaped control held on by only two screws.

Facing page, above. This three-quarters view of the first version of the Lambretta B is characterized by the light switch on the headlamp and by the wedge-shaped rear brake pedal. Looking closely at the right part of the handlebars, notice something that most Lambretta collectors fail to see: the black bakelite horn button, made by Argoradio of Varese, Italy, is in the form of a short cone and is attached to the handlebars by a small piece of nickel-plated metal.

Facing page, below. This lateral view of a second version of the Lambretta B shows how the boxy frame derived directly from the Lambretta A.

The Lambretta 125 B was the natural evolution from the A, but received much more fanfare at the magnificent unveiling ceremony in December 1948. The B boasted numerous mechanical and structural improvements and finally had the elastic rear suspension connecting with a joint from the transmission crankcase. To make for an even smoother ride, the front suspension was changed from the rubber ring model to two compressed cylindrical springs. The gear shifter was moved from the floorboards to the left handlebar which would spin to control the movement of the gearbox via a patented flexible "Teleflex" shaft. The wheel size was slightly enlarged to eight inches, giving a little more stability.

Other smaller changes made for a more functional scooter: moving the control cables outside of the tubes and making them much easier to change; a larger gas tank, allowing the rider to go further on one tank; and the position of the handlebars was changed and the saddle was raised, giving the driver a more comfortable ride.

With this model, Innocenti introduced metallic paint in four different shades for its scooters. Strangely, future models weren't offered with this option, and consumers had to wait until 1963 before they could get a metallic finish on their stock scooters. Since the Lambretta 125 B was very mechanically advanced compared to its nearest competitor, the Vespa, it drew a huge amount of interest both on the national market and in the international sector. The B was successfully exported to the most important markets outside of Europe: Australia, India, Egypt, South America, etc. The agents in these areas would be authorized in the 1950s and '60s to assemble and sometimes even construct their own Lambrettas under license from Innocenti.

During the 14 months of construction, the Lambretta B received a few slight improvements that were enough to classify two distinct versions. The first could be recognized by the same light switch as the Lambretta A, by the brake cover with the internal control, and by the wedge-shaped rear brake pedal. The second version was obvious because of the light switch by the gas lever, the brake cover with the external control, and the pointed rear brake pedal.

The Lambretta 125 B ushered in the real dawn of Italian scootering that would blossom in the 1950s: tourist groups or solo riders taking long trips, large scooter rallies of only one

68

Acquista una Lambretta
e spendi la differenza

brand, and the founding of the first Lambretta clubs. In 1949, the official Innocenti *Notiziario Lambretta* hit the shelves as the official newsletter of Lambrettismo in Italy and abroad. Each issue gathered technical information from experts and articles on the wildest Lambretta riders and their recent feats. In the racing arena, the B achieved numerous successes, especially in setting world speed and endurance records, which gave this little Lambretta the honor to adorn itself with the coveted symbol of speed "la freccia azzurra" (the blue arrow). The B was a success in the commercial sector as well. Finally, Innocenti was able to balance its books since the initial price of setting up the production line for the A model cost far more than initially thought. In spite of this success, it wasn't enough to prolong the brief life of the B longer than 14 months. A new completely redesigned series based on a well-planned market strategy took the B's place.

LAMBRETTA 125 C-LC

In 1950, Innocenti radically renewed the design of the Lambretta and offered, for the first time, two different versions to satisfy of the now huge scooter market. With the popular new C model, it became the most economic scooter on the national market, and still kept its sturdiness, reliability, and overall superior quality.

The steel tube frame was one of the principle esthetic qualities of the new Lambretta. The suspension was thanks to large springs with direct action integrated on both wheels, which were enlarged to 4.00 x 8 inches to further the comfort and road handling. The braking system finally had an overhaul and adopted the traditional system of brake lining mounted on the brake shoes and an aluminum drum that

Facing page, above right. The motor of the Lambretta 125 B incorporated the rear suspension of the wheel.

Below right. A small company from Milan built this curiously-shaped sidecar especially to be mounted on a Lambretta B.

Left. This painting was one of the most famous Innocenti ad campaigns to promote the Lambretta B.

This page, above. This pre-series Lambretta 125 C was photographed to help prepare publicity material to accompany the official commercial launch of the revised model.

Below. This Lambretta C has been completely restored and is obviously the first version because of the same gearbox as the previous model B.

Above left. Numerous accessories that were popular at the time are mounted on this Lambretta, including front and rear bumpers, front rack connected to the steering column, and dual saddles with the front one having a special seat cover.
Above right. Two more important options on this scooter were the spare tire rack with a protective wheel cover, the odometer, and tachometer.
Side. Peculiar characteristics of the second version of the Lambretta C were the shield-shaped gearbox and the handlebar levers that were far easier to use. This photograph shows the exact position of the rear fender before a license plate was required in Italy.

was tightly secured to help to disperse the heat.

The Lambretta C was immediately a favorite with the public, helped by its low selling price, and surpassed even the most rosy predictions of sales. People were lined up in front of the dealers to sign a reservation for a C; usually they had to pay installments before they were the bona fides owner. Production was finally able to keep up with demand. 3,000 units of the Lambretta B had been produced every month, but production of the C and LC soared to between 7,000 to 8,000 scooters monthly.

The success of these two new models was enormous

throughout Europe as well. So much that the German company NSU, one of the largest producers of vehicles in the world, asked Innocenti if it could produce Lambrettas under license for the German market. It's interesting to note that within Italy the C was by far the most popular scooter, while abroad the luxurious LC dominated sales even in poorer countries like Morocco and Egypt.

The LC had an elegant body with slender and aerodynamic styling that would protect the rider from the grime of the motor and the weather. The forced air from the fan helped the engine stay cool and give out constant power.

The production of the C series lasted about two years, during which time various technical modifications were introduced—such as the gear shifter and the handlebars. The first version could be identified because of the gear shifter box and the levers on the handlebar, which were both identical to the one on the B series. The second version shrunk the handlebar levers to make them easier to use, and the gearbox no longer had a boxy shape but resembled a small shield.

The choice of color schemes was reduced to just three shades, none of them metallic. Both versions of the C series came in a choice of blue, green, and tan; only a few of the very first Lambretta Cs to come off the assembly line were painted dark red like the 125 A.

Above left. The motor of the LC was identical to that of the C except for the air conveyer to force cool air and the air filter with external scoop.

Above right. Today, we would call this LC "loaded with options," which was prepared by a special accessory company for a motorcycle show. The rear glovebox is particularly useful since it doubled as the spare tire holder and takes advantage of the streamlining of the LC's bodywork, which couldn't be said for the economic C model.

Side. The Longhi company outside of Milan produced this elegant and luxurious sidecar to be mounted on a Lambretta through three solid bars anchored to the scooter's frame. This fun form of transportation could comfortably haul three people, and offered Italian families a valid substitute for the invincible automobile.

73

The plexiglass windscreen was no longer available, but at the same time other features were offered as options: a spare tire holder, extra floorboards for the passenger, and a large glovebox which replaced the little one on the Lambretta C.

The C series was the last Lambretta to be sold without a license plate holder in Italy since at the end of 1951, a new law was passed that required motor vehicles with an engine larger than 50cc to be licensed. For this reason, the rear fender wasn't designed to hold the plate until the D series was introduced. In November 1951, production of the C was halted after more than 100,000 units were made.

LAMBRETTA 125 D AND LD

After a couple of years of honorable service in the ranks of scooterdom, the Lambretta C was retired and the torch was passed on to a new model that had been thoroughly redesigned in terms of the mechanical system and the suspension. The new Lambretta was presented to the world on the 15th of December 1951 near the "Centro Studi" offices of the Innocenti factory by the engineering director Lauro and the son of the founder, Luigi Innocenti.

The selling points of the new D and LD versions were better suspension and comfort and more power and security. The lines of this new Lambretta were essentially the same as the preceding model, except that the whole scooter was lengthened slightly to make room for the new suspension system and other small modifications.

Facing page:
Above left. This pre-series Lambretta LC was photographed in the exposition hall of the *Centro Studi* at the Innocenti factory. An interesting feature is the rack attached to the rear in place of the pillion pad, but fitting with the lines of the scooter to keep the spare tire in its original position.
Above right. One of the most popular accessories mounted on Lambrettas was the air scoops on the side panels.
Below right. The opening on the right side panel accessed the gas tank and the air filter.
Below left. This photo makes it clear how the front legshield was stamped out in just one piece of metal.
This page:
Above. This first version of a Lambretta 125 D has been completely restored since its original construction at the beginning of 1952. This series can be set apart from the following version because of the rear rod brakes, the C-style seat, and the sleek covering of the front suspension.
Below. This example was built towards the end of 1952 and can be considered somewhere between the first and second versions since it already had the bowden rear brake cables, the front seat with the tube-shaped toolbox below it but still had the chrome handlebars and the little front brakes.

Side. The new D and LD series was presented to journalists from all over the world in December 1951 at the exposition room of the *Centro Studi* at the Innocenti factory. To make the scooter even more attractive, white sidewall tires were added, even though normal black tires were mounted when the scooter went into full production.

Below. This is the first version of the motor and suspension of the Lambretta 125 D. The engine acted also as the swing arm and was controlled by a torsion bar running crosswise from the frame. On the side of the rear brake covering can be seen one of the ends of the torsion bars covered by a rubber hood to protect it from dust.

The most important improvement is without a doubt the completely redesigned propulsion system. The transmission was simplified, and the cooling system was enlarged—to ensure the efficiency of the scooter even in the most difficult conditions—and was attached to the frame by a solid pivot pin which served also as the swing arm for the rear suspension. The rear wheel was positioned across from the engine and was held by a torsion bar crosswise to the frame under the motor, which gave a comfortable ride and variable flexibility.

To keep the swing connecting rod system for the wheel, a front shock was added on the front of the scooter. The springs were housed inside the tubes of the front fork and all the movable parts of the suspension were hermetically sealed in oil to be protected from water and dust.

The exhaust system was also revised by enlarging the muffler and changing the composition of the material inside, thereby reducing the overall noise of the scooter.

The D and LD series were certainly one of the most successful and most appreciated of all of Innocenti's production. Sales were exceptional and for many people, this series would remain the most perfect of all Lambrettas.

In 1953, the series underwent numerous mechanical improvements including an expansion of the front brakes, aluminum handlebars, plastic levers, motor supports made of rubber to dull vibrations, and control of the rear brakes by bowden cables.

Besides these technical modifications, the bodywork of the LD was revised with a small plastic shield placed on the front legshield, and oval-shaped grilles on the side panels to

Above. At the 1952 Milan Fair, Innocenti showed one of the first series of the Lambretta 125 LD. One of the highlights of the stand was the huge chrome wheel in the background, which would spin electrically and simulate the rough ground that the scooter would ride over to show the crowds how well the suspension worked.

Side. With one superficial glance, the new LD looks almost identical to the preceding LC, but many small things are in reality quite different. The front legshield is wider and stamped from two different pieces of metal. The two holes in the side panels have thinner edges and are set further apart, and the strips on the floorboard are now chromed with ridged pieces of rubber inserted to prevent slippage. A more radical evolution from the LC would be evident when the LD '53 was presented.

Side. By revising numerous esthetic details, the Lambretta LD became the LD '53 in 1953, but the very first of these new models still had the same two-holed side panels of the earlier version. Behind the front legshield, the hook for carrying the passenger's bag disappeared, but at the same time four holes were made, which made it possible to mount a large glovebox.

Below. The last version of the LD came at the beginning of 1954 with a few esthetic and functional improvements. The first was a larger green-colored seat with a closed front. The second change was to move the toolbox from under the seat inside the panels. Lastly, two rubber covers were applied to the handlebars to protect the cables. During this period, the D and LD series adopted molded plastic handle grips that would be used until the beginning of 1958.

Lambretta 125 ld/53

Razionale utilizzazione della potenza del motore
Frenatura pronta ed efficace
Stabilità del veicolo
in qualsiasi condizione di marcia

allow heat to escape. Innocenti also offered the possibility to mount a practical glovebox on the rear part of the side panels.

With these numerous modifications to the LD, this new version became officially known as the LD '53, whereas the D model didn't undergo any name change to identify the new model.

Strangely, the earlier LD from 1952 was offered in three different colors, gray, green, and tan, but the updated LD '53 was only available in gray. The more economic Lambretta D was still available in all three paint schemes.

Other changes that were introduced in 1954 mostly concerned the different color of the saddle, from brown to dark green, and two indicators on the handlebars for the clutch and the front brakes. Another added option offered in 1954

was the electric start via a 6 volt battery placed in front of clutch cover. A small plastic lever on the handlebars near the gear shifter controlled the ignition of the electrical system. On this luxurious model, larger and more comfortable seats were mounted as well as two gray plastic sheaths covering all the control cables. These improvements were soon introduced on the normal LD version as well.

It's interesting to note that during the first year of production, the economic D model was far ahead in sales, more than double that of the LD. In 1954, the tables had turned and the LD sold a few thousand more than the D. By the end of 1954, Innocenti introduced the new Lambretta D and LD 150, leaving the 125cc version to become the Lambretta F. At the same time, the fantastic production of the 125 D and LD ceased after three years of unbeatable sales records, which was a very important commercial success for Innocenti.

Above right. This present-day photo portrays a beautiful LD decked out with an electric starter. This is one of the very first produced of this version because it wasn't equipped with a key starter attached to the central section of the rear bodywork.

Above left. This advertising brochure announced the launch of the LD with electric starter.

Below left. The Innocenti *Centro Studi* development area had this six-volt starter motor built by the Becme factory in Genoa, Italy.

LAMBRETTA 125 E

The politics within the Innocenti company to lower costs as much as feasibly possible came to a head in 1953 with the presentation of the Lambretta 125 E, which was offered at the incredibly low price of only 108,000 Italian lira. To give an idea of the competition, however, we must remember that the 125 Vespa U model was selling for 130,000 Italian lira, and the very popular Motom moped was going for the respectable price of 102,000 Italian lira.

The long and difficult project finally put this super economic Lambretta on the road was the subject of many bitter discussions between the design department and the sales department. The commercial price of the E could under no circumstances surpass 108,000 Italian lira—an amount for which the design department said was impossible to produce a reliable scooter.

In the end the engineers were shown to be correct. The Lambretta E proved to be extremely delicate mechanically and the suspension (especially the front) was mediocre at best. Most of all, this technically inferior scooter darkened the Innocenti name, which had once been associated as a guarantee of high quality and reliability for its entire Lambretta line. Even if it looks stylistically similar to the 125 D, the E was a completely new design down to the smallest details. The legshield, the seat support, the rear fender and license plate

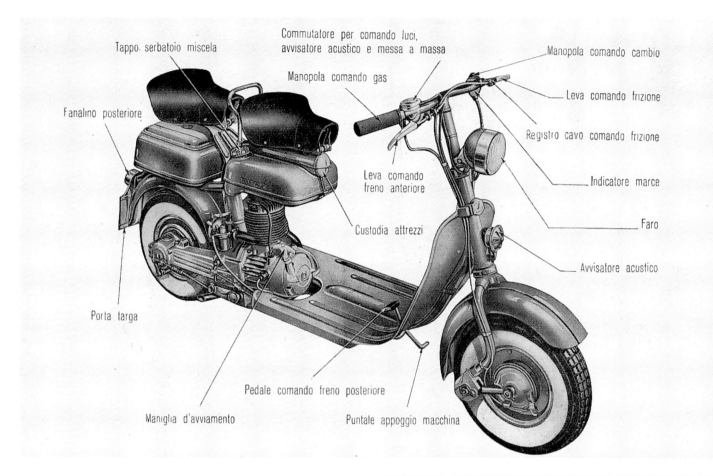

Tappo. serbatoio miscela

Commutatore per comando luci,
avvisatore acustico e messa a massa

Manopola comando gas

Manopola comando cambio

Leva comando frizione

Fanalino posteriore

Registro cavo comando frizione

Indicatore marce

Leva comando
freno anteriore

Faro

Custodia attrezzi

Avvisatore acustico

Porta targa

Pedale comando freno posteriore

Maniglia d'avviamento

Puntale appoggio macchina

Side. The user's main-
tenance guide showed
all the accessories and
the specific controls of
the scooter. To keep
production costs at a
bare minimum, the
electrical potential of
the magneto was low-
ered to the lowest level
allowed for motorcy-
cles, only 15 watt,
which caused the head-
lamp to constantly be
very dim.
Below. Close inspection
of the motor from the left
side shows an elegant
characteristic not typical
of economic motorscoot-
ers: a chromed exhaust
pipe. On the right of the
tube is the rubber bush-
ing which connected the
motor to the frame.

holder were all welded to the frame, which was formed by a
single steel tube. The dual arms of the front fork were angled
backwards, the shocks were redesigned with blade springs
wrapped around a split ring, and the wheel rims were made
out of one piece of stamped metal.

The most interesting part, however, was the engine mounted
with the shaft situated longitudinally that reduced the number
of transmission parts needed and improved the mechanical
performance at the same time. The pull-string starter was just
like an outboard motor. To start the engine, the driver would
have to pull the plastic handle upwards but be careful not to
tip the whole scooter off of its flimsy side stand. This complicated operation was too difficult for scooter novices or the delicate hands of a young lady, so many accessory companies soon
offered a conversion to turn the E into a kick-starting scooter.
The Achilles' heel of the Lambretta E was definitely its magneto and the starter. In the eleven months in which the E was
built, seven different types of magnetos were used and three
various spark plugs without ever definitely resolving the aw-
ful electrical system and the annoying tendency of the scooter to backfire upon starting.

Above left. This was one of the last Lambretta 125 Es built at the end of 1953 recognizable because of the glovebox with side hooks and the front tube that helped support the front fender to reduce vibrations.

Center. Two views of a Lambretta E from mid-1953 show the extreme simplicity of the construction of every part of the scooter to keep costs as low as possible.

Above right. Seen from the right side, the motor block and transmission shows this bare-bones longitudinal structure of the engine.

Below. This brochure folded out to show all the new models from 1953.

With all of these problems, the one highlight of the Lambretta E was its extremely good gas mileage; it could go more than 60 kilometers on a mere liter of mixed gas and oil. In a gas consumption test by *Motociclismo* magazine in 1954, an expert motorcyclist was able to drive an E getting 86 kilometers per liter of gas.

The initial enthusiasm that the Lambretta E garnered as "the scooter for everyone" was soon followed by numerous complaints and unsatisfied consumers who expected much higher quality from Innocenti. Because of the clamor against the E, the company was forced to take the model off of the market less than one year after its debut. The last batch of Lambretta Es were modified with a pedal starter and put on the market as the new version of the Lambretta F.

And so ends an ugly chapter in the history of the Lambretta, but one that was a warning to Innocenti and would help them learn to always strive for the highest quality in future models.

LAMBRETTA 125 F

Even after the Lambretta 125 E stunned Italy as a sensational commercial flop, Innocenti didn't give up with the idea of selling a super economic scooter. At the beginning of 1954, the Lambretta 125 F was presented to the world at the same low price of 108,000 Italian lira.

This new model was essentially a refurbished 125 E conserving all of its positive technical attributes, such as its high gas mileage and its performance. The outboard motor styled pull-start string was finally thrown out and replaced by a kick starter; the rear dual cones were mounted on ball bearings; and the shifting was smoother and more immediate due to an improved clutch. Most of the first 125 Fs off the production line were actually refurbished 125 Es, and its not uncommon

Two views of the second series of the Lambretta 125 F fitted with just a few updates compared to the first series to try and sell off the remaining early models, which were sitting in the warehouse and no longer produced. Besides the improvements written about in the text, the steering lock was now attached to the headlamp switch.

Right. The very first 125 Fs, like this one, were put on the market in 1954 and still used the same saddles as the E and the chromed handle behind the front seat for the passenger. For a very short time, the seats were redone in brown, but the color was soon changed to dark green on the same frame as before.

Below. Just a few months after its debut, the Lambretta 125 F received its first important improvement: more comfortable dark green seats that had already been thoroughly tested on the 125 D.

to still find the "E" written on the frame with the bottom line scratched off to look like an "F".

After just a few months, this new model was modified with a new elegant color, dark green, and the seat was changed to be the same as the 125 D.

At the beginning of 1955, to sell off the remaining stock in the factory, a second version of the 125 F was released calling it the second series. Coinciding with the debut of the Lambretta 48 moped, this new model was officially presented to the public in mid-1955 and had many technical improvements, more comfort, and a more reliable motor.

To perfect this model, Innocenti gave it the more efficient fork and front fender of the 125 D, the handlebars were raised slightly to improve the position of the driver, and the electrical system was made more powerful by adding a high-powered coil and condenser next to the magneto.

In spite of these important improvements to the Lambretta 125 F second series, it couldn't shed the unfortunate scar left by the ill-fated 125 E. Sales slumped, and the figures couldn't justify keeping the 125 F on the market. At the beginning of 1956, production was halted after less than one year from the F's debut.

LAMBRETTA 150 D AND LD

Since Innocenti was always listening to the demands of the ever-expanding scooter market, it chose the 1954 Motosalone Internazionale di Milano to unveil the new 150 D and LD, which derived from the ever-popular 125 D and LD. The new versions of this classic model were offered in the same two categories: the economic 150 D and the luxurious covered 150 LD.

The expanding displacement of the engine and the resulting power gain was a step forward for the Lambretta, especially the covered version since the weight of the sidepanels and its lack of wind resistance slowed it down considerably. The additional power of the 150 engine, now at approximately six horsepower, wasn't used to raise the overall speed of the scooter, but to improve the shifting of the

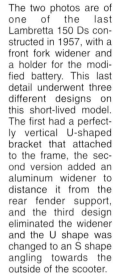

The two photos are of one of the last Lambretta 150 Ds constructed in 1957, with a front fork widener and a holder for the modified battery. This last detail underwent three different designs on this short-lived model. The first had a perfectly vertical U-shaped bracket that attached to the frame, the second version added an aluminum widener to distance it from the rear fender support, and the third design eliminated the widener and the U shape was changed to an S shape angling towards the outside of the scooter.

Near right and below. On the 1955 model, the exhaust system was equipped with an extra chromed, cylinder-shaped expansion chamber, which, apart from reducing the noise of the engine, angled the exhaust away from the scooter leaving the crankcase clean of grime. The central muffler was completely detachable to be able to clean the inside. Its covering was burnished, while the attached tube was completely chromed. The little round covering under the rear seat was the electrical rectifier that recharged the small six-volt battery.

Above right. The Lambretta 150 D first series was mostly recognizable because of the absence of the electrical current rectifier and the battery. Close observation of the motor reveals the different position of the hydraulic shocks and the different shape of the starter cover.

gears, the acceleration, and its power in climbing hills. The new and improved gear ratio allowed the scooter to make it up a 35% grade hill and pass most terrain without a problem.

The forced-air cooling system of the covered LD version was also put on the economic 150 D to ensure a constant temperature for the engine even in the worst weather conditions.

The characteristic rear suspension of the torsion bar attached to the swinging motor had already been thoroughly tested on the 125, but had the welcome addition of an efficient hydraulic, telescopic shocks that made the overall

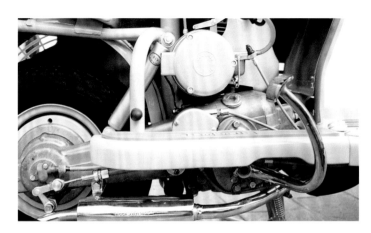

Above left. This close-up of the Lambretta 150 LD motor from 1955 shows that for the first time the crankcase wasn't painted in aluminum but left in its natural color. The only two remaining pieces that were still painted were the box that received the control cables and the air filter cover. All the little metallic odds and ends of the scooter were covered in cadmium, while the bronze oil plugs were still covered in nickel. The little black cylinder visible at the base of the tube above the floorboards was a rubber buffer to prevent vibration for the side-panels.

Below. In this side view of a 1955 LD, the plastic ivory-colored side air vent that released hot air from the engine can be seen. Later, towards the middle of 1956, other vents made of stamped or chromed metal were substituted but always kept the same shape. The taillight on the new 150 series was similar to the preceding 125. The light bulb holder, on the other hand, was no longer incorporated into the license plate holder but was now a separate piece. The hook to carry a bag located under the front seat was an accessory not made by Innocenti.

Above left. An English accessory company decked out this original Lambretta with an unusual fiberglass body. Above right. This top view clearly shows the protective coverings for the control cables. The glovebox on the 150 LD series was equipped with a tachometer, odometer, and a place to add a clock as an accessory. Bottom right. This rare 125 LD was derived from the 150 LD design, but received an inferior finishing compared to the larger model. On the example in the photograph, the rubber protection on the torsion bar is missing, and the muffler is from an LD '57.

The electrical schematics for the Lambretta 150 LD were improved because of the new electrical starter. One year after it was introduced, Innocenti revisited the battery-run electrical system because of so much demand from foreign markets. After the meager results of the first six-volt model in 1954, Innocenti preferred the twelve-volt system, which used dual six-volt, thirteen Ohm batteries. The two batteries were placed under the rear saddle and enclosed in a metal cover that was painted the same color as the body. The main switch was a key starter and was located in the middle of the glovebox behind the front legshield, while the electrical control was still on the left side of the handlebars.

handling more comfortable and safe even on the most uneven surfaces.

With the new 150 series, the Lambretta lost once and for all the Teleflex rod-shifting system and adopted the classic double bowden cables, which were universal for all major producers of motorcycles and scooters at that time. Innocenti also changed the exhaust system by adding an expansion chamber to further reduce the noise. A large air filter was put on the carburetor and another jet was added to aid starting. The gas control and electrical system was improved by control lights on the dash. Furthermore, the control for the opening of the gas tank and the starter were now positioned on the outside of the bodywork under the front seat. An option that was now standard was a convenient glovebox behind the legshield with a tachometer on the top and an optional clock.

In the slightly more than two years in which it was produced, the Lambretta 150 received numerous improvements almost monthly. The unfortunate part that tormented scooter drivers was undoubtedly the starter. Innocenti modified the whole system at least four times without ever being able to totally solve the problem.

To adapt to the new standards of the Italian highway laws, the Lambretta 150 was equipped with a six volt battery and rectifier at the end of 1955. Apart from being able to have

the headlights on while the motor was turned off, the new battery improved the overall performance of the scooter.

In the middle of 1956, the chromed expansion chamber on the exhaust was done away with and replaced with a more economic and robust muffler.

Also in 1956, a new version of the LD was offered with a 125cc motor but with the same overall structure as the 150 LD. Innocenti cut corners to offer this version at a more affordable, competitive price. The protective covers for the handlebar cables were eliminated, the electrical system was simplified by eliminating the battery, the glovebox behind the legshield wasn't standard, and cheaper seats were used. Even the 150 D version was built in smaller numbers, probably for the Swiss market.

The top-of-the-line, luxury 150cc version with electric start was requested by a few of the larger exporters in mid-1956 for the foreign market. Between 1956 and 1957, 5,000 units of a special version of the 150 LD were built just for the English market.

At the end of 1956 production of the 150 D stopped, which was the end of an era for Innocenti. It was the last "uncovered" Lambretta that saw the light of day, a tradition that began in 1947 with the 125 A. The LD, on the other hand, would continue to be built in a new version known as the LD '57.

LAMBRETTA 125-150 LD '57

The Lambretta 125 LD '57 shown here was one of the first produced since it still had the muffler with the short end from the 1956 version. Like the earlier models of LD, the finishing touches on the scooter varied in quality according to the size of the engine. The 125cc version was the most economical with aluminum molding and didn't have the odometer and the rear hydraulic shocks. It was offered in only one color, light gray, which was called "earth gray" in the brochures. Compared to its 150cc big sister, the 125cc had a reduced gear ratio and an 18mm carburetor as opposed to the larger 19mm. Perhaps most importantly, the smaller version didn't have the electrical system with a battery and current rectifier.

The latest version of the extremely popular Lambretta LD was presented to the press on the 2nd of February 1957 in the well-lit rooms of the *Centro Studi* area of the Innocenti factory. The two hostesses to launch the new model were film starlets Edy Campagnoli and Marisa Borroni.

During the introduction, the engineer and sales director Tomasi traced the entire sales records for the almost ten years of Innocenti's lead of the scooter world. At this point, more than one million units had been produced, of which 200,000 were export-ed around the world. More than 4,000 working machines to produce these vehicles were set up in the Innocenti industrial complex. The entire factory area measured one million square meters, all under the management of the president of the company, Ferdinando Innocenti.

With the nickname "'57," the LD would be the last shaft-driven Lambretta with dual cones produced, a design which stemmed from the very first Lambretta 125 A. Afterwards, Innocenti preferred the more simple and economic system of a chain-driven

transmission sealed in oil. The new LD '57 had the advantage of numerous mechanical and esthetic improvements, which made it an exceptionally reliable and elegant scooter. One important modification concerned the starter, which was completely redesigned using a epicyclical wheel with cylindrical gears that improved the ratio between the range of the kickstarter and the rotation of the motor. This new mechanical piece together with the larger kickstarter resolved once and for all the starting problems of the LD, which up until that point never worked well.

Above. The LD '57's motor was obvious because of the large, oval starter box of which there were two types: the first with oil lubrication, and the second lubricated by grease, and was situated next to the pivot for the pressurized lubricator. The only part of the engine that was painted in aluminum was the box that received the command cables, while the air filter cover remained its original metallic color like the rest of the engine block.

Side. With the new '57 LD series, the scooter lost the cute plastic Innocenti coat-of-arms that was attached to the front legshield. In its place, a more conventional chromed lettering was placed. A plastic "Innocenti" was added in the center of the front above the headlamp. The chrome "eyelid" above the front headlamp was stock, but this was the only time that Innocenti would add this slick accessory to its scooters.

Another interesting mechanical innovation on the LD was the air intake for the carburetor placed under the rear seat. This allowed the air to enter a small chamber before hitting the air filter and helped to diminish the obnoxious noise of the carburetor typical on the older models. The last but not least important of the improvements were a covering over the drum brakes to prevent them from getting dirty and a longer tube at the end of the muffler to further distance the motor from the exhaust.

The most noticeable modifications to the bodywork were the handlebars and the glovebox. The former was improved with an elegant aluminum finish that now contained the tachometer and the horn. The glovebox was shifted from behind the front legshield to behind the rear saddle and was incorporated into the frame.

The electrical system was improved as well with better-working and more efficient electrical switches, a larger taillight, and a chrome anti-reflective "hood" on the front headlamp.

The 150cc version was offered by Innocenti on the Italian market in an elegant two-tone paint scheme.

The base color of the scooter was still light gray, but the buyer could choose the color of the side panels, horn cover, and handlebars between: blue, red, beige, and green.

On the electric-starting version, the battery was placed in the now-useless rear compartment, so an extra glovebox was added behind the front legshield, like on the previous 150 LD model. The Lambretta 150 LD with electric start was only built for a few months, totaling 4,000 units mostly for the foreign market. Only 52 of the 125 LDs were built with an electric starter—probably for an important foreign dealer. The extremely low demand for the model with an electric starter convinced Innocenti not to offer it again as an accessory on the LD.

Production of the LD '57 ceased for good in July of 1958 after a total of 160,000 units had been produced of the two-sized scooters.

During the last period of production, Innocenti prepared a small number of unassembled LD motors to send to India in an effort to begin production of the first Lambrettas built under license in the Far East.

Facing page. The Lambretta 150 LD '57 claimed the title of being the first model offered in two-tone paint scheme on the Italian market. This page, above left. This original sidecar was constructed by an English firm especially for the Lambretta 150 LD '57. A series of these sidecars were built for the British police.
Above. This electric-starting Lambretta was destined for the German market since it had such a large license plate holder.

LAMBRETTA 175 TV

Once the powerful, speedy, and successful Vespa 150 GS hit the market, the management at Innocenti was forced to consider a super Lambretta to take on the supremacy of Piaggio in the field of racing scooters. With the release of a new model, Innocenti made a break from the past since the bodywork and mechanical system of this new Lambretta were completely redesigned.

On the 10th of April 1957, the new model was officially launched to coincide with the extremely modern exposition hall in the San Babila square in the center of Milan.

Surrounded by white and red azaleas revolving on a crystal platform, the Lambretta 175 TV immediately caught the public's eye at the fabulous presentation. Journalists from foreign magazines who had been invited for this event were especially thrilled since they had been waiting for a high-performance Lambretta for quite some time. With this new model, Innocenti opened a new chapter that would continue until the DL series of 1969.

The most notable change was the completely redesigned mo-

These two photos of a splendid Lambretta 175 TV were freshly restored and can be recognized as the first series since the controls are still on the handlebars, and it doesn't have the removable grille to access the horn. Notice the chromed edge of the wheel rims. In the beginning, the entire rim was chromed, but the locking nuts tended to come loose since the surface was too slick. Innocenti took the middle road and just chromed the outer edge while leaving the inside painted. The amount of chrome compared to the earlier LD was extremely modest, and the early 175 TV was only available in this ivory color with all the rubber mats and trim in light gray. A very small number of two-tone 175 TVs were produced with the front horn cover and the sidepanels in brown.

95

This prototype of the Lambretta 175 TV was nearly the final version. It was officially presented to the public in April 1957 at the avant-garde Innocenti exposition hall in the center of Milan in the Piazza San Babila. Only a few of this prototype were built, mostly to send to important foreign distributors to test and approve. Looking closely at the scooter reveals the interesting position of the starter control lever and the gas control lever on the side of the long saddle. Also the brake lever and clutch lever on the handlebars is ivory color plastic.

tor, which was a total break from the old version. The new motor had a horizontally-aligned cylinder, the transmission used a dual chain, and the four-speed gearbox was always engaged.

Even the frame was totally renovated to make room for the new motor and the various parts—such as the glovebox, gas tank, and air duct—which were shifted around. For the first time on a Lambretta, the wheels now measured 10 inches in diameter and 3.5 inches wide.

The suspension was radically changed. The front was simplified by mounting the springs right on the axle. The rear got rid of the costly torsion bar and replaced it with the more traditional hydraulic shocks with a helical spring, like on most motorcycles.

The slick lines of the outside of the scooter were perhaps the most interesting part: the front fender no longer turned with the front wheel; the cast aluminum handlebars now incorporated all the control cables; and the front headlamp was finally enlarged with a brighter bulb.

The last improvements, and equally as important, were the bench seat (which was obviously to make the scooter look more sporty), and the enlarged surface of the brakes for added

Side. The taillight on the TV was now rectangular, which can be seen clearly in this photo. The plastic cover for the taillight was divided in three sections by small pieces of aluminum. The outside sections were orange and were lit by two small light bulbs that signaled when the scooter was stopping, whereas the center section was red and worked as the brake light and running light.
Below. This right side view of the engine reveals the large rear shock that was painted the same color as the body of the scooter.

stopping power because of the overall increased performance of the new 175 TV.

Upon its debut, the TV was originally intended for export since foreign markets tended to prefer higher performance scooters. After all the intense interest in the new Lambretta in Milan, Innocenti decided to offer it on the Italian market as well.

During the time that the 175 TV was built, it underwent a few minor changes. Practical regulators with an internal pin were added on the handlebar levers for the brakes and clutch since they were so delicate (this feature wasn't included on the very last ones made). To access the horn, a small horn cover was added to the front. On the last 175 TVs produced, the rubber floormats were replaced by the more classic aluminum strips.

The expectations of the Lambretta 175 TV were achieved, but just a few months after it entered production already a few design flaws were revealed. Shifting was far too delicate and imprecise a process; the clutch was too small; and the transmission was too weak for the job. All these problems caused the premature halting of the production line after only a modest number of this scooter had been made.

LAMBRETTA 125-150 LI

The new LI series became an immediate success both in Italy and abroad after it was presented to the world in 1958. In being very careful about production costs, Innocenti was able to keep the price of the new 150 LI the same as the old 150 LD, while the 125 LI was actually 3,000 Italian lira cheaper—selling for a mere 132,000 Italian lira. The Vespa 125, meanwhile, was selling for 128,000 Italian lira, but lacked many of the superior qualities of its rival, the Lambretta.

Following the new path laid by the 175 TV, Innocenti radically renewed the LD model, which then became the LI available in the now classic sizes of 125 and 150cc. The new body was practically identical to that of the TV apart from the two single seats and the completely painted wheel rims. To differentiate the two-sized scooters, various chrome pieces were applied to each specific model. The 125 was sold in bluish-gray with the possibility of having dark metallic gray side panels. The 150, on the other hand, was available as a two-tone with a base of bluish-gray and a choice of red, blue, green or brown.

The mechanical system was conceptually the same as the 175 TV but was redesigned and simplified using a chain

The popular actors Lia Zoppelli and Enrico Viarisio testify in an ad for the new 150 LI which appeared in the Innocenti newsletter *Notiziario Lambretta* in 1958.

transmission. The gear shifter now used a smooth turning cross that was very reliable and efficient. These new features were applied with only slight changes on the LI and LD for the rest of their production.

As with the LD, the level of finishing touches depended on the size of the engine. On the 125cc version, the strips on the floorboards were made of stamped aluminum, some of the handles were just painted, and the odometer and rear seat were optional. On the 150, the strips on the floorboards also had strips of rubber, all the handles were polished, and the odometer and rear

Facing page, above. This pre-series Lambretta 150 LI was not yet equipped with all of the features that the final version would have.

Facing page, below. This beautiful blueprint shows the frame structure of the 150 LI drawn by Loiacono, the unequaled designer at the *Centro Studi* of Innocenti.

This page, above left. The top view of the 150 LI shows the aluminum handlebars that incorporated all the control cables.

Above right. An especially useful feature for everyday use is the rear rack built of chromed metal tubes and leaving enough room to slip the spare tire inside it.

Side. This Lambretta 125 LI was one of the first built since it had the two airducts on the front of the sidepanels, like those adopted on the first series of the 175 TV.

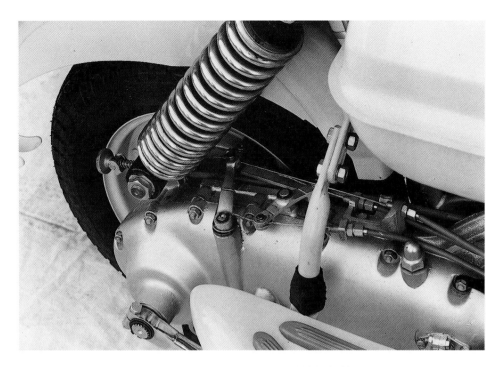

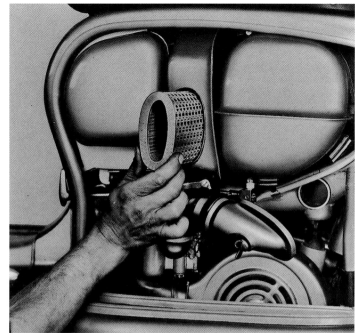

Above left. This close-up of the engine shows how the gear shifter system is set up on the new LI.

Above right. On the last version of the Lambretta LI, the air flow system was placed under the front seat.

Side. Upon opening the left side panel, the carburetor, the air flow system, and the electric box are all easily accessible. The electrical system consisted of the current rectifier, an electrical terminal, a fuse, and a coil.

Facing page, left. This Lambretta 150 LI was prepared for the German market since it had the long, dual-person bench seat, the spare tire, and the typical enlarged license plate holder.

Right. This beautiful photo of one of the early Lambretta 150 LIs was with the classic paint scheme of light gray from the first produced of this series.

seat were standard. Besides that, the 150 was equipped with an electrical current rectifier and a high-capacity six-volt battery.

Although this new scooter was radically different from its predecessor, the Lambretta LI was soon accepted by the huge scootering public and within a few months reached, but didn't surpass, the production levels of the glorious LD.

During the time of the LI's construction, constant but sometimes slight modifications were applied. Easily the most important change was the shift of the air duct for the carburetor below the front seat, the addition of a larger chamber for the air intake, and a paper filter like those on automobiles.

With ten-inch wheels and a four-speed gearbox, this speedy Lambretta LI became one of the best road-handling scooters with excellent acceleration and able to travel long distances without a problem.

The considerable power, ability to carry heavy loads, and exceptional mechanical reliability made the Lambretta LI the favorite for hauling heavy loads like gas cylinders and newspaper delivery. At the time of the introduction of the revamped LI second series in October 1959, the first LI would be identified as the first series.

LAMBRETTA 175 TV II SERIES

In this interesting cross-section, all the distinguishing characteristics of the new Lambretta 175 TV are visible: the motor directly derives from the 125-150 LI; the air filter system is different with the air duct located under the seat; and lastly, the shape of the handlebars is different and finally incorporates the headlamp, and turns with the front wheel. The construction of the muffler was improved significantly to reduce its noise with an efficient system of ducts aided by a sound muffling padding that lined the sides of the box.

Since Innocenti was extremely satisfied by the performance of the LI's motor, the new Lambretta TV was equipped with a larger version of that engine rather than trying to update the original TV motor, which didn't meet its original expectations. With this new engine and a few esthetic alterations, the Lambretta 175 TV became the Series II version and was officially inaugurated at the beginning of 1959.
Compared to its predecessor, this new version lost a little bit of power for a more functional shifting system even though

the actual displacement was increased from 170cc to 175cc by changing the size of the bore and stroke.
The new version was lighter—a sensible move to make the power to weight ratio more favorable—with the top speed over 100 km/h and a reduction in its gas consumption.
The air-flow system was considerably simplified by using a paper filter, which would need periodical changing.
The most interesting esthetic change was the return of the moveable front headlamp that shifted with the handlebars.

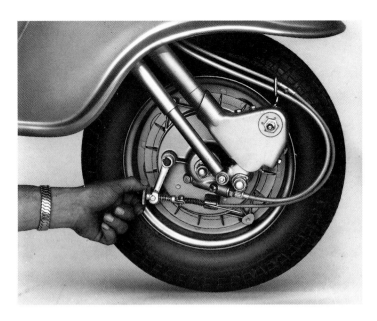

Above left. This close-up photo shows the front fork and hub of the TV Series II. To help reduce a brusque snap back of the suspension, hydraulic telescopic shock absorbers were mounted. This feature would remain on this model all the way through the 200 DL. To give the possibility to upgrade the smaller Lambrettas with this great feature, a few foreign companies and Innocenti offered a kit to adapt the front forks.

Above right and side. These two side views of the 175 TV Series II from the early stages of production, which can be recognized because of the smaller taillight and the round horn cover. Another interesting feature that isn't visible in the photo is that the rear frame contained a reinforcing plate that was welded to the entire length of the beam.

The first and most noticeable improvement given to the 175 TV Series II was the enlargement of the rear taillight. Later, the shape of the horn cover would be changed from round to oval to facilitate the replacement of the horn. To improve the sound of the scooter and reduce vibrations to the bodywork, some internal pieces were treated with an opaque black noise-dampening paint.

Beginning with the old 125 LC, Innocenti had decided that it preferred a staid front headlamp on all the fully-enclosed models, and not until ten years later did it realize that the moving headlight is safer and certainly more efficient than the fixed one.

With the introduction of this new handlebar unit, the brake and clutch levers were also modified to be the same as the LI series.

Probably to save expenses, the wheel rims were now completely painted the same color as the bodywork. Looking through the brochures of the time reveals that the actual price of the second series was reduced by 5,000 Italian lira compared to its predecessor.

As far as the paint schemes were concerned, the Italian market was offered two single colors, blue or mustard, and one two-tone version in sage and brown.

At the end of 1959, a bigger and brighter taillight was mounted to conform to the new Italian vehicular laws. At the same time, the horn was enlarged as well as the speedometer gauge. More than 40,000 units were sold, far exceeding expectations and making the 175 TV Series II one of the best-selling sporting scooters.

LAMBRETTA 125-150 LI SERIES II

Just a few days before the beginning of the 1959 *Salone del Motociclo* in Milan, Innocenti previewed the second series of the Lambretta LI in the nearby showrooms of the Minetti agency. The redone look of the LI followed in the footsteps of the already-introduced TV series II, and focused principally on the shifting of the front headlamp from the horn cover to the handlebars, so it would turn with the wheel and make driving at night much safer.

To conform to the new Italian vehicular laws, the second series of the LI improved the stopping power of the foot brake pedal. At this point as well, the odometer was made standard on both the 125cc and 150cc models.

A few mechanical improvements were made to the engine notably the piston being modified, so it would start more easily when cold and cut down on wear and tear. The connecting rod adopted a new system of enclosed tubular rollers on the top and bottom.

With these small but important changes, the Lambretta LI Series II could easily run on an oil-to-gas mixture of only two percent oil. But to avoid making a fool of yourself with a broken-down scooter, Innocenti recommended a hefty five percent oil-to-gas mix. Only after several months of testing did

The Lambretta 150 LI Series II was the best-selling model of the entire Innocenti production. In just a little more than two years, more than 162,000 units were constructed, with the record of producing 74 units per hour. The 150 was recognizable because of its elegant two-tone, which in certain cases didn't include the front horn cover. The base color remained "dawn gray" (light gray), while the side panels and horn cover could be in various hues: coral red, ruby red, "Nile green," and medium blue. Some versions of this scooter were also sold in just one color, "river gray." On the last of the second series of LI built, the air filter was held on by a long double spring.

Lambretta li 2ª serie

motore sezionato

INNOCENTI DIVISIONE MOTORI

Innocenti tell its dealers that the Lambretta could easily run on only two percent oil without any problems arising. This created a problem with the dealers of the first LI Series II and the reissue of this model since they were put in the embarrassing position of not knowing exactly what the correct oil-gas mix was supposed to be.

During 1960, the rear light was enlarged and made brighter and the horn was made louder. In 1961, the attachment of the air filter was simplified by mounting a double steel spring.

Once again, the finishing touches on the two-sized scooters varied, but this time the only difference was that the 125cc version had a single seat.

With more than 270,000 of the Lambretta LI Series II built, a new production record was set. The assembly line at Innocenti now put out 74 new scooters per hour.

Apart from regular production, Innocenti prepared parts that would be shipped to India, Brazil, Chile, and Argentina where they would be assembled by Innocenti factories there.

LAMBRETTA 125-150 LI SERIES III

Below. This Lambretta 150 LI Series III was cut in half to show the public the numerous good mechanical and structural qualities of the scooter at motorcycle expositions. Notice inside the gas tank the divisions to stop the fuel from sloshing around too much and compromising the stability of the scooter when the tank was full. This useful component, however, was also available on the preceding model. To help further reduce the noise of the engine, the muffler was enlarged, while retaining the same system of various chambers with sound dampening material on the walls.

In 1962, Innocenti radically revamped the Lambretta's lines and presented the third series of the LI in January of that year. With this new series, the Lambretta became more square yet still streamlined and much more modern and elegant. This was a classic example of industrial design applied to the production of an entire line of motor vehicles. Besides just showing the value of the Italian scootering "school of design," the new lines also helped solve many problems of aerodynamics that had presented themselves in earlier models.

The overall size of the bodywork was stylized and slightly smaller without making the scooter less comfortable or harder to handle. With this new bodywork, the Lambretta became

Be seen in the best places with the best people, be seen with the Lambretta 150 li - the scooter you **must** be seen with! Perfectly styled with sweeping aerodynamic lines. Fast, comfortable and economic. The 150 li has been designed for riding anywhere in the world - and the world is enjoying the 150 li! With this superb machine **power, performance** and **perfection** ride together.
Today the choice is Lambretta

known as the "scooter-lines," while in England it got named the "Slim Line."

Even the shape of the handlebars was smaller, but the size of the headlamp remained the same. The speedometer was now a trapezoidal shape and the shape of the electrical control box on the handlebars was reworked.

On the rear part of the scooter under the seat, the fake air duct was replaced with a plate that stated the model of the scooter and its emblem surrounded by an aluminum frame. The rubber runners on the floorboards now numbered four, down from six on the previous model, and the two outer ones were just plastic with the screws already inside of them.

Side. This Lambretta 150 LI Series III was completely restored to its original color of gray and "new blue." The seat is off of a 175 TV, which was the custom move that many scooterists used to do. Below. This folding advertisement of the LI 150 Series III was destined for the English market.

And when it comes to points of fashion - just take a look at these for the best in scooter-fashion!

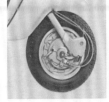

Expanding shoe brakes front and rear. Comfortable front suspension

Rear suspension comprising swinging engine unit with spring dampers

Stylish rear section with removable side panels

Streamlined front with latest handlebar design. Built-in illuminated speedometer

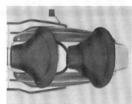

Safer, more comfortable riding positions for you and your passenger

The motor was essentially the same except for a small increase in the compression, which didn't raise the speed but gave the scooter a little more horsepower. The carburetor, on the other hand, was completely new with a central bowl that didn't use a conical jet, which improved the consistency of the performance of the engine and simplified its maintenance.

The last important mechanical change was the new larger capacity muffler that made the scooter much quieter without suffocating the engine and improved its performance.

With the introduction of the third series, the finishing touches on the bodywork were now identical between the two sizes of scooters, except for a few pieces that were polished aluminum on the 150cc version and painted on the 125cc model. As far as the paint schemes are concerned, the 125 was not offered as a two-tone. The consumer's color choices were sky blue or gray, and later light blue was added. The 150 came as a two-tone scooter with the side panels and the horn cover in "new blue," "coral red '63," and "sand beige," with the last two colors mostly for the foreign market. The LI Series III achieved the title as the most numerous Lambretta built, with production figures surpassing 480,000 in a little less than eight years (1962 to 1969). Proving how much experimentation and foresight went into this entire project, the LI Series III didn't receive any important modifications during its lifetime; only a few minor improvements to the assembly were ever changed.

Facing page, above. With the introduction of the third series, there were less differences of finishing touches between the two-sized scooters. The only remaining differences were the color schemes for the bodywork and a few pieces that were polished aluminum on the 150 and simply painted on the 125.

Facing page, below and centerfold. These two beautiful photos of the Lambretta 150 LI Series III are examples of some of the 140,000 units built between January 1962 and May 1967. It was certainly one of the most successful scooters, stylistically speaking. The bodywork wasn't excessive but was enough to keep the driver adequately protected from the elements.

Above. Opening the right side panel reveals how the entire engine was essentially the same as the preceding model.

LAMBRETTA 175 TV SERIES III AND 200 TV

With the slogan, "The one and only scooter in the world with disc brakes," the Lambretta 175 TV Series III became the sporting scooter known for excellence, brilliant performance, and extraordinary road handling. Even though there were numerous technical advancements compared to the second series, the selling price remained at 180,000 Italian lira, which showed how serious Innocenti was at competing in the marketplace. The two-tone paint scheme even included the front fiberglass mudguard. For aficionados of the single-colored scooter, Innocenti even offered an entirely white version, which can be seen in the ad on the facing page from a French brochure. It's important to remember that the extra front shocks on the third series were always painted in aluminum and not the color of the bodywork like on the first and second series.

Instead of following the tradition of first presenting the largest scooter of the line, Innocenti broke from the past and let the 125cc and 150cc Series III have their moment in the limelight before releasing the 175 TV version.

The bodywork of the new 175 TV Series III took the same lines as the smaller Lambrettas but with a few variations that made it even more sporty and elegant looking. The front fender was one of the most noticeable changes since it was more square and made of fiberglass. Other changes were the lowered horn cover, the octagonal-shaped headlight, and, as always, the long dual-passenger bench seat. Without a doubt the most interesting novelty was the mechanically-controlled front disc brakes that made the braking power adjustable and infinitely safer. This was a wise move since the front wheels on scooters were notorious for blocking up because the small diameter wheels didn't respond well to quick braking. With the new disc brakes, slowing down was much easier, and it became almost impossible for the brakes to freeze up.

The compression ratio of the motor was slightly updated, and the carburetor and the muffler were both enlarged. The overall performance of the engine was identical to its predecessor apart from a little better acceleration from a stop.

lambretta

175tv
le premier scooter au monde
équipé d'un frein à disque

Side. This drawing illustrates how the disc brakes made by Campagnolo for Innocenti work. The cast iron brakes remained suspended by three cylindrical columns, while the clamp was fixed to the side cover. On the opposite side, a resistance pad was mounted held by a lock bolt to keep it in perfect registration.

To satisfy the sporting market, a larger 200cc version of the TV was introduced in April 1963 in a few foreign markets (especially England). In some countries this new, high powered scooter was called the GT 200 but was identical to the TV 200. The 200cc version wasn't available at all in Italy, and impatient Italian Lambrettisti would have to wait until the beginning of 1966, when they could get their hands on a 200cc Lambretta.

Going back to the 175 TV, the side panels were changed

from the older model with new polished aluminum molding that were also put on the brand new 150 Special.

The old two-tone models—with a base of light gray and the side panels, horn cover and front fender in either coral red, light yellow, or dark gray—were no longer offered, but metallic blue was the only option.

At the end of 1965, the two sizes of the TV, 175cc and 200cc, were put out of production to make room for a new model that would be available exclusively as the 200cc version.

Facing page, below. Opening the left side panel reveals the unusual noise reducing treatment applied to the rear fender. To lessen the vibrations from the engine to the frame—particularly at high rpms—the engine holder was sensibly enlarged and attached to the outside of the crankcase. When replacing these, it's important to remember that the three holes in the rubber must be positioned very carefully.; the first one is in the lower part, and the other two towards the front of the scooter.

This page. These two beautiful photos are of the second version of the Lambretta 175 TV Series III. With this model, metallic paint was reintroduced that had previously been offered with the 125 B from 1949. The side panels with the polished aluminum ornaments were not in the least bit a novelty since they had already been tried on some pre-series versions in January 1962.

117

LAMBRETTA JUNIOR CENTO 125 THREE-SPEED AND 125 FOUR-SPEED

Below. Foreign markets received this promotional brochure for the Lambretta 125 Super Starstream.
Side. This scooter was almost the definitive version of the Lambretta Cento that was finished at the end of 1962. Only the very first to be released from the production line had dual seats like this one; later Centos had the more traditional dual-passenger single bench seat. The muffler on this version was painted black, while the actual stock version was aluminum colored.

To respond to the market demand for a simpler scooter with a cheaper price tag, Innocenti presented a completely new model of Lambretta in the spring of 1963 that would become the first in a series of economic scooters called "Junior."

For its conception, the design center at Innocenti was inspired by its competition at Piaggio. In fact, the whole frame of the scooter was conceptually very similar to that of the Vespa. The motor, on the other hand, was based on the LI, except that the cylinder was vertical rather than horizontal.

For the first time in Innocenti's history, a new model would be released with the unusual 98cc engine. Market research had revealed that this sized motor would be the right path to follow since it would satisfy different markets. Innocenti was soon proved wrong, and to attempt to fix the situation, soon offered a 125cc version as well. At first, the Cento was sold almost exclusively in foreign markets.

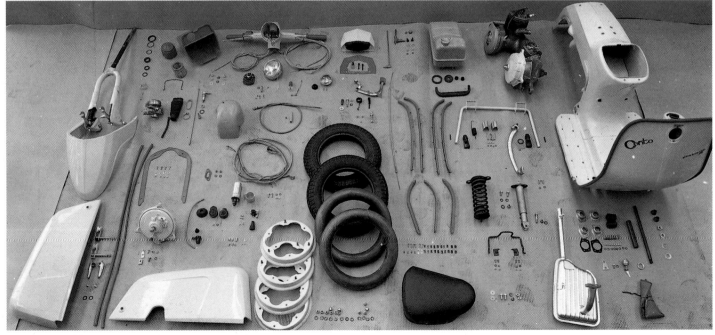

Above left. In this pre-production version of the Cento, the three-quarters view of the scooter reveals the "baby" emblem on the front legshield, which was used for some markets outside Italy. On the middle of the floorboards, the three rubber strips to prevent slipping were not yet mounted on the hump but would be applied as soon as the scooter went into production.
Above right. The rear part of the bodywork shows how square the lines were, especially compared to the central part of the scooter and the rounded shape of the front legshield.
Side. This interesting picture shows all the necessary components to make a Lambretta Cento.

Above left. Opening up the right side panel made all the principle parts of the engine accessible except for the magneto, which was on the opposite side. Large pieces of rubber were place inside of the rear shock to smooth the ride.

Above right and side. These are two views of the three-speed Lambretta 125 J in the classic metallic gray paint scheme. For this new model, Innocenti preferred to leave the look of the scooter exactly the same as the previous version—as if the selling of the 125 J were an effort to sell off the remaining stock of the relatively unsuccessful Lambretta Cento.

Later, perhaps because of a waning interest abroad, the scooter was sold also in Italy at the low price of 119,500 Italian lira.

The lines of the bodywork were based on the tried-and-true LI Series III, but at the same time some important differences separated the two models. The front horn cover of the LI was totally eliminated; the opening to the glovebox was moved under the seat; and the side panels were smaller compared to the size of the scooter.

The seats on the very first examples of the Cento put out by Innocenti were quadrangular but would soon be replaced by long, dual-passenger bench seats. To save on production costs for this model, Innocenti offered the scooter in only one color, light ivory.

As stated earlier, the motor derived from the LI but was further simplified. The primary transmission was a simplex chain and the gear ratio was reduced. The modest 4./ horsepower engine limited the performance of the Cento, so it couldn't even reach 80 km/h. The shoddy quality of the motor and the extremely fragile frame foreshadowed the premature end of the Cento in 1965 after only 17,642 units had been produced.

Facing page, above. This modern photograph shows a well-conserved, ivory-colored Cento. The long, classic bench seat complements the profile of the bodywork and can be raised to access the gas tank and the storage compartment.

Below. The new series of the four-speed Junior 125 with reinforced frame is pictured here on an alluring cover for a sales brochure.

This page. The Super Starstream was a very unique model since it was the first and only time in Innocenti's history that a certain model of Lambretta would be sold abroad without being at all available in its native Italy. The Super Starstream was based on the four-speed 125 J with an elegant two-tone paint scheme. The front fender turned with the wheel and the front horn cover looked like that on the TV and the Special.

Facing page. With the introduction in 1966 of the new reinforced frame for the 50 J, Innocenti also presented a new edition of the 125 J with the more sporty four-speed gearbox. This new version was nicknamed the *Stellina* (little star) because of the chromed star on the front legshield with the 125 emblem. The example in the photo has an enlarged front headlamp for lighting tests.

This page. Comparing the new Junior four-speed to the old version, this factory photo shows all the different shapes of the front legshields. The chrome writing on the four-speed version is not in its final form yet.

These two photos of a restored blue and white Lambretta 125 Super Starstream came from England. A red and white version was also sold but wasn't as popular as the former version.

To try and bounce back from unexpected commercial failure of the Cento, Innocenti presented a larger 125cc version in September 1964 with much improved performance both in the robust nature of the engine and its maximum speed of 80 km/h. The resilience of the motor was shown in the advertising campaign since the scooter was nicknamed *Superelastic* (Super resilient). Esthetically, the new 125 remained exactly the same as its little sister, except that a metallic gray color was offered.

To avoid the frame breaking, which happened all too often, the main internal tube was reinforced, but this didn't solve this grave defect once and for all. A final solution wouldn't see the light of day until 1966, when the frame would be entirely redesigned based on two years of research.

The Lambretta 125 Junior stayed on the assembly line for two years but was never able to reach the production levels that the successful LI had reached. Looking at the production figures suggests that 32 units of the LI were produced hourly compared to only 1/ of the Junior.

At the beginning of the summer of 1966, Innocenti debuted a new version of the 125 Junior with more aerodynamic and slick bodywork. The front legshield was smoother and therefore offered less wind resistance, while the rear was shaped to be more in uniform with the long seat. A small, chrome star was attached to the legshield with 125 written on it, which was the origin of the curious nickname *Stellina*, or "little star."

The performance of the engine was further improved. An extra gear was added allowing the *Stellina* to reach 87 km/h with ease.

As usual, the introduction of a new model called for a new paint scheme. The most common was the two-tone white and "ocean blue," but other colors were available mostly to satisfy the different tastes of the foreign market.

With the resolved structural problems of the frame and a more powerful engine, the Lambretta 125 J seemed sure to succeed, but once again was unable to catch the heart of the public. The overall disinterest in motorcycles and a selling price which was too near that of the larger model (the LI), probably added to this unsuccessful—but nevertheless attractive—scooter. In about three years of construction, only a few more than 16,000 were built.

To satisfy the specific requests of the English market, a small series of four-speed Lambretta Js were produced with a turning front fender and a small horn cover on the center of the legshield. This model was dubbed the "Super Starstream," while the normal version was simply called the "Starstream." Both versions were available in an elegant two-tone.

LAMBRETTA 150 LI SPECIAL AND X SPECIAL

Lambretta
INNOCENTI
150 li
SPECIAL

להנאה מלאה...

The cover of this Mideast-bound brochure shows the Lambretta 150 Special.

Just a little more than a year after the inauguration of the LI Series II "Slim Line," Innocenti presented a speedier version of the 150cc model at the 38th Salone di Milano motor show in 1963.

The new LI 150 Special was designed to satisfy the demand for a growing market of customers who wanted a fast and elegant scooter that stayed in the 150cc engine category.

With just a few important finishing touches to the bodywork, the Lambretta Special became a model that immediately conquered the critics' and public's heart both for its sleek and sporty lines and its top-ranked performance.

With a larger carburetor and modified distribution to the cylinder, the power of the scooter was increased without compromising the performance or fuel consumption. The gear ratios were slightly altered as well, so the Lambretta took off better from a stop and accelerated faster. These small but important modifications allowed the new Special to reach a considerable top speed of 92 to 95 km/h with the driver crouched down.

Another small mechanical innovation was the mounting of

Above left and side photos. "Every day and every Sunday drive with the 150 Special is a gift that you give yourself. A beautiful gift, elegant and refined, that you can also give to your girlfriend as you take her with you on a Lambretta painted those precious colors: silver and gold." With this text, Innocenti launched its 1965 ad campaign for the "Silver" and "Golden" versions of the well-tested Special 150.

Above right. A version of the 150 Special was prepared especially for the English market with two-tone side panels with metallic blue and "Pacemaker" written on the front legshield.

With the introduction of the X 150 version of the Lambretta Special, the paint scheme was no longer metallic but returned to the more conventional colors of "spring gray" and "field green." After an accurate test of the cylinder, the power of the motor was significantly increased to a record in its class of 9.39 horsepower. This compared to the more modest 7.1 horsepower of the Vespa 150 Sprint of the same period. Apart from the new chrome pieces on the front legshield, the Lambretta 150 SX adopted a different logo behind the seat by substituting "Special" with "Lambretta Innocenti" on a white background.

larger anti-vibrating supports to reduce to a minimum the engine vibrations to the bodywork. On the outside of the scooter, the lines were essentially those off of the 175 TV with: the octagonal headlamp, the more squared-off front fender, the slimmer and lowered front horncover, and the side panels decked out with polished aluminum decals.

For the first time on a 150cc model, the longer bench seat was standard. Although the seat is more uncomfortable than the single seats, racing scooterists preferred it. The last new feature was the new metallic paint schemes, which had originally been tested on the Lambretta 125 B but hadn't been used again on following models. To better identify the new model,

a chromed brass "Special" was attached to the right side of the front legshield, and the plastic plaque behind the saddle also had the new logo.

After three years of honorable service, the Special 150 was slightly revamped both in the bodywork and the engine. These small modifications were enough to change the name from 150 Special to X 150 Special.

The new version was presented to the media on the 26th of November 1966 near the *Centro Studi* Innocenti workshop in the Lambrate area of Milan. The voice of Doctor Rodecanati inaugurated the scooter with an exquisite gesture of camaraderie and these words, "I give my best wishes and saluta-

Side. This color photo of the 1963 Lambretta 150 Special was taken when it was released on the market. Offered at the especially low price of 163,000 Italian lira, the Special became, in just a short while, another success story for Innocenti. Taking the middle road between the expensive TV 175 and the economic LI 150, the Special 150 succeeded in conquering an important slice of the market that was already considered saturated. In its three years of production, almost 70,000 units of this scooter were produced in three versions: normal, "Golden," and "Silver."

tions to our loyal competitor Piaggio for the complete resumption of work that so honors our country."

Esthetically, the new X Special differed from its predecessor because of the horncover, a chrome piece on the front part of the sidepanels, and for the different writing on the front legshield. The metallic color was no longer offered—since it soon became obvious that it was such delicate paint—and the more normal colors of "spring gray" and "field green" were offered.

As far as the mechanical system was concerned, the engine was sensibly modified once again increasing its potential, reaching the remarkable amount of 9.38 horsepower at the same rate as 5600 rpms of the Special. With this improvement and a little retouching of the gear ratio, the Lambretta X 150 Special reached 98 km/h with the driver in an aerodynamic position. This velocity record kept it at the top of its category. During its entire production, which ended in January 1969, the scooter didn't undergo modifications apart from the substitution of the plastic front coat-of-arms with a chrome rectangular one. On the very last ones produced, the aluminum handles on the side panels were replaced with more economical spring-loaded hooks.

With more than 100,000 units produced, the 150 S and XS were certainly the last important commercial successes that Innocenti had (along with the DL, which couldn't be improved upon). In 1965, the scooters were offered in gold metallic paint, at which time the words "Golden" or "Silver" were mounted on the legshield above the "Special" logo according to the model.

Above. Another color snapshot taken when the scooter was released. This time it was the Golden version, which was advertised in 1965 with the enticing slogan, "What a flower this Lambretta is, and what a bouquet of colors! Golden and Silver."

LAMBRETTA 125 SPECIAL

Below and in the large photo. Using the same bodywork as the successful Special 150, Innocenti prepared a 125cc version at the end of 1965 aimed at the sixteen-year-old market. Unfortunately, its price of 150,000 Italian lira was too high compared to 139,000 Italian lira for the normal LI. Because of this, the 125 Special couldn't duplicate the success of its big sister and in its three years of production wasn't able to even surpass 30,000 units produced.

As the natural evolution of the 125 LI Series III, the Lambretta 125 Special was put on the market at the end of 1965 just in time for the annual motorcycle show in Milan. The new model was designed for a young audience that wanted a sporty scooter with outstanding performance and a "customized" look. The bodywork was essentially the same as the tried-and-true 150 Special, except for the metallic blue paint.

Apart from the long, dual-passenger bench seat, changes occurred to the light controls, the anti-theft key, and the modified writing to identify the model. With minor but important adjustments to the compression ratio and the cylinder, the power of the motor was raised above seven horsepower, which permitted the Lambretta to reach 86 km/h with the driver in an aerodynamic position.

To take advantage of the maximum acceleration possible, the gear ratio was slightly reduced without increasing the consumption of gasoline too much.

Side. Notice the fancy writing of "125" and "Lambretta" to show off that this is a new model. On the front of the last Specials produced, the central coat-of-arms was a quadrangular aluminum shield with "Innocenti" written on it.

In the three years that the 125 was produced, no relevant modifications took place apart from the glovebox changed to be made totally out of plastic and the Innocenti coat-of-arms being substituted with a rectangular chrome one.

The high 150,000 Italian lira price tag was certainly the main cause for the lack of success of the Lambretta 125 Special. To give an example of the difference in production numbers, only a few less than 30,000 units of the 125 Special were produced compared to the 146,000 of the normal LI.

Above. The motor on the new 125 Special was exactly the same as the normal LI except for the elastic supports to reduce the vibrations of the engine to the motor for higher overall performance.

LAMBRETTA 200 X SPECIAL

Following the positive experience of the Lambretta 200 TV on foreign markets, Innocenti decided to try the same size scooter on the Italian market. The new version would be essentially the same but would have the new name 200 X Special. Compared to its predecessor, the 200 TV, the new Lambretta's side panels were more square shaped and carried a polished aluminum arrow with the size of the engine written on it. For the first time on an Innocenti motorscooter, the saddle was "cardinal red."

The characteristics of the motor, however, remained unchanged. The power stayed at eleven horsepower and the maximum speed was 107 km/h, both aspects contributed to its road handling, which made the scooter much safer.

The Lambretta 200 X Special was the fastest and most-powerful scooter on the market. Thanks to its excellent road handling and braking power, it soon became the preferred means of transportation to the legions of sporting scooterists that partic-

Facing page. With just a few but wise improvements to the look of the scooter, the 1966 Lambretta 200 X Special was born. As the natural evolution from the TV series, the 200 X was different in that the paint scheme was completely white, the side panels were squarer, and the side emblems were redesigned to be shaped like an arrow. For the Italian market, the dual-passenger bench seat was recovered with elegant dark red fake leather. For export, the saddle was offered also in green, dark blue, and light blue. The example in the photo was recently restored, but the color of the saddle is too light and doesn't correspond to the original.

This page. This "Queen of the Road" showed off an SX 200 at the London motorcycle show in 1966. This exhibition was one of the most important in the world, so Innocenti showed off this special Lambretta with two-tone paint scheme just for the English market.

Facing page. Dating back to the time of its debut, this photo depicts the Lambretta SX 200. Notice the little openings on the left side of the front wheel hub that were protected by little plastic grilles. These would extract hot air and keep the front disc brakes cool. On the last SX 200s built, a chrome arrow was mounted on the fender and the horn cover from the Special X150 was used. Another finishing touch applied to the very last SX 200 Lambrettas was new hooks to attach the side panels like those used on the DL.

Side. Campagnolo, a company specializing in bicycle components and disc brakes for motorcycles, built these mechanically-controlled disc brakes just for the Lambretta. The little attachment bolts that held the long buffer on the suspension tube would soon be replaced with more economic wedge-shaped ones. All the small metallic pieces, including the brake lever, would soon be treated with a cadmium finish, while the front supplementary shock was painted in aluminum.

ipated in time trials and acceleration races.

Unfortunately, its high price of more than 190,000 Italian lira considerably limited the amount of people who could afford it. In its three years of production, only 20,783 units were built, and most of those ended up in England.

For the Italian market, the 200 XS was offered only in white, while for foreign markets different versions were available. In England, for example, one part of the side panels was painted "intense green" or other lively shades.

As with its little sister, one of the esthetic changes which occurred was the substitution of the front plastic coat-of-arms with a rectangular one made of chromed metal.

Above. The Lambretta 200 SX was the last model sold in Italy that still had an electrical rectifier and a battery. On the side of the glovebox was a sticker that listed specific instructions for good maintenance of the six-volt, eight-Ohm battery. In the beginning, the gear ratio remained the same as those on the 175 TV, but later these would be altered for maximum acceleration. Side. Under the left side panel, the air flow tubes and the regulating box for the electrical system were placed. To adjust the points, which was a rather complicated process, the carburetor, the side floorboard, and the magneto cover had to be removed. The glovebox was made of stamped metal, but would soon be replaced by one made of plastic.

LAMBRETTA JUNIOR 50, 50 IIS, 50 DE LUXE, AND 50 SPECIAL

Three years after its presentation at the Milan motorshow in 1961, the 50cc prototype was completely redesigned and finally hit the market at the end of 1964, exactly one year after its competition, the Vespa 50. The new Lambretta 50 was christened the "Junior" in honor of its young clientele. Apart from a few modest changes to the bodywork, the mechanical system and the suspension of the 50 Junior was sensibly improved compared to the 1961 prototype.

The specific changes to the motor were the switching of the rotating valves for a more traditional system and a completely overhauled gearbox with the introduction of a third speed. The front suspension was reinforced and became essentially the same as the Lambretta Cento, while an efficient hydraulic shock was added to the rear suspension. Even though the wheels were ten inches in diameter on the prototype, they were shrunk to only nine inches on the finally version.

This example of the pre-series Junior 50 based on the Cento was essentially the same as the version that would go into production. After three years of work and tweaking the design, the J 50 signaled the official entry of Innocenti into the world of small-engine scooters, which in Italy didn't even need a license plate.

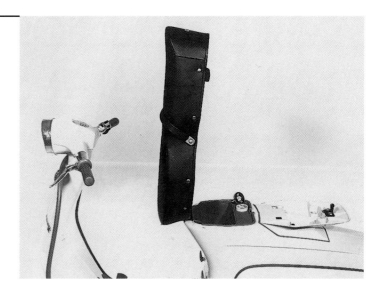

Above. The long, two-passenger bench seat was stock even though carrying a passenger on the smaller scooter was prohibited in Italy. Lifting the seat reveals the gas cap and the convenient glovebox; if the glovebox was then removed, the air filter could be accessed. There was space on the handlebars for an optional tachometer and an odometer.

Below. In this great photo the beautiful but simple lines of the Junior 50 can be seen. Although the price was slightly above its competition, the Vespa 50, the Junior didn't take long to win the hearts of the young scooterists in Italy thanks to its small size and above average power. Strangely, the J 50 was offered only in two color schemes: "snow white" and two-tone "light olive green" with dark green side panels.

As already seen on its big sister, the Cento, the frame of the J 50 soon revealed that it was far too fragile in the middle part, which caused customers to worry about the safety of the scooter.

To resolve this delicate problem, Innocenti totally redesigned the body and especially the structure. The rear section of the scooter was modified, and the front legshield was reduced. With these improvements, the Lambretta J 50 became the "Second Series" and was officially presented to the public on

November 26th of 1966 at the *Centro Studi* in the Lambrate area of Milan. In spite of these noteworthy improvements, the selling price remained unchanged at 109,000 Italian lira, but the new version was offered in two different colors: "aquamarine blue" and white.

The two different versions of the Junior 50 were remarkably successful but were never able to compete with the market supremacy of Piaggio in the area of small engine scooters.

To increase the appeal of the J 50, a new version dubbed the De Luxe was released in 1968 that had a more refined streamlining. Polished aluminum pieces in the form of arrows were mounted on the side panels (similar to those on the LI Special) and the rear section had a "De Luxe" emblem. Besides that, the connectors for the side panels were substituted with a spring-loaded hook that connected to the internal border around the main frame. Other modifications were

The new version of the Junior 50 with the reinforced frame was presented at the end of 1966. The important structural and esthetic modifications were to the legshield, the rear part of the scooter with the fake license plate holder made of aluminum alloy, and the shape of the saddle.

These three photos are of the 1968 Junior 50 De Luxe that replaced the 1966 version of the J 50. The new sidepanels with polished aluminum arrows and the words "de luxe" are evident in the snapshot above. The larger ten-inch wheels made the road handling of this little Lambretta far easier. From the top view, we can see that the new floor panel strips of aluminum holding rubber runners were the same as those on the larger Lambrettas. The new saddle was made of fake leather that was colored dark blue. On the rear part of the scooter a convenient rack made of stamped metal was placed, and a simpler rear section without the aluminum frame for a license plate that the 1966 series had.

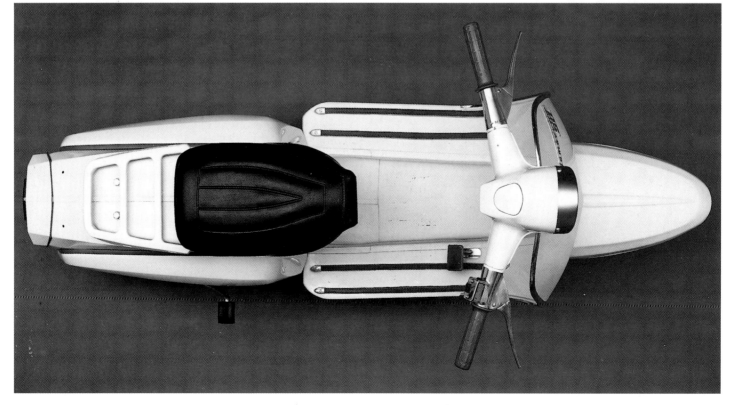

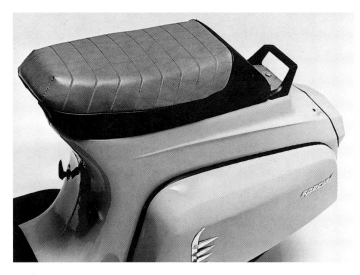

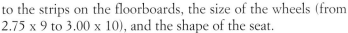

Above left. This is another photo of the 50 De Luxe; notice the large writing of "50" attached to the front side panel. Above right and the two photos below. The Lambretta 50 Special was the last 50cc model produced by Innocenti until the complete halt of the production line in April 1971. Even if Innocenti was already in dire straits, the 50 De Luxe was revamped in hopes of an unlikely turnaround in the market. The most notable differences were the shape of the saddle and the rubber floormats, instead of the classic aluminum strips. Many parts were now made out of plastic—including the handlegrips—and were tinted black like the DL series, but the strips along the edge of the front legshield were still polished aluminum.

to the strips on the floorboards, the size of the wheels (from 2.75 x 9 to 3.00 x 10), and the shape of the seat.

With this new version, Innocenti returned to the old tradition of painting the hubs and rims of the scooter in aluminum, while a shining "field green" was added to the gamut of colors offered. The last version of the Junior 50 appeared in the spring of 1970 alongside, but not replacing, the preceding model. With the nickname of "Special," this Lambretta would be the last 50cc model built by the Innocenti factory before the assembly line was transferred to the Indian government.

The new model had many new esthetic modifications. The covering for the floorboards was now a black rubber mat; the seat was now two tone and more slender; the arrow metal pieces on the side panels were modified; and a more practical handle was added, which helped to maneuver the scooter from when it was stopped.

Innocenti completely changed the list of colors available, which were definitely aimed at a younger clientele: red, turquoise, and "ochre yellow."

Unfortunately, the Special was never quite able to find its market niche, and less than 14,000 units were ever produced before production was halted in April 1971.

LAMBRETTA LUI 50 C AND CL

Below. The most notable part of the Lui was certainly the slim front legshield, which was characteristic of the entire frame of the scooter. Only a world-class designer like Nuccio Bertone could ever create such a true work of art.

Center. This top view of the Lui 50 CL shows the practical rubber floormats that were fastened with three rubber connectors and hid the screws that attached the whole front legshield. The molded aluminum head stock was made for a tachometer and odometer to be added as an accessory on the 50cc version but was standard on the 75cc model. On the example pictured, the handlegrips are squared, a feature that would be replaced with the more conventional cylindrical ones on the production model.

Facing page. This left side view reveals the black plastic covering of the magneto that keeps the styling cue of the horizontal slits just like on the handlebars and the optional rear rack. Attached to the cover is a little rectangular casing containing the connecting terminal for the two electrical cords coming out of the magneto.

The continuous search for new commercial frontiers caused Innocenti to push for a new little scooter/moped that had a 50cc engine. This super economical scooter would be sold alongside the Junior 50, but at a significantly reduced price.

The mechanical system and suspension were basically the same as the Junior 50, but the lines were significantly simplified with just the essentials remaining. The exposed motor, that wouldn't protect the rider from all the grease and grime, was similar to its well-known predecessors, the Lambretta C and D.

The qualifications of the prototype didn't convince the sales department at Innocenti; it preferred to entrust this important pro-

ject to the famous automobile designer, Nuccio Bertone. In a little more than three years, Bertone conceived a truly avant-garde scooter with young-looking lines but at the same time, elegant and enriched with styling cues that made this scooter one of a kind on the Italian scootering market.

The promising new model was dubbed with the pleasant name "Lui" for the domestic market, but was called "LUNA" for the export market. In the spring of 1968, the scooter was officially presented and received the highest possible critical acclaim and a lot of public kudos.

With the ad slogan, "All for Lui, and Lui for all," Innocenti began a huge advertising campaign that included not only magazine ads, but also printing school notebooks and ads in kids' magazines in an attempt to kick start the sluggish scootering market.

In response to the various markets, the Lui was offered in two distinct versions. The CL was the luxury version and was available in orange, turquoise, or "apple green." The more economical C didn't have as many finishing touches as the CL and was available in white or "ocean blue."

The frame of the scooter was mixed with the front area using

Following pages:
Left. To truly appreciate the beauty, a close-up view is necessary to see all the refined details of this one-of-a-kind scooter. First of all, there's the headlamp and handlebars made of three pieces of aluminum alloy that meld together to hide the connecting screws. Then, there's the gas tank that follows the lines of the frame and supports the elegant saddle of fake leather. Right. The more economic Lui C lost much of its character, so the price could be lowered. This orange paint scheme was only a pre-series color.

large sections of tubing, while the rear used stamped metal. The suspension was the same as the Junior since it had been tested for a few years now, except for the rear shock which was incorporated into the spring, probably just for looks.

The wheel rims and hubs were designed to give the scooter a sporty look and to make the Lui seem look even faster. For the first time on an Innocenti scooter, the hubs were made of a single piece of cast iron alloy, which was almost certainly designed to make the scooter heavier and handle better on the road.

The mechanical system of the Lui had all the general characteristics of the J 50 but with a different configuration for the crankcase that was better adapted to the scooter. Another difference was motivated by trying to make the scooter look sleeker; the plastic air scoop cover used the same artistic lines as the handlebars and the rear rack.

The economic C model was different from the CL in that the front and rear lights had a more traditional shape, and the handlebars were made of a chrome tube rather than aluminum alloy. The modest price difference between the two versions made the CL the best seller of the two. Even so, the ambitious sales predictions of the Innocenti directors was never fulfilled. After only fifteen months of production, the Lui ceased being construct-

ed after 27,000 units had been built. At this point, the only small engine Innocenti scooter still built that didn't require a license in Italy was the Junior 50, which would be made until the entire plant ceased production.

There were essentially two main reasons why the Lui wasn't a success: one, the futuristic lines of the scooter were never really comprehended by the general public; two, the motorcycle market had taken a steep downturn that took its toll even on the largest Italian motorcycle manufacturers such as Guzzi, Gilera, Bianchi, etc.

It's interesting to remember that the Lui was offered in a third version only for foreign markets. This model was called the "S" and was different from the CL in that it had a longer, dual-passenger seat, a raised muffler, and a rear license plate holder.

During the time that it was produced, the Lui underwent very few modifications. Undoubtedly the most important was the writing on the front legshield. On the very first models, the word "Lambretta" was mounted on the left side above the "50 CL" logo, while later the emblem was eliminated and replaced with a small, rectangular coat-of-arms with "Lui" written on it and attached to the center of the legshield.

On a few cases, it's possible to find above the coat-of-arms a little chrome "Lambretta" written, as on the Luna-Vega-Cometa series that were only for export.

LAMBRETTA LUI 75 S AND SL

With the presentation of the Lui 75 Lubematic, Innocenti achieved another first in the history of Italian scooter manufacturing: for the first time a mass-produced scooter had an automatic oil-gas mix.

A few months after the Lui 50 was presented to the world, Innocenti launched a new version of the scooter with a larger 75cc engine on the international market. This higher-powered model was aimed towards a clientele that wanted an economic scooter with high performance even when carrying a passenger.

The new model debuted with a lot of fanfare at the 15th Motor Show in Tokyo, where Innocenti was the sole foreign company. Two versions of the Lui 75 were prepared for the occasion that were painted white with a multi-colored floral pattern. After a period in which it was only available on the international market, the Lui 75 was offered in Italy in two different versions, the 75 S and the 75 SL.

The bodywork, the wheels, and the brakes were the same as the smaller model, but the electrical system was more powerful with the introduction of a high beam for the headlamp, a

The Lui 75 was presented at the 1968 Tokyo Motor Show with two different sets of decorations to test the reaction of the public before putting the scooter on the market. This was surely far too avant garde for the time, but nowadays this is considered standard when selling scooters to the youth market. The model pictured here isn't the original that was shown at the Tokyo Motor Show, but a repainted version based on a couple of color Polaroids found in the factory from 1968 before the Lui 75 was packed up and sent to Japan.

rear stop light, and all around larger lights. Other changes were the longer, two-passenger seat, a raised racing-shaped muffler, and a replaceable paper air filter.

With the increased displacement, the motor was made much more powerful. Its 5.2 horsepower and the new four-speed gearbox made acceleration quicker and hill climbing a cinch.

One of the differences between the SL and the S is the addition of an automatic oil pump to the SL, which kept the motor lubricated. The oil was contained in a separate compartment and was injected by a geared pump towards the piston and the moving parts of the engine. The amount of oil was automatically determined by the rpms of the motor. This was the first time that this mechanism was used on an Italian scooter and was called, "Lubematic."

For both versions, only two colors were available: orange and metallic gray. The only visual difference between the two scooters was the writing on the front legshield and the "Lubematic" written on the side of the gas tank. The 75 S was called the Vega and the 75 SL became the Cometa for foreign markets. Innocenti offered options of a rear rack and turn signals attached to the front headlamp.

With just a few more than 8,000 units produced, the Lui 75 was a commercial flop, especially considering the huge ad campaign by Innocenti to put the scooter on the international market. Even so, the Lui will go down in Italian scootering history as one of the most important examples of artistic expression on a mass-produced vehicle at a low price.

LAMBRETTA 125 AND 150 DL

With the slogan, "One design, three-sized engines," Innocenti put the new DL series on the market in the spring of 1969 with many changes to the bodywork and some improvements to the mechanical system. The only differences between the 125 and the 150 were the front logos and the color schemes. The 125 was available in white or turquoise, and the 150 came in red or white.

Following the positive collaboration with Bertone on the Lambretta Lui, Innocenti decided to entrust the famous designer with renewing the lines of the LI Special series without, however, changing its basic structure.

With just a few important modifications, the Lambretta became an elegant and modern scooter, while keeping its young and sporty look. Bertone's new design of the bodywork fit in perfectly with the old frame, and helped update the overall performance of the scooter.

The most noticeable alteration is without a doubt the larg-

er rectangular headlamp that looked similar to those used on several sport cars. Apart from that, the slimmer legshields now had a curious ink splotch, which was supposed to give an original touch to the new series.

Other changes to this new model were: the large saddle with sharper edges; the rear fender made totally out of plastic, and the black rather than gray molding.

Compared to the earlier version, the mechanical system was practically unchanged except for a slight adjustment to the low gears, which modestly increased the maximum

These modern-day photographs are of a Lambretta 125 DL that remained unsold for more than 23 years. On the first versions, the horn cover was made of aluminum alloy that was painted in opaque black, and would later be made in molded plastic.
Side. This two-tone Grand Prix version was built for foreign markets and is shown here in an Australian publicity photo.

Facing page. In this side view of the Lambretta DL, the square shape of the long seat is clearly shown. It was shaped like this to match the shape of the front fender. Unfortunately, design choices don't always conform to what is necessary since the DL seat—while elegant and sleek—felt more like a wooden plank.

This page. This close up of the handlebars reveals the new tachometer/odometer with "Lambretta" written on a black background. The settings are different according to the model; the 125 went up to 100km/h, and the 150 reached 120km/h.

Above right. To make the shape of the side panels seem less heavy, black sticker strips were applied half-way up with a fake plastic air scoop to boot.

Side. With a slight reworking of the engine and the carburetor, the Lambretta DL's performance was improved and kept the scooter at the top of its class. The clutch spring was also modified and now made of bronze. The attachments for the transmission cover were also changed since they just used bolts rather than screws. Just like on the SX, the DL's muffler had an extra 8mm connector for the exhaust pipe.

Left. For a few foreign markets, the Lambretta 150 DL was sold as the "Grand Prix" model with a checkered flag on the front legshield instead of the ink spot. This model was offered in a two-tone of white and blue or white and red, as well as the traditional paint schemes.

Right. On this rear view, the refined and aerodynamic shape of the bodywork can be seen. The only part that stuck out was the kick starter, which had been criticized since it could get caught on anything that it went near. Notice the return of the fake air scoop behind the seat like that of the second series.

speed. A new carburetor was added to the 150cc version with a diameter of 22mm, just like on the 200 DL.

With the revamped DL series, there were no longer any visual differences between the 125 and the 150 version except for the writing on the legshield and the different paint colors of white or turquoise for the 125 and red or white for the 150.

At the end of its run to keep production costs down, a few parts of the bodywork were made in plastic, and small safety balls were applied to the ends of the brake and clutch levers.

When construction of this model stopped in April 1971, Innocenti's adventure into the magical world of two wheelers came to a close after fourteen stellar years of innumerable successes and immense satisfaction. The Lambretta DL would live on in India, where the government rebuilt the complete production line.

LAMBRETTA 200 DL

At the same time as the debut of the 125 and 150 DL, Innocenti released on the market its new top-of-the-line scooter: the 200 DL. With this latest version, all the bodywork was the same as the smaller models. The only differences were the mechanically-controlled disc brakes, which were exclusively on the 200cc model, and the supplementary shock absorber on the front fork. In Italy, the only color available was "ochre," while export models came in different hues according to the destination.

The only improvements to the motor were the slightly tighter gear ratios and a new carburetor that allowed the Lambretta

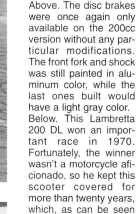

Above. The disc brakes were once again only available on the 200cc version without any particular modifications. The front fork and shock was still painted in aluminum color, while the last ones built would have a light gray color. Below. This Lambretta 200 DL won an important race in 1970. Fortunately, the winner wasn't a motorcycle aficionado, so he kept this scooter covered for more than twenty years, which, as can be seen in the photo, kept it in perfect shape.

Above left. At the 41st International Bicycle and Motorcycle Show in Milan, Innocenti presented its products to the public for the last time. The only new item was the Lambretta 200 DL with an electronic starter that was another first in a long string for Italian scootering world, and unfortunately the last for Innocenti. This modification came about because of a collaboration with the Ducati electronic department.

Above right and side. These two photos show the racy and elegant lines of the Lambretta 200 DL, the fastest, mass-produced scooter in the world (110.8 km/h).

200 to exceed 110 km/h and once again confirm the Lambretta's position as the fastest Italian scooter.

In 1970, an electronic version of the DL was proposed. Together with the *Ducati Elettromeccanica* system, the first Italian scooter with this system was produced. To identify this model, an oval stick with "Electronic" was placed where the ink blotch would have been.

The most successful foreign market was without a doubt the English, where the 200 DL always ranked first in time trials and races for the scooter category. A "Grand Prix" version of the 200 DL was produced almost exclusively for England with a different color scheme and a checkered flag on the front legshield rather than the ink spot.

On the last 200 DLs produced, many of the parts were made out of plastic rather than metal, and small safety balls were placed on the ends of the handlebars levers.

Even though the Lambretta 200 DL was an excellent example of a modern and fast scooter, it couldn't garner enough sales to stay in production, and production ceased in April 1971 along with the entire motorscooter production line at the Innocenti factory.

LAMBRETTA 125 f (FB) DELIVERY VEHICLE

Just a few months after the release of the Lambretta 125 B, Innocenti launched on the market a little, three-wheeled delivery van with the carrying section in the front. This set-up was used to take advantage of the mechanical system already used on the Lambretta 125 B, and therefore save on costs. In fact, the actual selling price was below the competition but didn't infringe on the reliability already associated with Innocenti products.

Three different versions of the three-wheeler were offered:
1. With a covered aluminum compartment.
2. With a covered wooden compartment.
3. With wooden panels reinforcing the edges.

The braking system for the three drums was mechanically controlled by a single pedal equipped with a gear that compensated for the three wheels to make the braking power steady on all three. Besides that, an extra lever on the handlebars controlled the rear drum brake.

To improve the cooling of the engine, an air duct was mounted above the magneto that sent air to the cylinder via a spiral vent made of stamped aluminum. The steering was typical of automobiles with a parallelogram shaped system that allowed the wheels to move free of the front compartment that was welded to the frame.

As far as the performance was concerned, it was hardly fantastic since the modest power and the small displacement of the engine couldn't handle loads heavier than 200 kilograms, and the maximum speed topped out at barely 45 km/h.

Even though the price of this little delivery vehicle was definitely affordable, the three-wheeled FB wasn't received well by the general public. After a little more than a year of production, it ceased to be built after just 2,000 units had hit the streets.

Above right and side. These two views of the three-wheeled Lambretta f feature the version with the wooden box that opened from the top. The delivery vehicle was also offered with a covered aluminum compartment or a wooden box with low sides. The interesting design made room for the engine block, but the gearbox had to be shifted from where it was on the scooter. The finishing touches of this delivery vehicle kept the frame tubing and the floorboard strips painted the same color as the bodywork, while the metal ends and the handlebars were chromed.

LAMBRETTA 125 FC DELIVERY VEHICLE

Center. With the introduction of the new FC model, a version was offered that had a two-door entry on the front of the compartment and the headlamp on top of the box. On following versions, the headlight would be moved down 20 centimeters but made to fit in better with the compartment.

Below. All the pieces of the two versions with the wooden box were exactly the same as those on the preceding model, the Lambretta FB. As with the motorscooters being built at the time, no license plate holder was built into the fender since the law didn't require one at the time. The electrical system was identical to the Lambretta FB except for the light switch, which was now triangular shaped and made out of black plastic with the grounding wire situated above the covering.

After a six month break from producing delivery vehicles to sell off old stock, Innocenti introduced a new version of the three-wheeler using the new and improved mechanical system of the C and LC scooters.

The general structure remained almost identical, and the modest performance also stayed the same. The most interesting change was the new hydraulic braking system that made stopping and controlling the vehicle much easier than before.

The rear bodywork derived from the Lambretta C, while the motor and the air cooling system came off the Lambretta LC. Other changes were to the exhaust, the gearbox, and the wheels were widened to four inches so they could grip the road better and provide for better stability when carrying a full load.

Apart from the three different versions of the compartment as on the preceding model, the FC delivery vehicle was also offered as the "chassis" version without any compartment to satisfy the numerous requests from companies that adapted the three-wheeler to their own needs.

Even this latest version of the three-wheeler didn't sell very well, probably because the front compartment size was fairly small, especially if a company needed to carry large loads.

LAMBRETTA 125 FD DELIVERY VEHICLE

In the renovation plans for production in 1953, Innocenti didn't neglect its delivery vehicle. In fact, by the beginning of the year, a completely revamped version of the three-wheeler was already previewed that was nothing like the FB or FC versions. The most important change without a doubt was the shifting of the compartment to the rear of the vehicle, and the motor and driver moved forward. With this new model, Innocenti conformed to the classic and traditional Italian transport design of having a single wheel in front that steered the vehicle and two rear wheels to hold the cargo. This design was in response to the numerous requests by loyal customers to alter the position of the compartment.

The new model was dubbed the 125 FD since it used most of the same mechanical parts off of the D and LD scooters, especially the motor, the wheels, the handlebars, and the entire front section. The frame was formed by a single large section of tubing that was

Above. This exposed view reveals the entire structure of the new Lambretta 125 FD three-wheeler. The rigid rear axle was supported by two long leaf springs without the help of shocks, and the structure contained the dual cones, the differential, and the axle shaft all in an oil bath. There are no cardan attachments, but only two rubber connectors between the motor and the differential. The license plate holder and a tail lamp are situated at the extreme left rear of the frame, while the right rear doesn't have a light.

Side. Undoubtedly the most popular of the Lambretta 125 FD models was the one with the wooden compartment and low sides shown here. To protect the driver from the elements, the front legshield from the LD was used.

165

The 125 FD three-wheeler came with either an aluminum- or wooden-enclosed compartment that were usually built by outside companies specializing in these boxes.

Innocenti would then attach then to the frame at the factory. To minimize the vibrations, Innocenti put rubber buffers between the frame and the compartment.

Facing page, above. These two 125 FD three-wheeled vehicles were used to deliver the mail in the city of Milan, Italy. Notice the complete covering for the driver from the weather. Below. This Innocenti delivery vehicle was designed specifically to transport metal bins. Thanks to all the possibilities that metal tubing offered in the 1950s, Innocenti vehicles were adapted for all sorts of different tasks, from bringing ladders to stores, to firetrucks, to carrying people.

attached through various welds to the rectangular tubes and stamped metal that made up the base of the compartment. The result was an extremely rigid frame that didn't weigh much.

The front expansion brakes were controlled by the handlebar lever and the hydraulic rear brakes were activated by a foot pedal. The brakes were enlarged compared to the scooter to give efficient and even stopping power.

With the new position of the mechanical system, the transmission used a shaft drive and the differential and the axle shaft were incorporated into the rear axle just like on normal automobiles.

As on the previous model, four different versions were offered: just the frame, with a wooden compartment and low sides, and an enclosed compartment made of aluminum or wood. As with the earlier models, the most popular of all was the short-sided wooden pickup version since the cost was low and it was by far the most flexible version.

With this model, Innocenti was finally able to sell a good number of its three-wheelers and break into the difficult market sector of transport vehicles dominated by Guzzi and Aermacchi. Customers also found it a good alternative to Piaggio's three-wheeled Ape.

LAMBRETTA 150 FD DELIVERY VEHICLE

Below. The frame structure of the 150 FD three-wheeler was sensibly reinforced compared to the older versions with the 125cc engines. The main tube of the frame was lengthened in the rear section connecting to a supplementary beam that strengthened the rectangular structure. Besides that, the internal leverage of the front suspension was enlarged and the helical springs with variable pitch were strengthened. Notice the automobile-style muffler that significantly reduced the amount of noise made by the engine and released the exhaust far away from the vehicle's body.

Just three years after it was born, the FD three-wheeler now had improved performance and could carry much heavier loads. In the autumn of 1955, Innocenti put a new series on the market with a 150cc engine that appealed to a serious commercial market base.

The new version used the engine from the Lambretta 150 D with an external high-tension coil and the dual-cable shifting system. The brakes, the tires, and the general structure remained the same.

In response to the increased load able to be carried by the FD, the front suspension was significantly reinforced with stronger springs and the pivot pins at the joints, while the rear suspension stayed, for all intents and purposes, the same.

Besides the traditional models offered, the FD was also available with a low-sided metal compartment in back with an "X" pattern along the stamped metal. This would be far and away the most popular version.

With this model, Innocenti's delivery vehicles reached a high level of reliability and exceptional weight-to-power ratio.

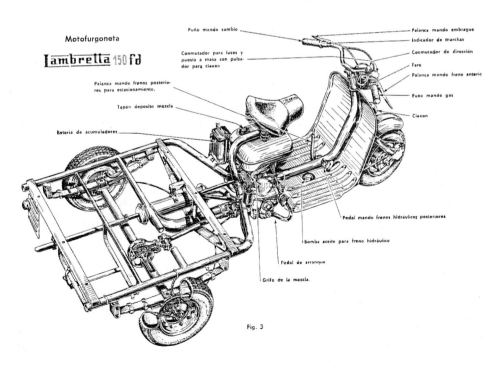

Motofurgoneta

lambretta 150 fd

Puño mando cambio

Conmutador para luces y puesta a masa con pulsador para claxon

Palanca mando frenos posteriores para estacionamiento.

Tapón deposito mezcla

Bateria de acumuladores

Palanca mando embrague

Indicador de marchas

Conmutador de dirección

Faro

Palanca mando freno anterior

Puño mando gas

Claxon

Pedal mando frenos hidráulicos posteriores

Bomba aceite para freno hidráulico

Pedal de arranque

Grifo de la mezcla

Fig. 3

In the large photo. This Lambretta 150 FD was put to work inside the Innocenti factory to deliver spare parts to dealers. The rear aluminum compartment was modified so that the doors opened on the side rather than the rear. A complete ribbed covering was applied over the driver for protection against the elements, although this wasn't an official Innocenti product.

Side. These two pictures show the metal compartments offered by Innocenti for the Lambretta 150 FD delivery vehicle. The FD with the low sides was by far the most popular both for the its lower price and for its extreme versatility in carrying all sorts of different loads. The lights mounted on the sides of the compartment served both as running lights and turn signals.

This improved performance allowed the FD to be used in the most diverse climates and countryside: from the Tunisian desert to the Finnish prairies, from the Italian Alps to the grassy plains of Argentina.

In the four years that it was built, the FD received many improvements, especially to the starter which proved to be the Achilles' heal of the D series. The modifications paralleled the D series, especially the epicyclical gears used for the starter just like on the LD '57 series. As for the frame, the only important change was the increase from three to four connectors for the wheel rim to the hub.

With more than 16,000 produced, the 150 FD three-wheeler would be the most popular vehicle with vertical cylinder produced.

LAMBRETTA 150 FD/C DELIVERY VEHICLE

With the 150 FD/C delivery vehicle, Innocenti offered for the first time a true automobile-style cab for the driver, complete with an opening sunroof and doors (optional). The frame remained the same as the previous model, except for, of course, the support structure for the cab. Even the wheels, the springs and the suspension stayed almost identical. All the controls for the vehicle were inside the cab, from the steering control to the gas tank and the six-volt battery. To reduce the problem of the sharp angle of the front fork, an adjustable steering column lock was mounted.

Facing page, above left. Only a few dozen of the *Giardinetta* (little garden) model, designed by Ghia, were built to transport passengers.

Above right. The entirely enclosed compartment of this version was finally appreciated once the covered front cab of the FD/C was introduced. The access to the rear compartment was through two doors in the rear.

Below. This curious, and a little bit pathetic, "firetruck" was designed for the FD/C three-wheeler by the Innocenti Corporation of New York City. It's unknown how many fires were put out and how many kitties were saved from trees, but it was a good example of how versatile the Lambretta three-wheelers were.

Just a few days after the beginning of the 35th Motorcycle Show in Milan, Innocenti's new evolution of the successful FD delivery vehicle was presented at its new luxurious exposition hall in downtown Milan's Piazza San Babila. The most noticeable difference of the new model was the large area for the driver to sit that finally protected him from the elements and significantly improved his comfort in any season.

The whole mechanical system was now conveniently protected by a stamped metal structure that also offered the support for the large seat, which could accommodate two people.

The perfect visibility was thanks to a curved plate glass windscreen with manual windshield wipers, while the roof of the cab was covered with a canvas sunroof that could be opened for better air flow.

Another new innovation was the addition of a reverse gear to be able to maneuver the vehicle better and now made the little three-wheeler nearly a full-fledged automobile. This reverse system allowed there to be three forward gears and three reverse gears.

With this latest version, the compartment built in wood was abandoned for an aluminum one, which was cheaper and quite a bit stronger. Three different versions were now offered: with only the frame in back, with a covered stamped-metal compartment, and a low-sided pickup. The doors on these models were considered optional.

In the spring of 1958, a new version was offered that could carry three passengers on a plaid couch in the back of the vehicle. The three-wheeler was dubbed *Giardinetta* (little garden) and was conceived by the famous bodywork designer Ghia. In case of bad weather, a rainproof cover, just like on spider convertibles, could be extended over the passengers and attached to the body of the vehicle by a series of automatic buttons.

Even thought the lines of the Giardinetta FD/C were elegant and modern, only a few dozen were built since it didn't strike a chord with the public. In the future, Innocenti preferred to totally abandon its brief foray into the world of transporting passengers. A few of the Giardinettas were used at the Olympic games held in Rome in 1960 to move service personnel around the Olympic Village.

When the production of the FD/C three-wheeler ceased, so did the evolution of the vertical cylinder and dual-cone system. In its place, the second part of Innocenti's mechanical revolution took over with the horizontal cylinder and the four speeds of the LI gearbox.

LAMBRETTA 175 LI, 175 LI II SERIES, AND LAMBRO 175 DELIVERY VEHICLES

Compared to the preceding model, the new Lambretta 175 LI delivery vehicle didn't receive any changes to the outside bodywork apart from a small horncover. The inside, however, was modified quite a bit, especially the handlebars with the control cables inside, the design of the instrument panel, and the braking mechanism. Two hydraulic shocks were finally mounted on the rear axle to smooth the bumping of the wheels to the body, but the rear lights remained the same with a single taillight attached to the left side that doubled as both a running and a brake light.

Facing page, lower left. This close-up shows the entire mechanical system of the LI 175's motor. Except for certain aspects, the motor was quite different from that of the motorscooter. Notice the primary transmission with helical gears, the conical gear starter, and the reverse gear mechanism driven by a simplex chain.

During the summer of 1959, Innocenti radically renewed its production of three-wheeled vehicles with a new model that derived directly from the Lambretta LI from the previous year. The most noticeable modifications were to the mechanical system and therefore the overall performance was improved. The new horizontal cylinder used a four-speed gearbox and was attached to the frame with special elastic buffers that significantly reduced the amount of vibration transferred.

The enlargement of the engine displacement to 175cc and the resulting power increase, expanded the market for Innocenti's delivery vehicles all the way to the mountains, which were traditionally thought of as far too difficult a terrain for three-wheelers. The bodywork was practically identical to its predecessor, apart from a small horncover and a license plate holder. At the beginning of 1960, a few months after the second series was introduced, a kickstarter was now used to start the engine as just one of the many technical and esthetic improvements for the three-wheeler.

The front suspension was entirely redesigned similar to that of the Lambretta LI, and both the covered and uncovered com-

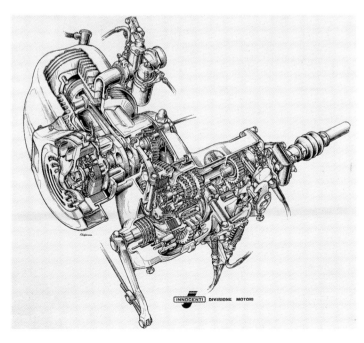

partments were considerably enlarged. The weight of a load that the three-wheeler could now carry reached 400 kilograms. Another improvement was the electrical system shift from 6 volt to 12 volt, which improved the overall lighting and provided enough power to light the new side turn signals mounted on the front part of the cab.

With the introduction of the second series of Lambretta delivery vehicles, the optional convertible roof was strangely no longer offered as an accessory on any future models. At the beginning of 1964, the LI three-wheeler received a few more modifications to the cab, and the possibility to mount an electric dynamotor starter. For this new version, the name "Lambretta" was abandoned for "Lambro," which had already been used on the 200cc series.

Of the three different versions offered, the LI 175 delivery vehicle would be the most popular model of three-wheelers produced by Innocenti. In the nine years of production, more than 82,000 units were produced that were exported around the world and even built under license in a few foreign countries.

Above left. This is an example of the 175 LI second series three-wheelers since it had the running and braking lights mounted on the side of the cab and the front fork with a different spring set up compared to its predecessor.

Above right. With the covered compartment model, the amount of load able to be fit into the box was reduced by ten percent, but the maximum weight stayed at 350 kilograms.

Left center. The Lambro 175 model built in 1964 was different from its predecessor in that it had an inverted door opening, and a large plastic emblem mounted on the front.

LAMBRO 200 DELIVERY VEHICLE

This snapshot includes all the components necessary to make a new Lambro 200 delivery vehicle. Notice in the back of the photo, the structural elements to piece together both the frame and the floor boards, which are made up of both tubing and stamped metal. The rectangular box located next to the cab is a practical glovebox that would be mounted on the front right side of the compartment.

Fifteen years after its first three-wheeler hit the streets, Innocenti finally decided to give a name to its well-known form of transport. This time as well, the little river that wanders through the factory was the inspiration for the name of the vehicle, and in a short while "Lambro" became synonymous with three-wheeler.

The first model to receive the new name was the 200cc version of the classic LI 175 Series II. The official debut was in the summer of 1963 in the two traditional versions of pickup-style with the opening trunk, and the enclosed compartment version.

For this new vehicle, Innocenti designed a mixed frame of both tubing and stamped metal, which was extremely light weight but very robust at the same time. Also the front suspension and the wheels were revamped on the new model.

Thanks to a practical increase in the volume of the rear compartment, the size of the load was significantly enlarged and the maximum weight now reached the impressive 500 kilogram mark. The mechanical system was basically a derivation of the tried-and-true 175cc version, with only minor changes and a new gear ratio to help keep the three-wheeler as fast as before. The bodywork of the vehicle remained the same as the 175cc model, even the color scheme stayed, as always, "Lambro gray." In spite of the improved weight and size capacity of the load, the Lambro 200 wasn't able to duplicate the success of its little brother, and after less than three years would be substituted with a new model with a profoundly new mechanical system.

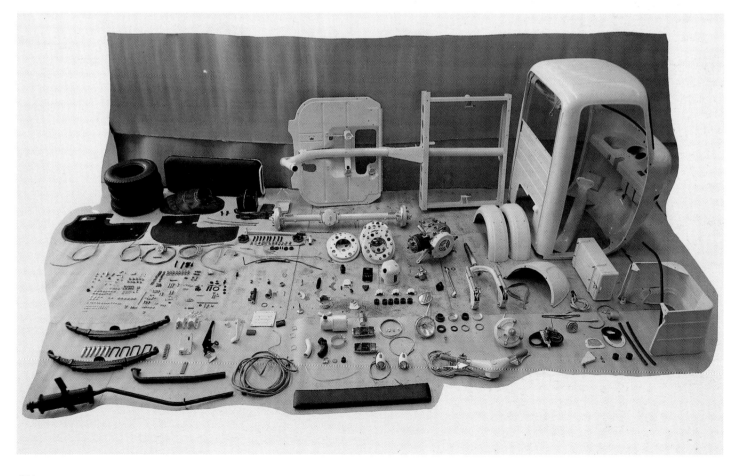

Above. This version of the stripped-down Lambro 200 was made available only to body-work companies that would fit them with specialized compartments for a multitude of possibilities. Because of this tactic, the Lambro 200 now entered into sectors that had previously been impossible for a little three-wheeler. For example, it worked in the mines of South Africa running on train tracks.

Below. With the introduction of the bigger 200cc engine, even the rear compartment was enlarged and the weight capacity now reached 500 kilograms. When the delivery vehicle was equipped with the covered compartment, the maximum load decreased to 475 kilograms because of the weight of the box.

175

LAMBRO 450 DELIVERY VEHICLE

Even though it had a smaller engine, the Lambro 450 had a larger enclosed rear compartment than the one mounted on the 200cc version. The open air version and the pickup model stayed the same.

Using the same frame and body as the Lambro 200, Innocenti presented a new edition of the successful LI 175 with the new name of Lambro 450 in 1965.

Compared to the previous model, the rear compartment was enlarged both in the covered and uncovered versions. The wheel rims were bigger, and the front fork was considerably stronger and equipped with two hydraulic shocks.

Thanks to the new frame structure, the maximum weight load was increased to 450 kilograms. At the same time, a slight tweaking of the engine raised its power, and thereby increased the performance of the three-wheeler.

This model received a few improvements to the cab as well. Innocenti finally included stock electric windshield wipers and the control panel was redesigned with the square odometer that had already been used on the Lambretta LI Series III.

An option on this model, as well, was the electric Bosch dynamotor starter with a larger 25 Ohm battery.

The Lambro 450 was built for less than two years with a total of 9,500 units produced, and would be the last Innocenti delivery vehicle with only one headlamp.

LAMBRO 550 DELIVERY VEHICLE

At the end of 1965, Innocenti renovated its top-of-the-line three-wheeler. The Lambro 200 became the Lambro 550 with the number in the name no longer meaning the size of the engine but the maximum weight load instead.

The most noticeable difference compared to the previous version was the dual, wider dimension headlamps for better night vision and safer driving. This important improvement would soon be applied to all of Innocenti's three-wheelers, and would become a distinctive sign between the Lambro and its competition. Other changes were the stamped metal wheel rims, which were typical of automobiles of the day; the new

light inside the cab; and a small increase in the engine's power.

Other improvements that were no less important were the maximum weight load of 550 kilograms, the further-enlarged rear compartment, and the improved braking system adapted to the increase in power of the engine.

To promote the new model, Innocenti launched a huge ad campaign using every means possible: daily newspapers, weeklies, movies, posters, and personal letters.

In the sales history of delivery vehicles, this was certainly the first time that a company mounted such a huge and intense

The official presentation of the Lambro 550 took place near the Innocenti factory behind the *Centro Studi* design building. The main character at the event, apart from the three-wheeler, was a cute, blow-up red elephant that accompanied the Lambro 550 for its entire promotional campaign. With the sales pitch of "Carry more than an elephant," the Lambro 550 entered Italian homes through advertisements in daily newspapers, magazines, movies, and posters.

promotional campaign towards all social classes. In the windows of every Innocenti dealer, a large blow-up red elephant was displayed to demonstrate the incredible sturdiness of the three-wheeler. Thousands of little inflatable elephants were made to give out to the public at town festivals.

With the slogan, "Carry more than an elephant," the Lambro 550 (also known as the "Super") succeeded in winning the public's heart and therefore having considerable commercial success in Italy and abroad. An interesting fact was that of the 34,000 units produced, almost 17,000 were sent to Turkey and Vietnam.

Above. With the Lambro 550, the rear compartment was further enlarged to 1420 mm long, 1250 mm wide, and 1015 mm high for a total volume of 2.2 meters cubed.

Below. This photo reveals the new headlights that add character to the Lambro 500 and make driving at night far safer. The electrical system substituted the dynameter for an alternator with a transistor regulator.

LAMBRO 550 N AND 550 A DELIVERY VEHICLES

Innocenti took a big step forward in its production of delivery vehicles when it presented its new Lambro 550 N three-wheeler in mid-1967. The most important novelty was the transfer of the motor from under the seat inside the cab to outside under the front of the compartment. This new technical innovation was introduced to reduce the noise level inside the cab, lower the heat from the engine, and therefore to improve the safety and comfort of driving.

Four elastic supports were now used to hold the motor in place, and were situated symmetrically on the frame. Another improvement was the larger muffler and the modified clutch and brake ratios to improve the performance. An air scoop was placed on the front of the cab and two air deflectors on the doors that made the air flow for the driver very comfortable. The front windshield as well was improved and made sleeker with a chromed frame.

The flexibility of the leaf springs of the rear suspension were improved, which made the entire vehicle far more useful. The maximum weight load and the amount of space

The lines of the new Lambro 550 N three-wheeler were practically identical to the earlier model, apart from a few modest alterations inside the cab. The most interesting change was the shift of the entire motor out of the cab to under the front part of the compartment. This picture shows the engine head, the exhaust manifold, and the air intake all painted black. The flexible tube that peeks out from above the engine brings hot air into the cab when the heater is activated.

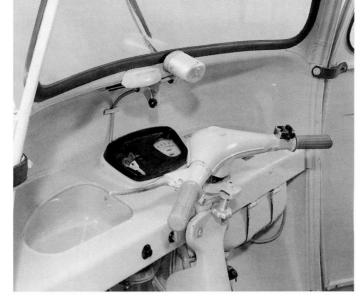

Above. The Lambro 550 N was the first Innocenti three-wheeler to have standard electric start. To activate it, the little black button on the left side of the dashboard near the starter lever had to be pushed. Below. To easily get at the motor and to facilitate carrying loads, the rear compartment was hinged in the back. Notice all the holes in the stamped metal frame to make the vehicle lighter.

in the trunk were identical to the earlier Lambro 550. At the beginning of 1968, the Lambro 550 N was also offered with a longer rear compartment with low sides to transport large, but light weight loads. This different version was named the Lambro 550 A (in which the "A" stands for *allungato*, or lengthened).

While technically the Lambro 550 N was advanced, the design of the body was definitely dated. Even so, it was a commercial success, especially the enclosed rear compartment version.

LAMBRO 500 L DELIVERY VEHICLE

As the direct heir to the successful LI 175 series, the Lambro 500 L debuted in the middle of 1967 to take the place of the dated Lambro 450, which had already served its purpose.

In putting together this new model, Innocenti took the entire design of the larger three-wheeler that it had put out a few months prior. In essence, the Lambro 500 L was absolutely identical to its big brother apart from the size of the rear compartment. Even though this model was aimed towards a more modest customer, all the finishing touches of the bigger version were applied to the 500 L.

The most interesting characteristics of the Lambro 500 L were the shifting of the motor from inside the cab to under the front

Above. This close-up shows the new external position of the motor on the Lambro 500 L. To reduce the amount of noise, an extra muffler was mounted along with the already existing one. Notice the shape of the wheel hubs made of aluminum alloy, which were the same as those on the 550 N version.
Below. The Lambro 500 had a smaller rear compartment than the 550 N but was still bigger than its predecessor, the Lambro 450.

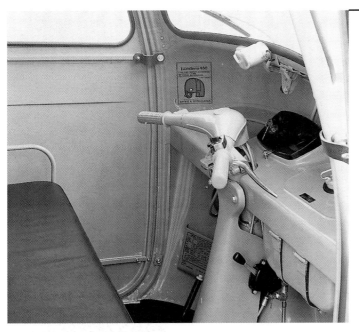

Above. The internal cab mirrored exactly that of the larger 550 N version. To the left of the gas tank, notice the control box for the reverse gear clutch, while the command lever for the heater is attached under the right part of the dashboard (not visible in the photo).

Below. This covered version of the Lambro 500 L seen from behind shows the large rear doors with a centralized locking handle. The U-shaped stamped metal bracket that can be seen behind the license plate holder was used to attach a spare tire.

part of the compartment, the addition of a second exhaust to muffle the engine's noise, and a second headlamp to improve driving at night.

Even though the maximum load was increased to 50 kilograms, the performance of the vehicle was improved even with a full load. The top speed was raised a few kilometers per hour, and the climbing power of the three-wheeler was improved due an adjustment of the gear ratio.

The slight price difference between this model and its larger brother was certainly the main cause for its weak sales record. After not even two years of production, only 8,000 units were produced.

LAMBRO 550 M, 550 V, AND 550 ML DELIVERY VEHICLES

Innocenti had a boom year in 1969. In the scooter sector, the new DL series was launched, replacing the LI/S series; and in the world of three-wheelers, the new 550 M and V were presented and immediately went to the top of the small delivery vehicle world because of their advanced technical and esthetic features.

The famous Bertone was entrusted with the design of the bodywork since he had already collaborated with Innocenti on other successful products. The simple design helped transform the three-wheeler into an elegant yet modest custom-built delivery vehicle. It's certainly rare in the field of transport cars that one comes along with avant-garde lines like this one.

The basic concept of this new three-wheeler was to offer its users the comfort and modern look of the automobiles of the day, but at the same time keep all the ease of driving, the performance, and the versatility typical of delivery vehicles.

The driver's cab was spacious and perfectly furnished. The bottom seat had springs inside and measured 97 cm wide. The back of the seat as well was loaded with springs and anatomically designed for maximum comfort even with a passenger. The instrument panel had many indicator lights and a large tachometer.

The braking system was completely revamped as well with a single pedal that stopped all three wheels at the same

The extremely modern lines of the revamped 550 series earned the Innocenti factory another technological first in the Italian motorized world. This was the very first time that a vehicle in this category was offered with a steering wheel just like on automobiles. Besides that, the ample space inside the cab also set a record for comfort. The economic version is pictured here with the lower sides for the trunk, measuring 1,700 mm long and 1,400 mm wide for a total load of 2.38 square meters. The covered version had a much larger compartment with two openings, a sliding door on the side, and two doors on the rear. With this model, Innocenti offered for the first time special versions for different types of loads. Models produced were for the transport of: water and drinks, frozen food and meat, fruit and vegetables, and loose material like gravel or leaves (in which case the trunk had a hydraulic lever to dump the load).

time. The hand lever of the emergency brake, on the other hand, worked only on the rear wheels. The 550 V version didn't use handlebars but a steering wheel that controlled the wheels via a system of gears that lessened the torque. On this version, the gas and brakes were run by

pedals—just like on normal automobiles—while the shifter control used a long lever situated in the center of the cab.

To facilitate the routine maintenance of the motor, the hinged rear compartment could be raised when empty and held up at 45 degrees by an automatic lever.

At the beginning of 1970, the Lambro 550 was also offered with a low-sided rear compartment measuring 170 by 140, and was dubbed the 550 ML.

At that point, the other two versions were available only with an enclosed rear compartment with a sliding side door and two rear doors, which were usually hinged.

In spite of all its advancements, the Lambro 550 delivery vehicle wasn't as much of a commercial success as the Innocenti management had hoped it would be. The probable cause for the relative failure of this three-wheeler was inside the Innocenti management, who at that time didn't know how to properly promote the new Lambro.

Above. The driver's area on the new 550 series was spacious with a large windshield and an instrument panel just like on automobiles. Unfortunately the handlebars hid the large tachometer and odometer in this photo. On the 550 ML version, the tachometer and odometer were more economical like that on the 500 ML. The glovebox was now made out of plastic and could be removed to make cleaning easier.

Below. Lifting up the rear compartment makes the motor easily accessible for routine maintenance. The box could be lifted up when nothing was left in it, and could be held in place at a 45 degree angle by a hinged metal bar.

LAMBRO 500 ML DELIVERY VEHICLE

In the autumn of 1969, Innocenti put an economic version of the luxurious Lambro 550 M and V three-wheeler on the market. This new model had a slightly smaller rear compartment, more spartan finishing touches, and became known as the Lambro 500 ML.

To keep the selling price down, a few features had to be eliminated. The door panels weren't included, as were the front grille, while the dashboard and all the controls were the same as the old 450 series.

The maximum load was 500 kilograms, even though the motor and its performance were identical to its big brothers, the Lambro 550 M and V models.

At first, the Lambro 500 ML was only offered with a 200cc engine—certainly the most appropriate size for a three-wheeler—but was soon accompanied by a 175cc version, which eventually was the only one available.

In response to a specific request from the French market at the beginning of 1971, a small series of the Lambro were built with a 125cc engine that could still carry a maximum load of 500 kilograms, but its performance wasn't nearly as good.

The economic version of Innocenti's three-wheelers was called the 500 ML, and could be recognized because of the smaller rear compartment, the smaller maximum load of 500 kilograms, and more modest finishing touches. The size of the wheels remained unchanged from its predecessor. The windshield squirter was now only offered as an option.

LAMBRO 600 M AND 600 V DELIVERY VEHICLES

The last creation of Innocenti in the field of delivery vehicles saw the light of day in January of 1970. The Lambro 600's two versions of M and V were the last delivery vehicles produced before the finally closing of the Innocenti factory and the subsequent sale to the Indian government.

This three-wheeler can't be considered a truly new vehicle since it basically took most of the characteristics of the 550 series, enlarged the rear compartment, and improved a few of the mechanical characteristics.

The significant size of the trunk, 2000 mm x 1510 mm, increased the amount of load that the Lambro could carry and therefore the overall versatility for many different forms of transport. Besides setting a new record of size for three-wheelers, the Lambro 600 became a future point of reference for the competition.

As far as the mechanical improvements are concerned, the only real changes were the new synthetic clutch plate and slight expansion of the wheelbase to about 200 mm. This model wasn't offered with an enclosed rear compartment, but only as a

pickup version with low sides. The rear could easily be covered, however, with metal ribs and a canvas or plastic cover.

As with the 550 model, the Lambro 600 was available in two different versions: the 600 M used a manubrio (or handlebars), and the 600 V used a volante (or steering wheel).

It's interesting to note that most customers preferred the steering wheel compared to the handlebars, which is without a doubt due to Innocenti's innovation in having the first three-wheeled delivery vehicle with a steering wheel. In an effort to increase sales in all sorts of different areas, special versions of the Lambro were prepared for specific uses. With the help of other companies, the rear compartment was prepared to carry drinks, to clean streets, to transport fresh food, and to conserve fresh fruit and vegetables.

As hinted at earlier, the Lambro 600 meant the end of the motor vehicle history of the Innocenti factory. In fact, the last vehicles put off the production line were 72 Lambro 600 Vs produced at the very beginning of January 1972.

The specialist Lojacono drew this splendid drawing inside the Innocenti factory to help us appreciate all the constructive details of the modern Lambro 600 V three-wheeler. The steering mechanism is especially interesting with a box of gears mounted on spherical heads that lessened the torque of the steering wheel. Notice the large area under the seat, which was now open since the engine had been moved to the rear of the vehicle. The heating tube for the cab and the air duct had been shifted compared to the 550 M and the 550 V models.

TRI-LAMBRETTA

The last vehicle that Innocenti would design was the Tri-Lambretta. 760 units total were produced in 1970, and were available just as the frame-only version. The model shown on these pages was a prototype found at the Innocenti factory that was built as a demonstration model to eventually be sold to the Far East market. As can be seen in the photo, the rear part of the vehicle was exactly the same as the Lambretta DL.

To satisfy requests from the Far East market, especially India, Innocenti produced an odd little three-wheeler in 1970. The characteristics of the Tri-Lambretta recalled the very first Innocenti delivery vehicles, the FB and the FC versions built in the 1940s and '50s, in that the rear looked exactly like a scooter with the motor situated under the driver and the front carried the load.

This setup had many distinct advantages. The first was the ability of the driver to control the merchandise while driving. Other reasons were because the price was lower since the rear differential was unnecessary and many more basic scooter parts could be used. In building the Tri-Lambretta, the rear of the scooter was the same as the Lambretta DL without any substantial changes. Even the same wheels were used, but the handlebars obviously had to be adjusted for the new design.

This original three-wheeler came in only one version without any front compartment since the local distributors would add accessories as they sought fit for their customers. To further cut the sales price, the brakes were all mechanically controlled with bowden cables, all the instrument control panels were eliminated, and a single adjustable seat was placed on the rear.

Strangely enough, the Tri-Lambretta was never presented to the international press to hopefully be able to sell in Europe.

The entire production, albeit modest, was sent to the Far East, and only two different prototypes were left behind in Italy.

One of these was set up to transport passengers on a comfortable spring loaded seat with an ample front area to rest their feet, which doubled as a safety legshield.

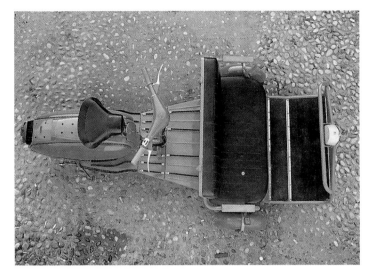

The top view of this Tri-Lambretta shows all the space available to the passengers on the luxurious faux-leather couch with springs in the back rest. A large area in front of the steering column was designed to store the baggage of the passengers. The model that actually went into production was different than this prototype in that the strips under the driver's feet were reconfigured and the front suspension used springs mounted on a cross beam, similar to those on automobiles. Since this vehicle was a cross between a scooter and a car, the driver had to be especially adept at keeping this bizarre three-wheeler on the road.

LAMBRETTA 48

This example of the Lambretta 48 was similar to the one presented at the 1954 Motorshow in Milan. Compared to the final version that went into production, this one differed in that this one used steel bars for the rear rack as opposed to stamped metal, and for the rubber seat in place of the classic fake leather saddle with a horizontal spring.

The first moped with large wheels built by Innocenti was shown for the first time at the 1954 Milan motorshow to gauge the reaction of the public. Actual production of the vehicle wouldn't take place until a long time afterwards, in the autumn of 1955.

Innocenti surprised the moped world when it decided to throw its hat into the ring with this sleek motorized bicycle at a very affordable price.

In building the Lambretta 48, the Innocenti design department was inspired by the most famous moped in the world, the Quikly built by NSU.

To keep the cost down, the entire frame was built out of stamped metal, including the springs and the rack. The suspension and the adjustable seat gave a surprising amount of comfort to the driver on any type of street, whereas the brakes proved to be a little weak for the peppy 48cc motor.

The large 22-inch wheels helped make the moped perfectly stable, even over the most unpredictable roads. The motor was miraculously quiet and ran without any hassle. The large muffler reduced the engine sound to less than 80 decibels, and the air filter built into the frame completely eliminated any sound from the air intake.

Thanks to close study of the spark plug, the little motor

was extremely frugal in its use of gasoline. With one liter, the Lambretta 48 could travel 80 kilometers, and could hit a top speed of 50 km/h.

Behind the seat was a solid carrying rack built of stamped metal that could carry up to 25 kilograms of baggage.

In case the moped broke down, it was possible to disengage the motor with a special button and just use the pedals. It was also possible to activate the two gears, so the speed and power of the bike could be adjusted if going uphill. In the six years of production, the Lambretta 48 was

Above. Innocenti mechanics and time trial racers gather around the little Lambretta 48. It was nicknamed "Ribot" at the end of the race around the Monza track because it ran 100 hours without any problems. Notice the enlarged gas tank to reduce the amount of stops to refuel.

Side. This 1958 model was a transition between the first and second series since it already had the internal high tension-coil but still had the decompressor mounted on the cylinder head. The polished rear shocks and the aluminum carburetor cover had already been introduced towards the end of 1956.

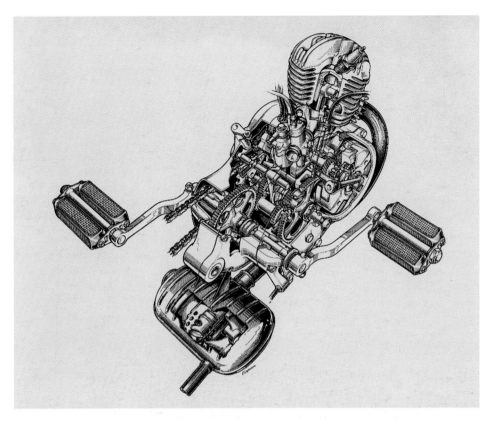

Above left. In this drawing of the transmission and the motor, the difference between this motor and its competition can be seen: First of all, the single-disc clutch was placed close to the engine shaft; second was the two-speed gearbox with a smooth coupling; and finally, the small diameter magneto with the coil placed outside of the rotor.

Above right. This pre-series version still had the rear rack made of metal bars, but at least the seat was made out of fake black leather like those on the final production models.

Side. This second series of the Lambretta 48 can be distinguished because of the two-cable shifting system, and the lack of the decompressor on the cylinder head and the high tension coil mounted on the outside of the bike.

This is an original photo of the Lambretta 48 prototype that was shown at the 1954 Milan Motorshow to test the reaction of the public to the possibility of Innocenti entering the world of mopeds.

always offered in only two colors, gray and red. Apart from that, it received many mechanical improvements, which made for two distinct series of the moped.

The first had only one control cable to shift gears, a high-tension coil attached to the frame, and a decompressor on the cylinder head. The second had two cables for shifting gears, the coil was incorporated into the crankcase, and the decompressor was eliminated.

On the very first examples produced, the left crankcase cover had a small curved chromed Innocenti emblem mounted on it, but later models put the writing right on the crankcase.

At the end of its production life, the handlebar controls were substituted with more conventional ones produced by a company that specialized in them.

In April of 1957, Innocenti ran an interesting test to demonstrate how solid and reliable the little 48cc

Lambretta motor was. The test was run right before Easter, and the Lambretta was supposed to drive 100 hours straight and cover about 6,000 kilometers at the Monza racetrack.

The gas tank of the Lambretta 48 was enlarged for the occasion, and another seat was placed on top of the carrying rack, so the racer could have two different positions when driving. The little Lambretta was driven by seven different factory racers that brilliantly ran 4,433 laps at top speed without any mechanical problems. In the end, the seven racers nicknamed the Lambretta "Ribot" in honor of the famous Italian colt. In spite of the high marks for reliability and road handling, the Lambretta 48 never won the hearts of the general public. Maybe it was the high seat, or the two-speed gearbox, which never worked quite as well as it should have.

Nevertheless, production numbers topped 63,000 units in the six years that the Lambretta 48 was built.

LAMBRETTINO 39 AND SX AUTOMATIC

The Lambrettino 48 SX was the one-and-only Innocenti product ever built with a continuously shifting transmission. The technology supposedly originated in France with the motor connected to the secondary transmission via a chain and a trapezoidal belt with two pulleys that varied in diameter according to the number of rotations of the wheel and the speed of the engine. The white plastic cover over the muffler protected the magneto from the elements and was easy to unhook by lifting the little tongue that stuck out on its right.

The Lambrettino signaled the return of Innocenti to the world of mopeds when it was first previewed at the 1966 London Motorshow. For the first time in history, Innocenti didn't produce the motor in-house but looked to another famous Italian company, Motom, to help them out. Motom's little one-speed engines were one of the most reliable on the market and because of their small 39cc displacement, they hardly used any gasoline.

The frame that this little engine received was built out of squared-off metal with a quadrangular shape that had a built-in air duct in the front to keep down the annoying noise of the carburetor. The rear of the moped didn't have any sort of suspension apart from the springs under the seat.

Many accessories were built out of plastic to keep costs down including the gas tank, the lights, the engine covering, and the toolbox. A large luggage rack was placed behind the seat, and a little plastic floorboard between the rider's legs left room to carry a small bag.

The wide range of colors available were: "sand," "ocean blue," dark green, medium green, turquoise, and "island

This was one of the first prototypes built in the Innocenti factory that used the 39cc engine built under license at Motom. Its frame was almost identical to the final version, but the front fork and the gas tank attached to the carrying rack didn't stand up to the severe trial tests.

This left-side view gives a good shot of the automatic transmission of the Lambrettino SX. Ballast was inserted into the front chromed flywheel that would shift to the outside of the wheel little by little with centrifugal force and move the two pulleys. This way, there were an infinite amount of gears, with a maximum of .0469 to a minimum of .0788. On the large aluminum-painted pulley a special transmission release was inserted that allowed the driver to conveniently just use the pedals in case of an emergency.

blue." The plastic pieces were all colored light gray.

In case of emergency, all the driver had to do was hit a little button and the engine disengaged from the rear wheel, so the moped could be used as a bicycle.

In the autumn of 1967, the more luxury version, called the "SX Automatic," was presented with a gradual automatic shifter, as the name insinuates. On this new version, the en-gine displacement was enlarged to 50cc to improve both the acceleration and its hill-climbing ability. The valuable addition of the automatic shifter used two pulleys that varied in diameter and were attached by a rubber trapezoidal belt. The diameter of the pulley varied according to the speed of the wheel, which essentially made for an infinite number of gears. The frame remained almost exactly the same as the basic ver-

sion, except for the crankcase chain and the muffler. The colors available for the SX were: olive, light violet, yellow-orange, blue, and dark green.

The obvious difference in price between the two versions of almost 20%, gave the basic version a distinct advantage in sales. Even so, it never was very successful and only stayed in production for one year.

Towards the end of its life, the Lambrettino 39 was sold under the name "Debramatic" with the only difference being a slight increase in the amount of oil in the engine.

These are two photos of the Lambrettino 39 that was built between November 1966 and December 1967 with a total production number of 15,677. The motor was completely different from the SX version in that it didn't have the automatic shifter but only a single-gear centrifugal clutch. The magneto was positioned on the left of the moped while the clutch was almost hidden by the pedal gear wheel on the right side. The enclosed-oil crankcase was incorporated into the motor and contained the gears for the primary transmission.

RACING LAMBRETTAS

On the following pages are a several of the finest specimens of racing scooters in the history of Innocenti. Obviously these aren't all the racing bikes that Innocenti produced in the few years that it built them since very few were actually built by hand. Each example has its own story and evolution according to what use it was put.

LAMBRETTA 125 A 1948

This model was specially prepared for closed circuit racing, and was put together by a private party using Innocenti parts directly from the factory, like the large gas tank and the aluminum manifold. The enlarged cylinder head, on the other hand, was made by an outside company called "Vortex."

To improve its road handling, the gear ratio was widened and eight-inch hubs replaced the original seven-inch ones. The large metal T frame piece attached to the center of the frame allowed plenty of air around the engine to keep it cool and also to keep down the amount of vibrations. The long saddle was surely a cutting edge design for 1948.

To lighten the bike, all the original bodywork on the rear was stripped and replaced with an extremely light chromed steel tube.

The carrying rack, the starter system, and parts of the electrical system were eliminated as well.

LAMBRETTA 125 C 1950-1951

The version written about here was the first racer built on the C frame especially for time trails and long-distance racing. The motor's identification number was ES 29 1R, which meant that it was from the first group of the number 29 experiment.

Compared to the normal Lambretta C, the entire structural and mechanical system were altered. The steering column and the handlebars were significantly shortened, while the gas tank and front brakes were enlarged. The front legshield was slimmed down to make driving on uneven terrain easier.

As far as the mechanical system is concerned, the carburetor was an SS 27 C made by Dell'Orto. The large air filter could be used in two different positions depending on the conditions; when the hatch was open the air flow was free and when closed, it purified the air.

The huge muffler and exhaust system were made out of light stamped iron and the above-average length made it a sort of expansion chamber. An inspection plug was placed on the front part of the exhaust to clean out all the dirt.

The cylinder was bored out as much as possible and positioned to avoid any problems to the crankcase pump. The connecting rod was carefully placed and a bronze footing 16 mm in diameter was mounted as opposed to the standard 14 mm one.

To reduce friction to the gearbox, the gears and the transmission pivot pin rotated on roller bearings. The diameter of all the teeth on the gears were enlarged to help resist the stress placed upon them during races. A large gas filter was placed on the left side behind the cylinder that used an extremely fine steel mesh filter.

Other modifications were to the firm seat covered in soft brown leather and the easily accessible spare tire. On this version, the CO_2 cylinder isn't attached to the floorboards, which was used to put out fires or to pump up tires.

This model won Innocenti the most races of any bike,

such as the 1951 Milan-Taranto race, the 1951 Six Days In Italy race, and the 1951 Liège-Milan-Liège race in the scooter category.

The Innocenti long-distance driver that knew how to get the most out of the Lambretta C racer was Ernesto Longoni, who unfortunately passed away recently.

LAMBRETTA 125 BITUBO 1951-1953

Built for circuit races and just pure speed, the Lambretta Bitubo (dual tube), was the apex in the evolution of Innocenti racing scooters. Even though the Bitubo was originally conceived to put the Lambretta's implacable enemy, the Vespa, in its place, it ended up competing with the rising star, MV Agusta. This new competition could often rank first in the scooter racing category, and it was busy preparing a mini four-stroke version of its famous

bialbero Grand Prix motorcycle.

The Bitubo was a very special model that basically had nothing to do with the stock Lambrettas of the time. The gearbox had four speeds that were shifted via a foot pedal, and a torsion bar fit snugly inside the pivot arm to make up the very original suspension system.

Even the cylinder was extremely original with two backwards exhaust portals. The air intake was enlarged to make up a special sort of cone facing forward that allowed a huge amount of air into the carburetor. This ideal carburetor system helped the scooter surpass 100 km/h, but also required a driver that was extremely attentive to not drown out the engine.

The frame was more similar to a motorcycle than a scooter, and there was no more trace of legshields, a glovebox,

LAMBRETTA 125 D 1954

The Lambretta 125 D pictured on this page has a unique history that must be told. Deriving from the basic 1954 Lambretta D, its owner, Richard Piciulin, decided to modify the little scooter. Piciulin was hired as an expert metal worker at Innocenti, in fact the bodywork of all the prototypes and even the record-setting Lambrettas were his handy work.

The beautiful shape of the gas tank designed by Piciulin incorporated the spare wheel and contained a good twelve liters of gas.

The same kind of gas tank was mounted on the Lambretta 150 D for the around-the-world trip of Cesare Battaglini. With this Lambretta, Piciulin participated in all of the most important Lambretta rallies in the 1950s, including the very first Milan-Taranto race of 1959.

At the beginning of the 1970s, this Lambretta had seen better days and a solid rack was placed on the rear behind the glovebox to help a postman deliver the mail.

Piciulin hadn't forgotten about his creation, though, and when the mailman was moving to a new town, he convinced the postman to give him the scooter back.

The Lambretta D stayed in Piciulin's hands for the rest of his life. It was placed in a corner of his metal workshop that he kept going constantly right up until his death at age eighty.

Today, this Lambretta is making its new owner happy, and is still run regularly across all Europe.

Center. This example of a recently restored Bitubo was prepared in a very unusual way, probably to participate in light motorcycle races. In fact, the frame was "closed," which wasn't allowed for regular racing in the scooter class. The "V" superimposed above the Lambretta writing is how the decal really was, unfortunately the original logo couldn't be saved, therefore this is a reproduction.

Above. The design of the Lambretta D was sketched out by Mr. Piciulin with the predominant feature being the large gas tank that fits in perfectly with the rest of the elegant bodywork. The differences in this engine compared to the normal stock version were small; two sparkplugs were used and a longer air duct was added that was similar to the 150cc version. Notice the position of the front headlamp that was attached to the handlebars, so it would move with the front wheel.

or little wheels. In fact, the aluminum wheels were enlarged to twelve inches for better handling.

The front fork and the rear of the Bitubo were extensively streamlined, and the saddle was positioned in such a way that the driver would have to be in a position like the Grand Prix racers.

The performance of the Bitubo was fantastic both in acceleration and for its top speed. With the special Innocenti-designed fuel with an alcohol base, the Bitubo could easily reach 150 km/h and was unbeatable in flat-out acceleration races in its category. A few of the Bitubo were also built with a normal cylinder and single exhaust, which were made for several important foreign distributors to help spread the word about Innocenti at local competitions.

LAMBRETTA 125 B AUTOMATIC

The example of the auto-matic-shifting Lambretta pictured here is probably the only one that has survived in perfect condition. It was discovered at the house of a relative of the technician who originally tuned up the delicate automatic-shifting system. It has now been completely restored and works perfectly. The bodywork and the frame are identical to the regular series Lambretta B, except for, of course, the elimination of the shifter and clutch levers on the handlebars. On the rear section of the engine, the tachometer/odometer is attached with the dial then being mounted above the front head-lamp. The unusual *Cambio automatico* (Automatic gearshift) written on the side of the glovebox was painted by hand and is exactly the same as the original.

Towards the end of the 1940s, a German engineer, Mr. Krais, patented a new automatic shifter that he shopped around to various automobile and motorcycle manufacturers in Europe. Innocenti was seriously interested in using the remarkable patent and to begin studying the possibility of equipping its Lambretta with this new automatic shifter.

The working of this mechanism was extremely simple and used a different automatic clutch plate for each gear that engaged at a certain number of rpms. When shifting into a higher gear, the lower one would automatically disengage by a patented freewheel, which reduced the amount of pieces actually moving at any given time. It was possible to keep the scooter in low gear for climbing steep hills to maximize the complete potential of the engine without having to continually change speed.

Two Lambretta Bs were especially prepared to test out the new mechanism, and the frame and the whole mechanical system wasn't significantly altered from the stock Lambrettas. Unfortunately, the hill-climbing tests didn't give the desired results since the gear oil wasn't able to keep a steady temperature and overheated to the extent that the working of the automatic gearbox was compromised. Furthermore, the cost of using the automatic shifter ended up being higher than originally thought, so the entire project was prematurely abandoned.

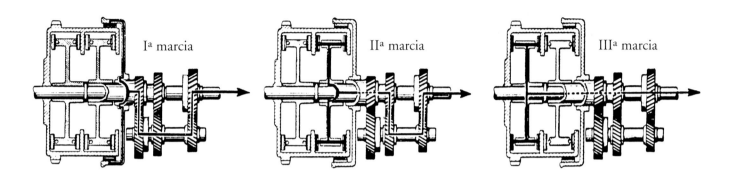

I^a marcia   II^a marcia   III^a marcia

Above. These diagrams show how the Krais automatic shifter works using a centrifugal clutch. The three drawings reveal how the three different gears are engaged according to the speed of the engine. The moment that it shifts into a higher gear, the lower gear is disengaged through a freewheel designed by Krais. By adjusting the strength of the clutch springs, it was possible to vary when the gears engage according to the rpms of the motor.

Below. Only on the Lambretta, the three centrifugal clutch plates (one for each speed) were positioned differently: two were placed in the front section and the other in the space usually occupied by the gearbox. The long chromed lever on the front cover had three positions: neutral, first gear, and second gear. The last two positions could be for descending long hills to use all the braking power of the motor.

RACING AND TOURIST MOTOLAMBRETTA 125

These two beautiful photographs with the brick wall background of the Innocenti factory show the MotoLambretta 125 Tourist model in all its glory. The most interesting part is without a doubt the telescopic front forks made of stamped metal that close up look not unlike the wheels used on the undercarriage of airplanes. The front spring system is incorporated into the shaft, while the mechanical shocks are attached to the outside, similar to the shape of the rear of the bike. Notice the position of the taillight, which is exactly the same as the C and LC series that doesn't leave room for a license plate holder since Italian law didn't require vehicles under 125cc to be licensed.

High off the remarkable success of the Lambretta 125 B, Innocenti did a surprise move by throwing its hat into the light motorcycle ring with the presentation of a racing cycle at the 1949 Milan motorshow. With the name "MotoLambretta," the new Innocenti product was the star attraction at the show because of how its original design set it apart from the competition.

Compared to its little scooter brother, the MotoLambretta used basically the same motor with slight modifications to the engine block, the connecting rods, and the primary transmission, but the gearbox was expanded from three to four gears to take advantage of the engine's potential for racing.

The gear shifter was controlled by a foot pedal that was built into the right side of the gearbox. The final transmission to the rear wheel was via a long shaft and dual cones with the crown-wheel axle attached to the wheel hub. The rear suspension was particularly original with the large oscillating fork. The suspension joint was attached directly to the rear part of the engine block, while the elastic part

Just a few months after a notice appeared in the magazine *Motociclismo* on June 23rd 1949 announcing the imminent entrance of Innocenti into the motorcycling world, the racing MotoLambretta 125 was presented to the world at the Milan motorshow. Surrounded by myriad Lambrettas, the new Innocenti creation was the hit of the show, both with the public and the international press.

MOTO Lambretta 125 2/
TIPO COMPETIZIONE
CHASSIS 04 02
IL MOTORE DELLO SCOOTER TIPO RECORDS DEL MONDO A MONTLHERY
SOSPENSIONE ANTERIORE - A FORCELLA TELESCOPICA
SOSPENSIONE POSTERIORE - A FORCELLA OSCILLANTE
CON BARRA DI TORSIONE
TRASVERSALE
TRASMISSIONE MOTRICE - A BARRA DI TORSIONE
CON COPPIA CONICA
POSTERIORE
CAMBIO DI VELOCITA - A QUATTRO RAPPORTI
CON COMANDO A PEDALE

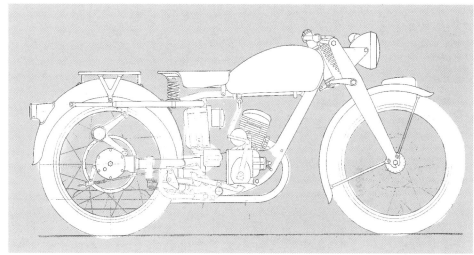

formed a special torsion bar under the joint and connected to the fork with two jointed arms. The frame of the MotoLambretta was a mixed construction of both tubes and stamped metal with the engine built into it as an essential part of the structure.

A more traditional approach was used for the 21-inch wheels with side brakes and friction shocks on the rear.

Besides this model, the Innocenti design team envisioned other light racing motorcycles with a four-stroke engine or a two-stroke engine with dual pistons and different layouts for the suspension. It's very probable, however, that the MotoLambretta was the only bike that Innocenti seriously developed to enter into the 125cc racing motorcycle market.

Based on this original blueprint, Innocenti displayed a 125cc tourist version of the MotoLambretta at the 1950 Milan fair, declaring that the motorcycle would be on the market any day.

Besides having a regular electric system, the new tourist model was different from the racing version because of the telescopic front forks and suspension similar to those used on airplane wheels. This bike as well was stopped by the company management for some unknown reason, and no more Innocenti motorcycles would ever be displayed again.

This sketch was for a different tourist MotoLambretta. This time it was equipped with a traditional parallelogram front fork, similar to those used by most of the light motorcycle manufacturers in Italy. In this example, the taillight was positioned to allow the owner to mount a license plate holder on the rear fender.

207

RACING MOTOLAMBRETTA 250

For the 1951 *Fiera di Milano* motorshow, Innocenti built an impressive stand full of novelties. Besides the Queen of the Show, the racing Lambretta 250, a Lambretta that had set a distance record was displayed, as well as a mechanical robot that showed how easy it was to drive an Innocenti scooter. A movie filmed inside the factory describing how a Lambretta was born was continually projected on the screen behind the stand. This photo shows the lap counter built into the gas tank and the fuel plug in a very unusual position.

Exactly one year after the presentation of the two-stroke MotoLambretta 125, Innocenti displayed a new 250cc racing motorcycle at the 1951 Milan motorshow.

The event was extremely important because it was the first time that Innocenti built such a technically-advanced racing vehicle that was in direct competition with the most important international motorcycle manufacturers, especially with the Italian company that dominated the 250cc class, Moto Guzzi.

To complete this very original motorcycle project, Innocenti engineer Torre managed the engineer Salmaggi, who was temporarily hired for the project and should have been allowed to participate in the initial design, the development of the prototype, and test runs. Unfortunately for Salmaggi, he often had to submit to the decisions of Torre for the construction of the bike, and eventually had to leave the project prematurely since the two of them didn't get along.

Unfortunately, it was impossible to discover how much Salmaggi contributed to the project and the building of the prototypes compared to Torre. But it's almost certain that the

initial design and the first prototype were Salmaggi's work, while its evolution and improvements were the work of Torre. The impeccable lines and the powerful dual-cylinder, four-stroke, V-shaped engine made the Lambretta 250cc the most admired motorcycle at the Milan show. It received the most enthusiastic remarks from motorcycle critics from all over the world.

The engine had single-shaft distribution controlled by a series of cones and small hermetically-sealed shafts in oil, while the lubrication was pressurized with an external recovery reservoir attached next to the rear wheel.

The clutch was a single dry disc just like those used on automobiles, and the gearbox had five speeds. The control of the shifter was surely original since the first four gears were acti-

Above. When the Lambretta 250 was displayed at the Milan motorshow, the crowd was thick around the stand. The motorcycle didn't look as much like a stripped-down racing bike, but like an elegant sport motorcycle aimed at a richer clientele.
Below. This official Innocenti photo clearly shows the extra lever mounted on the rear foot peg to put the motorcycle into fifth gear. Another visible feature is near the central section of the motor where the oil reservoir is mounted close to the rear wheel. The cycle shown here was one of the first examples of the Lambretta 250 with the magneto enclosed in the front nose-shaped cover.

vated by a right foot lever. To get into fifth gear, the driver had to hit a small pedal on the left-side that was situated on the rear foot pegs, so he had to be in an aerodynamic position on the straightaway to switch it.

The frame had a central beam made out of a steel tube that curved towards the rear. The engine block was held at two spots on either side by triangular brackets that looked like those used on airplanes.

The rear suspension used an oscillating fork that incorporated the transmission shaft on the left side and was controlled by a torsion bar made out of special steel. The shocks were a little more traditional with the typical adjustable friction model.

The 22-liter gas tank was especially original in that it incorporated a lap counter in the front part and a foam rubber cushion in the middle to rest on when in the aerodynamic racing position.

For the test runs on the racetrack and the delicate tuning of the bike, the two drivers Romolo Ferri and Nello Pagani were hired. They alternately tested the bike innumerable times on the Monza racetrack for all of 1952 and 1953.

Even though the maximum power of the bike hit 28 horsepower at 9,500 rpms, the Lambretta 250 was unstable and difficult to steer especially around sharp turns. Other problems were the unexpected gear shifts due to the longitudinal rotations of the engine shaft and the transmission with cardan joint that created the well-known wipe-outs on the track.

To improve its road-handling, the frame was continually modified. The rear friction shocks were substituted with hydraulic ones, but later the torsion bar was replaced with normal telescopic shocks, helical springs, and the wheel diameters were shortened to only 18 inches.

To increase its power, dual cam cylinder heads were used and the lubrication reservoir was moved under the engine to lower the center of gravity. The electrical system was radically altered with the single magneto inside the crankcase replaced with two external magnetos placed between the V of the cylinders. Finally, a specially-constructed single magneto was used.

The official debut of the MotoLambretta 250 happened at the French racetrack at Bergerac at the end of May 1952 with

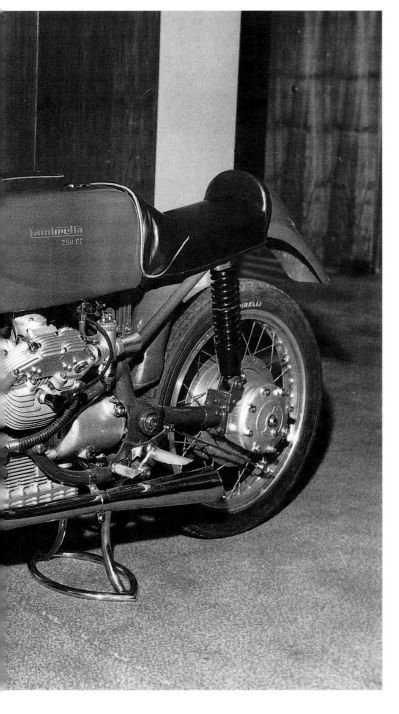

Above. This was the second to last version of the Lambretta 250 with the dual-cylinder motor still equipped with two magnetos. To improve the cooling of the oil in the engine, an aluminum duct was placed under the crankcase with a large air intake.

Center. This was the next version of the Lambretta 250 that was presented at the 1951 Milan motor-show.

Below. The third version of the Lambretta 250 was built in the second half of 1952, with many changes to the body-work and engine of the motorcycle. To increase its power, dual-cam cylinder heads were mounted and two mag-netos were used rather than one.

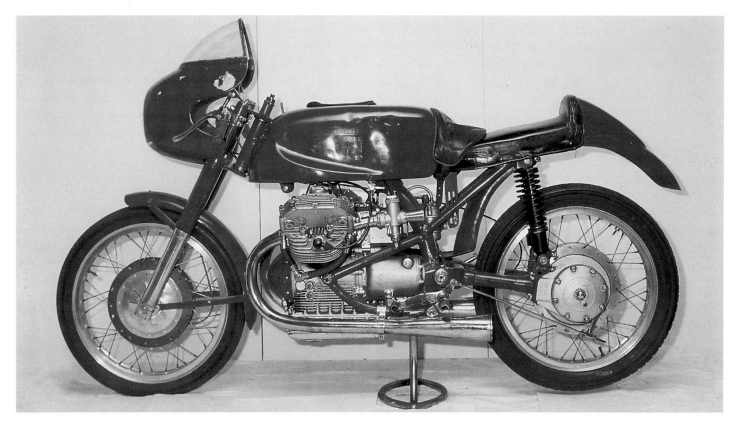

More than thirty years have passed since the photo on the preceding page and the one pictured here, but the motorcycle is identical. Although it now has a few dings and scrapes, it is still in excellent shape with the chrome shining and its original racing red paint glowing. Now this example of the racing Lambretta 250 can be found at the Museum of the Lambretta Club of Italy.

the two drivers Pagani and Ferri. The first contact with the difficult world of racing proved promising. Ferri got a big head start on the others and was immediately a few lengths ahead of the competition. For seventeen laps he stayed in the lead, but unfortunately the gear selector broke and he was forced to call it quits. The Pagani team, on the other hand, had to withdraw before the race had even begun because of a broken distributor gear.

A short-while after this promising debut, Innocenti hit the racetrack again at the Grand Prix of Locarno in September 1952. The same drivers, Pagani and Ferri, would race but with engines and transmissions that had been radically revamped.

Unfortunately, this time was doomed as well since neither bike was able to finish the race due to the fragile mechanical systems. Even so, both showed an impressive top speed dur-

ing the race.

After that, Innocenti participated in several more races that were not quite as important in an attempt to fix all the quirks of the engine and perfect the geometry of the suspension. The MotoLambretta was continually developed for all of 1953, but finally the company decided to quit trying to solve all the difficult problems posed by this motorcycle. Instead, Innocenti decided to concentrate all its energy on new motorscooters.

The Lambretta 250 still remained a valid testimonial to the high level that Innocenti was able to reach in the difficult sector of motorcycling after just a few years of experience.

In honor of this entire project, a Lambretta 250 was completely restored and displayed in the offices of the Innocenti workshop *Centro Studi* for all of the 1970s until the end of scooter production.

1950 LAMBRETTA 125 C PROTOTYPE AND 1957 LAMBRETTA D MILITARY PE

At the beginning of 1950, Innocenti decided to take a plunge into the world of supplying the military by designing a miniature folding scooter that could easily be used for parachuters. Once on the ground, the soldier could hop on the Lambretta with all the necessary equipment and scoot over any sort of land scape.

Just for this purpose, a special version of the brand-new Lambretta 125 C was given a little hinge right in the middle of the frame that allowed the scooter to be folded up, which significantly reduced its volume. To avoid having any parts jutting out, the handlebars as well folded up, and the floorboards and front legshield were completely eliminated with a small crossbar mounted as foot pegs.

To further reduce the volume of the scooter, the front steering column was shortened, and the glovebox and the rear side panels were abandoned.

The mechanical system remained essentially the same as the Lambretta C, except for the exhaust, which was raised to a higher position on the frame to protect it from water and bumps.

Unfortunately, little more is known about the development of this interesting prototype and the only real information that remains is two photographs taken at the factory.

Six years later, the development department at Innocenti revisited the design of the folding Lambretta in response to a specific request from N.A.T.O. for a folding parachuting scooter to help the air force.

A very interesting prototype was prepared for this task that was extremely versatile since it could be used in almost any climate or condition.

The frame was made up of strong steel tubes that were hinged at

This secret photo of the tactical parachuting scooter based on the Lambretta 150 D production model was presented to the N.A.T.O. Commission. The left side view shows the bare-boned torsion bar system since the elastic element is connected inside the pivot pin that supported the motor like on the Lambretta E and F.

Above. The parachuting Lambretta was folded up and ready to be launched from the heavens. The handlebars were unhooked from the steering column and its clamp was used to attach the parachute. Notice the original locking frame with the spherical clamp in the middle of the bike.
Below. The entire engine block is visible from the right side and very similar to that of the Lambretta LD '57. The only important differences were the starting mechanism using epicyclical gears and the aluminum cylinder to reduce the overall weight of the machine. Strangely, the engine displacement was only 125cc with a MA 18 carburetor from older models.

the center with a patented clamp (patent number N.003.P.0097) that more than cut in half the amount of space that the scooter took up.

The front suspension with oscillating connecting rods used a more simplified design that would be used on regular production Lambrettas as well from 1957 to 1972. The rear suspension, however, was the same torsion bar that was just like those mounted on the Lambretta E and F series.

On the front handlebars, an adjustable clamp was attached, so it could support an automatic light machine gun. It was also possible to equip the Lambretta with a lighting system that was shielded against radio waves.

The motor derived directly from the one used on the 125 LD '57, with the only alteration being the elimination of forced ventilation and the substitution of the heavy cast iron piston with a

lighter aluminum one with a chromed barrel.

To improve its hill-climbing ability, the gear ratios were reduced and the spark plugs were adjusted to increase the resilience of the motor in low gear and reduce the amount of fuel used.

The prototype weighed in at around 55 kilograms, but as the official presentation explained, the weight could be reduced to about 48 kilograms if a lot of super-light material was used. If special tires were mounted, the overall weight of the scooter would be one kilogram less.

A particularly interesting feature of this scooter was the possibility to attach a hook to the rear of the scooter to tow a little trail-

This Lambretta was recently found at an important Innocenti dealership in the Emilia-Romagna province of Italy. Unfortunately, not even the owner remembered the story behind this particular civilian model. This Lambretta was almost certainly created inside the Innocenti factory as an experiment, not as a customized version by its owner. Close inspection of this vehicle reveals just a few differences between this version and the military prototype, especially as far as the frame was concerned.

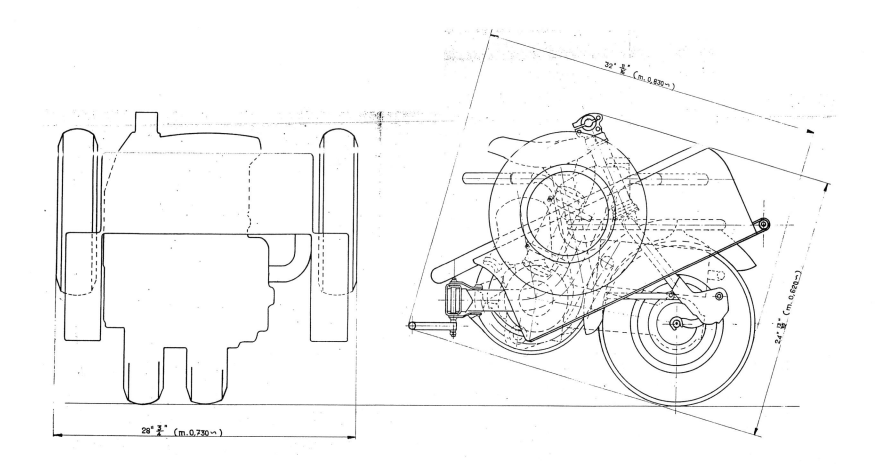

Above. This drawing showed exactly how much volume, in inches, the folding Lambretta would take up. In this case, a little ammunition trailer was incorporated that used the same wheels as the scooter.

Side. The first design of the folding military Lambretta used the frame from the 1950 Lambretta 125 C series. In this case, the handlebars didn't come off, but instead they folded with two hinges attached to the center clamp.

er that could be dropped from planes in the same box as the Lambretta.

During all of 1957, the parachuting Lambretta was tested both inside the factory and outside. The scooter was dropped many times near the Linate airport in Milan to find out how much damage it would receive when it landed and then used on difficult terrain.

Not much more is known about the development of this scooter as well, but probably the folding Lambretta didn't pass the strict tests to make it satisfactory for N.A.T.O.

A civilian version was built as well based on this last prototype but with an electrical system and painted in an unusual orange color. Unfortunately, it's unknown whether this model was built because of a request from a foreign market, or if it was just a fantasy scooter built by some workers in the Innocenti factory. At least its known that this prototype never went into any sort of full production.

LAMBRETTA LI "GHIA" PROTOTYPE

In 1959, Innocenti decided it was time to rework the lines of the Lambretta LI second series. For this difficult task, a designer outside of the Innocenti development team was called up for some modern and avant-garde ideas.

The job went to the famous designer Ghia, who had already worked on the development of the beautiful Ducati Cruiser scooter. Showing a lot of interest, Ghia prepared two different wooden models right away, so Innocenti could get a 3D view of the project. After the better of the two designs was approved, a metal prototype was built and then tested using the technical and mechanical system of the normal Lambretta LI.

For the first time in Innocenti's history, it used the monocoque structure and thereby imitated its bitter rival, Piaggio, who had always been a strong supporter of the single unit frame. Other interesting novelties of the prototype were the moveable front fender—like on the old LD—and the attachment of the wheel hubs with three connectors rather than four.

This interesting project was never completed since Innocenti preferred to redo the bodywork without changing the tried-and-true single tube frame that it had always used.

Side. This wooden model came from the Ghia bodywork company in Turin, Italy as an idea for the redesign for the Lambretta LI series. Notice that handlebars and the saddle are off of the Lambretta LI series II to make the model look more realistic.

Below. The final metal version of the Lambretta designed by Ghia didn't have particularly "happy" lines since the front of the scooter was squared off, while the rest of it kept the round shape of the II series. Notice the decision to reduce the size of the side panels compared to the size of the frame, a styling cue which would be adopted for the new Junior series of 50, 100, and 125cc scooters.

217

LAMBRETTA LI PROTOTYPE WITH MONOCOQUE FRAME

This close-up photo of the rear of the mono-coque-frame Lambretta LI Series III shows another alternative to the time-consuming construction of the tubular frame with bolted on bodywork. Besides the classic glovebox under the driver's seat, another triangular storage area was placed behind the gas tank, which was intended to keep tools and vehicle documents. Notice the different position of the bolts that held on the air flow system, a design that would be adopted for the Lambretta Junior series.

In an effort to keep down the costs of the brand-new Lambretta LI Series III, an interesting new frame and bodywork design was proposed in 1962 that would replace the expensive welded and bent tubes with a monocoque frame.

Using the knowledge garnered from the Lambretta J 50 series, the designers were able to put together a test model of the new model in just a short while.

The bodywork of the new prototype used the same shape as the LI series III, except for the slimmer foot rest, which was definitely uncomfortable for the driver. Besides that, the wheel hubs now only had three points of attachment to the rim.

The entire mechanical system, the suspension, the seat, and the handlebars all remained the same, but the shape of the muffler was altered to fit in with the new floorboards and the kick starter.

The testing of this new model gave glorious results, so it seemed that this new prototype would be put into regular production. For reasons unknown, the Innocenti management blocked its construction, keeping the old tube frame design for which the Lambretta was famous.

BODYWORK DESIGN OF THE SX 200

This project dated October 1966 featured an attractive, slender design for the Lambretta SX 200 (which had already been released at the beginning of that year) with larger twelve-inch wheels.

Apart from the square lines, the project had the interesting idea of placing the glovebox behind the front legshields. The front fender swiveled along with the wheel, just like on the earliest Lambrettas, and would be used on the little J 125 Super Star Stream for the English market.

It's probable that this project was envisioned in preparation for the forthcoming super Lambretta with a dual-cylinder 200cc engine.

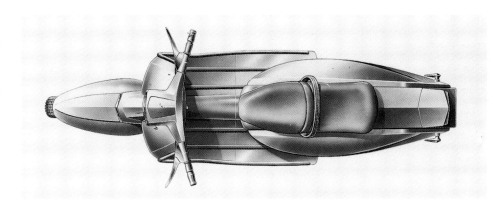

This rather squared-off design was proposed for the Lambretta 200 SX, but wouldn't go beyond the drawing board. Instead, the Bertone Studio was entrusted with coming up with a new design for the top-of-the-line Lambretta.

DUAL-CYLINDER LAMBRETTA 200 PROTOTYPE

The dual-cylinder Lambretta 200 number 10 (the prototype test number) had mounted a practical glovebox behind the front legshield in place of the one under the driver's seat to make room for the airflow system and the battery. The large extra cover over the transmission crankcase kept the lubrication system separate. On the front part of the scooter, notice the special disc brakes with the internal floating clamp and the disc attached to the sides of the wheel hub.

The enormous success of the Lambretta 200 on foreign markets, especially in England, caused Innocenti to prepare an exclusive model with outstanding performance to satisfy the most demanding clientele who wanted a scooter that was at the top of its class in power and speed.

For this reason, an interesting two-stroke, dual-cylinder motor was designed that used a properly enlarged transmission and gearbox off of the SX 200. The engine displacement of the two cylinders was kept within the 200cc area, so the Lambretta could still compete in the scooter category.

The motor was designed in such a way as to not take up too much room, so it could still fit in the SX series frame. Since the carburetor and the air intake system were enlarged, the glovebox was shrunken and the air duct was shorter.

For road tests, two prototypes, numbered 10 and 11, were prepared with slight differences. Special characteristics of the number 10 prototype were the aluminum cylinder with chrome parts, the mechanical lap counter, and the possibility to mount twelve-inch wheels. The number 11 had a cast iron cylinder, an automatic oil pump that mixed the gas and oil, and an interesting glovebox placed behind the legshield

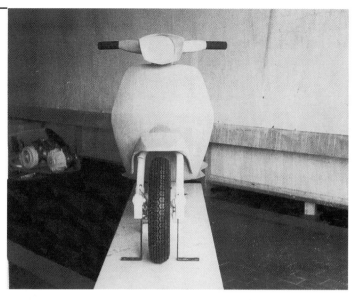

These three shots of a wooden model for the bodywork of the dual-cylinder super Lambretta were taken inside the Bertone laboratory. The partially-squared shape was similar to the Lui, but had a personality all its own and a unique sporty style.

instead of the one under the seat. Even during the very first trials by the expert tester Cereda, the dual-cylinder Lambretta showed its strong racing personality and its excellent reliability. Even so, the fine tuning of the scooter that was required to eventually put it into production proved to be a long and laborious process lasting more than a year.

One of the persistent problems was the electrical system since the magneto wasn't able to supply the right amount of current fast enough to the two external electrical coils, causing unforeseen drops in power. To improve the efficiency of the magneto, an electrical starting system designed by Ducati especially for this model was tested. In the end, Innocenti returned to the points and condenser system.

One of the very interesting attributes was the disc brakes made especially for this model. The brakes were still mechanically controlled, but its overall braking power was increased by enlarging the diameter of the disc and by bringing the braking clamp inside the mechanism. In doing this, the disc was attached to the edges of the wheel hub and the clamp remained floating inside to adjust to the wear on the device. Strangely, this new brake design was never used on production models, and the smaller disc brakes with a fixed clamp were still used.

While the trial runs continued nonstop, Bertone was called up to draw an avant-garde bodywork design that could handle the large dual-cylinder engine.

For this scooter's new "clothes," Bertone looked back on the brand-new Lui scooter which had just been designed. Soon a wooden model was prepared to give a 3D view of Bertone's vision. The front headlamp was undoubtedly similar to the Lui, while the unusual rear section was more square and large enough to hold the dual-cylinder engine.

Unfortunately, the impending scooter market crash blocked the development of this fascinating project, even if the English importer Peter Agg had already shown interest in purchasing 10,000 of them. The sales department at Innocenti decided that the "Super" Lambretta wouldn't be profitable to enter into production and indefinitely set aside the design.

FOUR-STROKE MOTOLAMBRETTA 98

The mysterious four-stroke MotoLambretta 98cc was built in conjunction with Motom at the end of the 1960s. This one-and-only example was rediscovered inside the Innocenti factory, unfortunately none of the workers at the factory could remember the exact history of this motorcycle. The prototype seems almost ready for production, but a few parts were badly designed and simply attached to get an idea of what the bike would look like. For example, the side panels wouldn't allow access to the carburetor to activate the starter, the side covers on the gas tank were made out of wood, and the taillight still had "Yamaha" written on it!

Following the successful collaboration with the Italian company Motom in the construction of the Lambrettino moped, Innocenti considered taking advantage of Motom's knowledge of this market and therefore entering into the business of selling motorcycles as well.

From this train of thought, the MotoLambretta was born (as pictured below). Obviously the design of this prototype wasn't completely finished, but it could still function perfectly.

Technically, this model derived from the light 1962 Motom 92 motorcycle, but the body was completely new, even if it looked like the first Japanese bikes brought into Italy at the end of the 1970s.

This example was discovered in an abandoned hangar at the Innocenti factory. Unfortunately, it was impossible to find any documents that could help us understand the history and character of this interesting motorcycle.

48 AUTOMATIC MOPED PROTOTYPE

One of the last Innocenti projects to try to revitalize its sales was developed with the collaboration of the engineer Micucci, who was famous for having designed the unforgettable Guzzi 65 (*Guzzino*).

The 49cc moped was intended to be put on the market to replace the unfortunate Lambrettino 39 which had a horrible sales record.

For this new model, Micucci designed a new frame made of two large sections of tubes that formed a robust structure that wouldn't twist. The motor and the transmission were attached to the frame with stamped metal plates that also helped support the rear fork.

The gas tank was especially interesting with a practical indicator to show how much fuel was left with a transparent tube inserted into the metal work and attached to the tank that would fill up with exactly the amount of gas in the tank.

The little two-stroke 49cc engine was fueled with a rotating valve, while the entire final transmission used a belt for the primary transmission, a reduction gear sealed in oil with a dry clutch for the secondary, and a chain for the third.

In the first few months of 1971, a final and definitive prototype of the moped was prepared in hopes of bringing it to the upcoming Milan motorshow. Unfortunately, the difficult economic situation at Innocenti didn't allow the new moped to be put into production or properly publicized, and therefore the project was indefinitely abandoned.

The prototype of the 48 Moped was finally ready by the spring of 1971, just when the Lambretta assembly line was about to be closed indefinitely. Even though the lines of the 48 Moped were attractive and young looking, it never got out of the prototype phase since Innocenti was completely abandoning its motorcycle production. A small cylindrical button was placed on the center part of the foot rest that when hit, unhooked the transmission and allowed the pedals to be used.

PROTOTYPES

Side. These two three-wheeler designs to carry passengers remained only at the planning stage and were never developed. The first drawing was based on the mechanical system of the Lambretta 125 A, while the second used that of the 125 LC model. Below. In 1949, the *Centro Studi* design department at Innocenti developed this interesting little car using the motor of the FB delivery vehicle. The design was then passed on to another company, Cimen, that made a prototype based on Innocenti's schematics that was almost totally functional. Known by the cute name *Girino* (tadpole), the little car didn't win the hearts of the general public when presented at the Milan motorshow in 1949. No more than a few dozen were ever built.

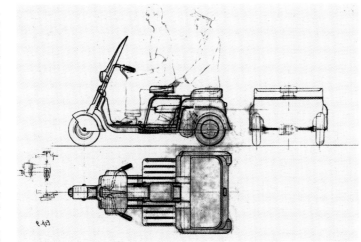

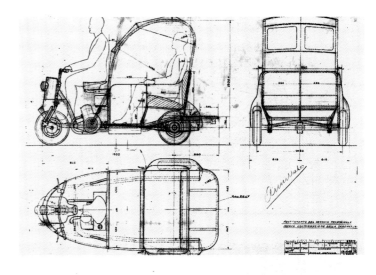

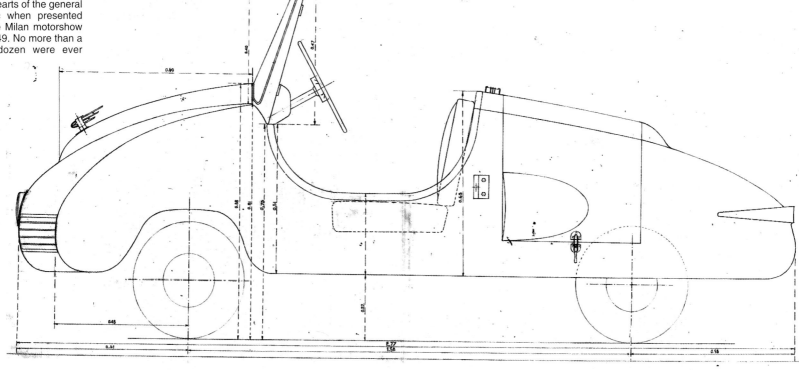

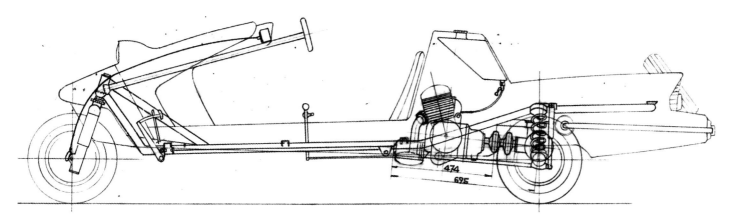

Side. This project placed the FD delivery vehicle's motor into an avant-garde little car with a typically American design built by a company called Basson.

Below. As one of the very first designs for a super economic moped to accompany the renowned scooter production, this beautiful prototype saw the light of day in 1953 with very innovative technical solutions to design problems. The motor was a little mechanical masterpiece since it was perpendicular to the frame and used a shaft-driven transmission. The crankcase acted as the rear oscillating fork for the rear suspension. An outboard-engine-style pull starter was used to get the engine going; unfortunately, it's missing from this photo. The front suspension derived from the one used on the Lambretta 125 E but was mounted backwards, and the boxes containing the leaf springs were made out of stamped metal. Even the frame was made the same way, out of stamped metal, as well as the wheel hubs and all the attachment brackets. In this case too, production didn't go beyond just a few trial prototypes.

225

Side. Using the most possible parts from the Lambretta 48, this drawing showed a passenger-carrying moped. Unfortunately, it was impossible to determine if this project was ever completed in Italy, or if it was just drawn by request for a Far-East importer (and perhaps built there).

Below left. This experiment dated 1957 used a variable pulley system for the automatic gearbox on the economic model of Lambretta. The primary transmission was positioned on the right side using a trapezoidal belt, which incorporated an automatic variator. Located on the left side, on the other hand, was the final chain-driven transmission that went right up close to the edge of the wheel rim and was distinguished by a particularly high ratio with the wheel.

Right. The 1956 experiment 109 was a new motor design with a chain-driven transmission in a crankcase sealed in oil. Notice the hinged rear section to facilitate the access to the engine. Besides that, this was the first time that the headlamp was streamlined into the horncover and the handlebars.

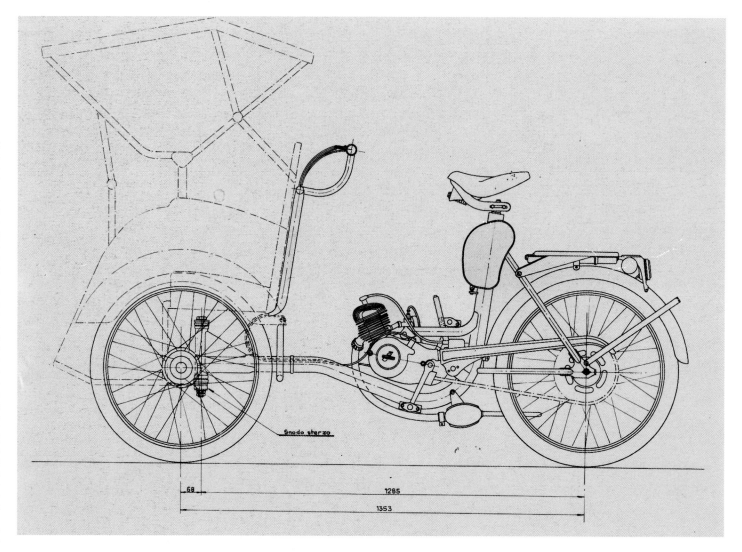

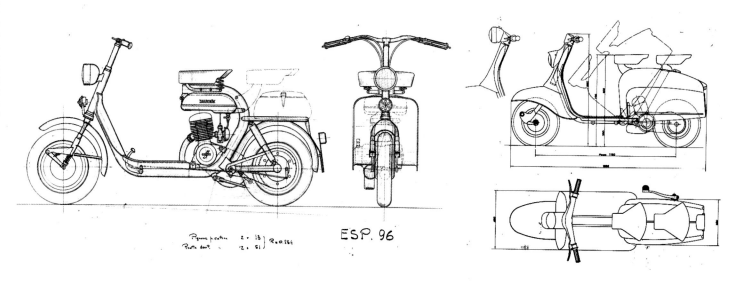

ESP. 96

226

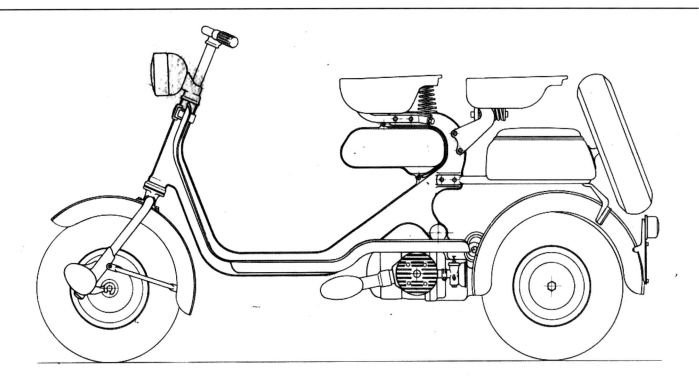

These two designs from 1956 and 1957 were an attempt to replace the popular 150 D model with a new super economic Lambretta. Some of the ideas were taken from the 1953 48cc moped, such as the motor positioned under the floorboards with the cylinder laid out perpendicular to the frame, and the longitudinal shaft-driven transmission with dual cones. Between the two drawings shown here, the best is without a doubt the top one, with bar-boned lines that are still modern and elegant.

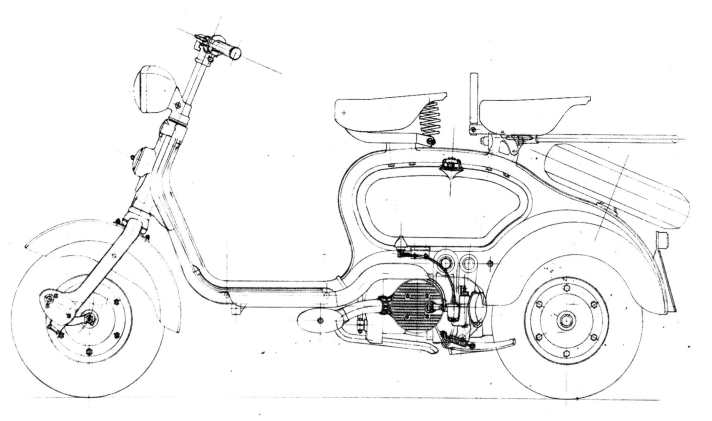

Once again, the experiment 109 is shown with its interesting front suspension and the final chain-driven transmission enclosed in the crankcase that also acted as the oscillating fork for the engine block.

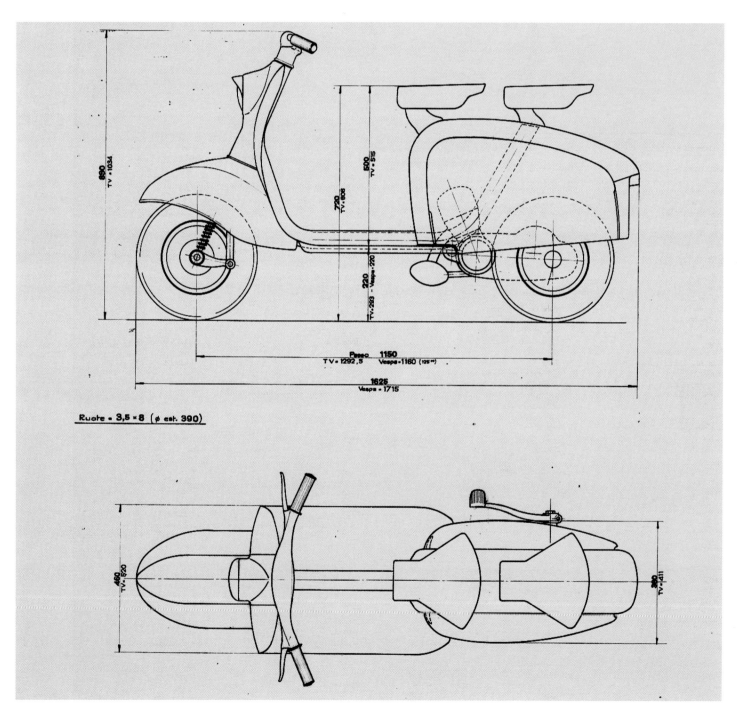

TECHNICAL CHARACTERISTICS

Lambretta 125 m (A) 1947-1948

Amount Produced Beginning at Number	9,669 from no. 5,000
Engine	123cc, two-stroke, 52x58 mm
Power and Rate	4.3 hp at 4,200-4,500 rpm
Compression Ratio	1:6
Head and Cylinder	aluminum and cast iron
Engine Cooling	air
Ignition	Filso or Marelli magneto
Spark Advance	26° 33 mm on the circumference of the flywheel
Point Settings	.40-.50 mm
Carburetor	dell'Orto MA 16
Carburation	maximum jet of 65, minimum jet of 55, valve of 55
Starter	pedal
Crankcase Oil	Mobil Oil A 180 grams
Transmission Oil	Mobil Oil A 200 grams
Oil/Gas Mix	5% with Mobil Oil A
Clutch	multiple discs in oil bath
Gears	3 speed with foot shifter
Primary Transmission	gear
Secondary Transmission	shaft
Frame	1220 mm stamped metal
Front Suspension	movable parallelogram with rubber coupling
Rear Suspension	absent
Wheels	dismountable wheels
Tires	3.50 x 7 Pirelli
Tire Pressure	front .8-1 ATM, rear 1.8-2 ATM
Brakes	drum
Dry Weight	about 60 kg.
Km. per Gallon	1 liter per 50 km.
Gas Tank Capacity	6 liters plus .8 liter reserve
Maximum Speed	65-70 km/h
Initial Price	135,000 Italian lira
Electrical System	6 volt
Sparkplugs	Bosch 225, short thread

Lambretta 125 B 1948-1950

Amount Produced Beginning at Number	35,014 from no. 00001
Engine	123cc, two-stroke, 52x58mm
Power and Rate	4.3 hp at 4,200-4,500 rpm
Compression Ratio	1:6
Head and Cylinder	aluminum and cast iron
Engine Cooling	air
Ignition	Filso or Marelli magneto
Spark Advance	26°-28° 33-35 mm on the circumference of the flywheel
Point Settings	.40-.50 mm
Carburetor	dell'Orto MA 16
Carburation	maximum jet of 65, minimum jet of 45, valve of 55
Starter	pedal
Crankcase Oil	Mobil Oil A 180 grams
Transmission Oil	special grease 130 grams
Oil/Gas Mix	5%
Clutch	multiple discs in oil bath
Gears	3 speed with hand shifter
Primary Transmission	gear
Secondary Transmission	shaft and gear
Frame	1250 mm stamped metal
Front Suspension	movable parallelogram with helical springs
Rear Suspension	joint attached to the motor with hydraulic shock absorber
Wheels	dismountable wheels
Tires	3.50 x 8 Pirelli
Tire Pressure	front .7-.8 ATM, rear 1.75 ATM
Brakes	drum
Dry Weight	about 68 kg.
Km. per Gallon	1 liter per 50 km.
Gas Tank Capacity	7 liters plus .8 liter reserve
Maximum Speed	65-70 km/h
Initial Price	135,000 Italian lira
Electrical System	6 volt
Sparkplugs	Bosch 225, short thread

Lambretta 125 C-LC 1950-1951

Amount Produced Beginning at Number	C 87,500/LC 42,500
Engine	123cc, two-stroke, 52x58mm
Power and Rate	4.3 hp at 4,200-4,500 rpm
Compression Ratio	1:6
Head and Cylinder	aluminum and cast iron
Engine Cooling	air (C), forced air (LC)
Ignition	Filso or Marelli magneto
Spark Advance	26°-28° 33-35 mm on the circumference of the flywheel
Point Settings	.40-.50 mm
Carburetor	dell'Orto MA 16 or Zenith 18 MCT
Carburation	MA: maximum jet of 65, minimum jet of 45, valve of 55/18 MCT: maximum jet of 80/84 minimum jet of 40
Starter	pedal
Crankcase Oil	Mobil Oil A 180 grams
Transmission Oil	special Mobil grease no. 4
Oil/Gas Mix	5%
Clutch	multiple discs in oil bath
Gears	3 speed with hand shifter
Primary Transmission	gear
Secondary Transmission	shaft and gear
Frame	steel tubing of strong1240 mm sections
Front Suspension	oscillating connecting rods
Rear Suspension	joint attached to the motor
Wheels	dismountable wheels
Tires	4.00 x 8 Pirelli
Tire Pressure	front .7-.8 ATM, rear 1.75 ATM

229

Brakes	drum
Dry Weight	C: 70 kg./LC: 80 kg. (without accessories)
Km. per Gallon	1 liter per 50 km.
Gas Tank Capacity	5.6 liters plus .87 liter reserve
Maximum Speed	65-70 km/h
Initial Price	C: 125,000 Italian lira/LC: 166,000 Italian lira
Electrical System	6 volt
Sparkplugs	Bosch 225, short thread

Lambretta 125 D and LD 1951-1955

Amount Produced Beginning at Number	D: 123,141, LD 131,615 from no. 0001
Engine	123cc, two-stroke, 52x58mm
Power and Rate	5 hp at 4,600 rpm
Compression Ratio	1:6.5
Head and Cylinder	aluminum and cast iron
Engine Cooling	air (D), forced air (LD)
Ignition	Filso or Marelli magneto
Spark Advance	Marelli 34-36.5mm, Filso 32-34 on the circumference of the flywheel
Point Settings	.40-.50 mm
Carburetor	dell'Orto MA 18 B2/MA 18 B3/Zenith 18 MA 18B2 maximum jet of 75, minimum jet of 40, valve of 50 MA 18 B3 maximum jet of 70, minimum jet of 45, valve of 75/ Zenith 18 maximum of 102
Starter	pedal, optional electric starter on the LD
Crankcase Oil	Mobil Oil A 400 grams
Transmission Oil	Mobil Lube GX140 100 grams
Oil/Gas Mix	5%
Clutch	multiple discs in oil bath
Gears	3 speed with hand shifter
Primary Transmission	gear
Secondary Transmission	shaft
Frame	steel tubing of strong 1281 mm sections
Front Suspension	oscillating connecting rods
Rear Suspension	torsion bar attached to the motor
Wheels	dismountable wheels
Tires	4.00 x 8 Pirelli or Ceat
Tire Pressure	front .7-.8 ATM, rear 1.75 ATM
Brakes	drum
Dry Weight	D: 70 kg./LD: 85 kg. (without accessories)
Km. per Gallon	1 liter per 50 km.
Gas Tank Capacity	5.6 liters plus .7 liter reserve
Maximum Speed	70-75 km/h
Initial Price	D: 135,000 Italian lira/LD: 166,000 Italian lira
Electrical System	6 volt/with 6 volt battery and electric starter
Sparkplugs	Bosch 225, short thread

Lambretta 125 E 1953-1954

Amount Produced Beginning at Number	42,352 from no. 000001
Engine	123cc, two-stroke, 52x58mm
Power and Rate	3.8 hp at 4,500 rpm
Compression Ratio	1:6.3
Head and Cylinder	aluminum and cast iron
Engine Cooling	air
Ignition	Filso, Nassetti or Marelli magneto
Spark Advance	25° 24.5 mm on the circumference of the flywheel
Point Settings	.40-.50 mm
Carburetor	dell'Orto MU 14 B1
Carburation	maximum jet of 68, minimum jet of 268 B1, valve of 50
Starter	pull string
Crankcase Oil	Mobil Oil A 300 grams
Transmission Oil	Mobil Lube C 140 100 grams Oil/Gas Mix 5%
Clutch	multiple discs in oil bath
Gears	3 speed with hand shifter
Primary Transmission	gear
Secondary Transmission	shaft
Frame	steel tubing of strong 1280 mm sections
Front Suspension	oscillating connecting rods
Rear Suspension	torsion bar attached to the motor
Wheels	dismountable wheels
Tires	4.00 x 8 Pirelli or Ceat

Tire Pressure	front .7-.8 ATM, rear 1.75 ATM
Brakes	drum
Dry Weight	58 kg. (without accessories)
Km. per Gallon	1 liter per 60 km.
Gas Tank Capacity	5.9 liters
Maximum Speed	70 km/h
Initial Price	108,000 Italian lira
Electrical System	6 volt
Sparkplugs	Bosch 225, short thread

Lambretta 125 F 1954-1955

Amount Produced Beginning at Number	32,701
Engine	123cc, two-stroke, 52x58mm
Power and Rate	3.8 hp at 4,500 rpm
Compression Ratio	1:6.3
Head and Cylinder	aluminum and cast iron
Engine Cooling	air
Ignition	magneto
Spark Advance	25° 24.5 mm on the circumference of the flywheel
Point Settings	.40-.50 mm
Carburetor	dell'Orto MU 14 C1
Carburation	maximum jet of 72, minimum jet of 270, valve of 40
Starter	pedal
Crankcase Oil	Mobil Oil A 300 grams
Transmission Oil	Mobil Lube C 140 100 grams Oil/Gas Mix 5%
Clutch	multiple discs in oil bath
Gears	3 speed with hand shifter
Primary Transmission	gear
Secondary Transmission	shaft
Frame	steel tubing of strong 1280 mm sections
Front Suspension	oscillating connecting rods
Rear Suspension	torsion bar attached to the motor
Wheels	dismountable wheels
Tires	4.00 x 8 Ceat
Tire Pressure	front .7-.8 ATM, rear 1.75 ATM
Brakes	drum
Dry Weight	58 kg. (without accessories)
Km. per Gallon	1 liter per 60 km.
Gas Tank Capacity	5.9 liters
Maximum Speed	70 km/h
Initial Price	108,000 Italian lira
Electrical System	6 volt
Sparkplugs	Bosch 225, short thread

Lambretta 150 D and LD 1954-1957

Amount Produced Beginning at Number	150 D: 54,593 from no. 5001/150 LD 109,344
Engine	148cc, two-stroke, 57x58mm
Power and Rate	6 hp at 4,750 rpm
Compression Ratio	1:6.5
Head and Cylinder	aluminum and cast iron
Engine Cooling	forced air
Ignition	Filso, Nassetti or Marelli/Marelli or Filso magneto
Spark Advance	24°-26° 31.4-34 mm on the circumference of the Marelli or Filso flywheel
Point Settings	29.6-32 mm on the Filso magneto 0140/.40-.50 mm
Carburetor	dell'Orto MA 19 B4
Carburation	maximum jet of 72, minimum jet of 40, valve of 75
Starter	pedal
Crankcase Oil	Mobil Oil A 500 cc
Transmission Oil	Mobil Lube GX 140 100 grams Oil/Gas Mix 6%
Clutch	multiple discs in oil bath
Gears	3 speed with hand shifter
Primary Transmission	gear
Secondary Transmission	shaft
Frame	steel tubing of strong 1281 mm sections
Front Suspension	oscillating connecting rods
Rear Suspension	torsion bar attached to the motor
Wheels	dismountable wheels
Tires	4.00 x 8 Pirelli or Ceat
Tire Pressure	front .7-.8 ATM, rear 1.75 ATM
Brakes	drum

Dry Weight	D: 75 kg./LD: 88 kg. (without accessories)
Km. per Gallon	1 liter per 50 km.
Gas Tank Capacity	D: 5.6 liters plus .7 liters reserve/LD: 6.4 liters plus .7 liters reserve
Maximum Speed	75-80 km/h
Initial Price	D: 130,000 Italian lira/LD: 150,000 Italian lira
Electrical System	6 volt, II version with 6 volt battery
Sparkplugs	Bosch 225, short thread
Differences for the 125 LD	52x58, 5 hp at 4,600 rpm/compression ratio of 1:6.3 Carburetor MA 18 B4, max. jet of 70, min. jet of 40, valve 70/maximum speed 70-75 km/h, price of 135,000 Italian lira

Lambretta 125-150 LD '57 1957-1958

Amount Produced Beginning at Number	44,665 125cc from no. 300,001/113,853 150cc from no. 200,001
Engine	123cc, two-ströke, 52x58mm/148 cc, two-stroke, 57x58mm
Power and Rate	125 5 hp at 4,600 rpm/150 6 hp at 4,600 rpm
Compression Ratio	125 1:6.3/ 150 1:6.5
Head and Cylinder	aluminum and cast iron
Engine Cooling	forced air
Ignition	Filso, Nassetti or Marelli/Marelli or Filso magneto
Spark Advance	24°-26° 4-4.6mm before the mark on top
Point Settings	.40-.50 mm
Carburetor	dell'Orto MA 18 B4
Carburation	maximum jet of 70, minimum jet of 40, valve of 75 150 MA 19 B4/maximum jet of 75, minimum jet of 40, valve of 75
Starter	pedal with helical electrical/gears available by request
Crankcase Oil	Agip-Energol SAE 30 540 gr.
Transmission Oil	Agip-Energol 140 120-130 gr. Oil/Gas Mix 6%
Clutch	multiple discs in oil bath
Gears	3 speed with hand shifter
Primary Transmission	gear
Secondary Transmission	shaft
Frame	steel tubing of strong1281 mm sections
Front Suspension	oscillating connecting rods
Rear Suspension	torsion bar attached to the motor
Wheels	dismountable wheels
Tires	4.00 x 8
Tire Pressure	150 front 1.00 ATM, rear 1.90 ATM/125 .8, rear 1.75
Brakes	drum
Dry Weight	125: 86 kg./150: 90 kg. (without accessories)
Km. per Gallon	125: 1 liter per 100 km./150: 2.1 liters per 100 km
Gas Tank Capacity	6.4 liters plus .7 liters
Maximum Speed	125: 70-75 km/h/150: 75-80 km/h
Initial Price	125: 135,000 Italian lira/150: 150,000 Italian lira
Electrical System	125: 6 volt/ 150 6 volt with battery/ 150 electric start 12 volt with 2 6 volt
Sparkplugs	Bosch 225, short thread

Lambretta 175 TV 1957-1958

Amount Produced Beginning at Number	10,089 from no. 01,000
Engine	170cc, two-stroke, 60x60mm
Power and Rate	8.6 hp at 4,600 rpm
Compression Ratio	1:7.6
Head and Cylinder	aluminum and cast iron
Engine Cooling	forced air
Ignition	Filso magneto
Spark Advance	26°-28° 32-33mm on the circumference of the magneto
Point Settings	.35-.45 mm
Carburetor	dell'Orto MB 23BS5
Carburation	maximum jet of 105, minimum jet of 45, valve of 70
Starter	pedal
Crankcase Oil	Agip-Energol SAE 30 1,000 cc
Transmission Oil	-
Oil/Gas Mix	6%
Clutch	multiple discs in oil bath
Gears	4 speed with hand shifter
Primary Transmission	duplex chain

Secondary Transmission	gear
Frame	steel tubing of strong 1290 mm sections
Front Suspension	oscillating connecting rods with hydraulic shocks
Rear Suspension	torsion bar attached to the motor with a single shock
Wheels	dismountable wheels
Tires	3.5 x 8
Tire Pressure	front 1.00 ATM, rear 1.50 ATM with only 2.50 between the two
Brakes	drum
Dry Weight	120 kg. (without accessories)
Km. per Gallon	3.2 liters per 100 km./
Gas Tank Capacity	8.5 liters
Maximum Speed	103 km/h/
Initial Price	185,000 Italian lira
Electrical System	6 volt with 6.7 amps battery
Sparkplugs	Bosch 225 or 240 with short thread

Lambretta 125-150 LI 1958-1959

Amount Produced Beginning at Number	125: 47,747 from no. 500,001/150: 108,984 from no. 700,001
Engine	123cc, two-stroke, 52x58mm/148 cc, two-stroke, 57x58mm
Power and Rate	125 5.2 hp at 5,200 rpm/150 6.5 hp at 5,300 rpm
Compression Ratio	1:7
Head and Cylinder	aluminum and cast iron
Engine Cooling	forced air
Ignition	Filso, Ducati, or Marelli magneto
Spark Advance	22°-24° 32-33mm on the circumference of the magneto
Point Settings	.35-.45 mm
Carburetor	dell'Orto 125 MA 18 BS5/150 MA 19 BS5
Carburation	MA 18 maximum jet of 93, minimum jet of 35, valve of 50/MA 19 B4 maximum jet of 96, minimum jet of 40, valve of 65
Starter	pedal with helical electrical gears available by request
Crankcase Oil	Agip-Energol SAE 90 600 cc
Transmission Oil	-
Oil/Gas Mix	4%
Clutch	multiple discs in oil bath
Gears	4 speed with hand shifter
Primary Transmission	duplex chain
Secondary Transmission	
Frame	steel tubing of strong 1290 mm sections
Front Suspension	oscillating connecting rods
Rear Suspension	torsion bar attached to the motor with a single shock
Wheels	dismountable wheels
Tires	3.50 x 10 Pirelli or Ceat
Tire Pressure	front .9 ATM, rear 1.25 ATM and only 2.25 total
Brakes	drum
Dry Weight	105 kg. (without accessories)
Km. per Gallon	125: 2.1 liters per 100 km./150: 2.2 liters per 100 km
Gas Tank Capacity	8.5 liters
Maximum Speed	125: 75-77 km/h /150: 84-86 km/h
Initial Price	125: 132,000 Italian lira/150: 150,000 Italian lira
Electrical System	125: 6 volt/ 150 6 volt with 4-5 amp battery
Sparkplugs	Bosch 225, long thread

Lambretta 175 TV II Series 1959-1961

Amount Produced Beginning at Number	43,700 from no. 100,000 later no. 200,000
Engine	175cc, two-stroke, 62x58mm
Power and Rate	8.6 hp at 6,000 rpm
Compression Ratio	1:7.6
Head and Cylinder	aluminum and cast iron
Engine Cooling	forced air
Ignition	Ducati magneto
Spark Advance	22°-24° 32-33mm on the circumference of the magneto
Point Settings	.35-.45 mm
Carburetor	dell'Orto MB 23 BS5 and later MB 21 BS5
Carburation	MB 23 BS 5 maximum jet of 110, minimum jet of 40, valve of 70/ MB 21 maximum jet of 88, minimum jet of 40, valve of 70

Starter	pedal
Crankcase Oil	Agip-Energol SAE 90 600 cc
Transmission Oil	-
Oil/Gas Mix	4%
Clutch	multiple discs in oil bath
Gears	4 speed with hand shifter
Primary Transmission	duplex chain
Secondary Transmission	-
Frame	steel tubing of strong 1290 mm sections
Front Suspension	oscillating connecting rods with hydraulic shocks
Rear Suspension	torsion bar attached to the motor with a single shock
Wheels	dismountable wheels
Tires	3.5 x 8 Pirelli
Tire Pressure	front .9 ATM, rear 1.25 ATM with only 2.25 between the two
Brakes	drum
Dry Weight	115 kg. (without accessories)
Km. per Gallon	2.3 liters per 100 km./
Gas Tank Capacity	8.5 liters
Maximum Speed	104 km/h/
Initial Price	180,000 Italian lira
Electrical System	6 volt with 8 amp battery
Sparkplugs	Bosch 225 or 240 with long thread

Lambretta 125-150 LI Series II 1959-1961

Amount Produced Beginning at Number	125: 111,087 from no. 700,001/150: 162,040 from no. 900,001
Engine	123cc, two-stroke, 52x58mm/148 cc, two-stroke, 57x58mm
Power and Rate	125 5.2 hp at 5,200 rpm/150 6.5 hp at 5,300 rpm
Compression Ratio	125: 1:5.2/150: 1:6.5
Head and Cylinder	aluminum and cast iron
Engine Cooling	forced air
Ignition	Filso, Ducati, or Dansi magneto
Spark Advance	22°-24° 32-33mm on the circumference of the magneto
Point Settings	.35-.45 mm
Carburetor 1960	125 MA 18 BS5 maximum jet of 73, minimum jet of 35, valve of 50/ MA 19 BS5 maximum jet of 78, minimum jet of 40, valve of 50
Carburetor 1961	125 MA 18 BS7 maximum jet of 73, minimum jet of 35, valve of 50/ MA 19 BS7 maximum jet of 78, minimum jet of 40, valve of 50
Starter	pedal
Crankcase Oil	Agip-Energol SAE 90 600 cc
Transmission Oil	-
Oil/Gas Mix	2%
Clutch	multiple discs in oil bath
Gears	4 speed with hand shifter
Primary Transmission	duplex chain
Secondary Transmission	-
Frame	steel tubing of strong 1290 mm sections
Front Suspension	oscillating connecting rods
Rear Suspension	torsion bar attached to the motor with a single shock
Wheels	dismountable wheels
Tires	3.50 x 10 Pirelli or Ceat
Tire Pressure	front .9 ATM, rear 1.25 ATM and only 2.25 total
Brakes	drum
Dry Weight	125: 104 kg./ 150: 105 kg. (without accessories)
Km. per Gallon	125: 2.1 liters per 100 km./150: 2.2 liters per 100 km
Gas Tank Capacity	8.5 liters
Maximum Speed	125: 75-77 km/h/150: 84-86 km/h
Initial Price	125: 132,000 Italian lira/150: 150,000 Italian lira
Electrical System	125: 6 volt/ 150 6 volt with 8 amp battery
Sparkplugs	Bosch 225-240, long thread

Lambretta 125-150 LI Series III 1961-1967

Amount Produced Beginning at Number	125: 146,734 from no. 125 LI 1001, from 7/63 125 LI IV 95,001, and from 9/67 125 LI IV 148,000/150: 142,982 from no. 150 LI 600,001
Engine	123cc, two-stroke, 52x58mm 148 cc, two-stroke, 57x58mm

Lambretta 175 TV Series III and 200 TV 1962-1965

	125 5.5 hp at 5,200 rpm/ 150 6.6 hp at 5,300 rpm
Power and Rate	
Compression Ratio	125: 1:7/150: 1:7.5
Head and Cylinder	aluminum and cast iron
Engine Cooling	forced air
Ignition	Filso, Ducati, or Dansi magneto
Spark Advance	
Point Settings	.35-.45 mm
Carburetor	dell'Orto 125 SH 1/18/150 SH 1/18
Carburation	125: maximum jet of 98, minimum jet of 42, valve of 1 150: maximum jet of 105, minimum jet of 45, valve of 2
Starter	pedal
Crankcase Oil	Agip-Energol SAE 90 600 cc
Transmission Oil	-
Oil/Gas Mix	2%
Clutch	multiple discs in oil bath
Gears	4 speed with hand shifter
Primary Transmission	duplex chain
Secondary Transmission	-
Frame	steel tubing of strong 1290 mm sections
Front Suspension	oscillating connecting rods
Rear Suspension	torsion bar attached to the motor with a single shock
Wheels	dismountable wheels
Tires	3.50 x 10 Pirelli or Ceat
Tire Pressure	front .9 ATM, rear 1.25 ATM and only 2.25 total
Brakes	drum
Dry Weight	125: 104 kg./ 150: 105 kg. (without accessories)
Km. per Gallon	125: 2.1 liters per 100 km./150: 2.2 liters per 100 km
Gas Tank Capacity	8.5 liters
Maximum Speed	125: 77-79 km/h/150: 84-86 km/h
Initial Price	125: 139,000 Italian lira/150: 150,000 Italian lira
Electrical System	125: 6 volt/ 150 6 volt with battery/150 from frame no. 650,001 without battery
Sparkplugs	Bosch 225-240, long thread

Lambretta 175 TV Series III and 200 TV 1962-1965

Amount Produced Beginning at Number	175: 37,794 from no. 500,001/200: 14,982
Engine	175cc, two-stroke, 62x58mm/198 cc, two-stroke, 66x58mm
Power and Rate	175: 8.75 hp at 5,300 rpm/200 10.75 hp at 5,700 rpm
Compression Ratio	1:8
Head and Cylinder	aluminum and cast iron
Engine Cooling	forced air
Ignition	Ducati Filso Marelli magneto
Spark Advance	
Point Settings	.35-.45 mm
Carburetor	dell'Orto SH 1/20 and later MB 21 BS5
Carburation	175: maximum jet of 106, minimum jet of 50, valve of 1/200: maximum jet of 108, minimum jet of 48, valve of 1
Starter	pedal
Crankcase Oil	Agip Rotra SAE 90 600 cc
Transmission Oil	-
Oil/Gas Mix	4%
Clutch	multiple discs in oil bath
Gears	4 speed with hand shifter
Primary Transmission	duplex chain
Secondary Transmission	-
Frame	steel tubing of strong 1290 mm sections
Front Suspension	oscillating connecting rods with hydraulic shocks
Rear Suspension	torsion bar attached to the motor with a single shock
Wheels	dismountable wheels
Tires	3.5 x 10 Pirelli or Ceat
Tire Pressure	front .9 ATM, rear 1.25 ATM with only 2.25 between the two
Brakes	rear: drum/front: mechanically-controlled disc
Dry Weight	110 kg. (without accessories)
Km. per Gallon	2.3 liters per 100 km./
Gas Tank Capacity	8.6 liters
Maximum Speed	175: 104 km/h/200: 107 km/h
Initial Price	175: 180,000 Italian lira/200 not sold in Italy
Electrical System	6 volt with 8 amp battery
Sparkplugs	Bosch 225 with long thread

Lambretta Junior Cento-125 Three-Speed and 125 Four-Speed 1964-1969

Amount Produced Beginning at Number	100: 17,642 from no. 100 LB 000001/125 3-speed 21,651/ 125 four-speed 16,052
Engine	98cc, two-stroke, 51x48mm/122.5 cc, two-stroke, 57x58mm
Power and Rate	100 4.7 hp at 5,300 rpm/125 5.8 hp at 5,300 rpm
Compression Ratio	100: 1:7.5/125: 1:7.45
Head and Cylinder	aluminum and cast iron
Engine Cooling	forced air
Ignition	Ducati magneto
Spark Advance	23°-25° 2.4-2.8 mm before the point on top
Point Settings	.35-.45 mm
Carburetor	dell'Orto 125 SHB 18/16
Carburation	100-125 3-speed: maximum jet of 70, minimum jet of 40, valve of 1/125 4-speed: maximum jet of 72, minimum jet of 40, valve of 1
Starter	pedal
Crankcase Oil	Agip Rotra SAE 90 360 cc
Transmission Oil	-
Oil/Gas Mix	2%
Clutch	multiple discs in oil bath
Gears	100-125 3-speed: 3 gears/125 4-speed: four gears with hand shifter
Primary Transmission	simplex chain
Secondary Transmission	-
Frame	single body frame 1190 mm
Front Suspension	oscillating connecting rods
Rear Suspension	torsion bar attached to the motor with a single shock
Wheels	dismountable wheels
Tires	3.00 x 10 Pirelli or Ceat
Tire Pressure	front 1.3 ATM, rear 2 ATM
Brakes	drum
Dry Weight	90 kg.
Km. per Gallon	100: 1.87 liters per 100 km./125 3-speed: 2 liters per 100 km./125 4-speed 1.98 liters per 100 km.
Gas Tank Capacity	6.2 liters
Maximum Speed	100: 76 km/h/125 3-speed: 86.7 km/h/125 4-speed: 87 km/h
Initial Price	100: 119,500 Italian lira/125 3-speed: 125,000 Italian lira/125 4-speed 133,000 Italian lira
Electrical System	6 volt
Sparkplugs	Bosch 240, long thread

Lambretta 150 LI Special and X Special 1963-1969

Amount Produced Beginning at Number	Special: 69,529 from no. 150 LIS 200,001/ XS 31,238 from no. SX 150 750,001
Engine	148cc, two-stroke, 57x58mm/
Power and Rate	Special: 8.25 hp at 5,590 rpm/XS 9.38 hp at 5,600 rpm
Compression Ratio	Special 1:7.5/XS 1:7
Head and Cylinder	aluminum and cast iron
Engine Cooling	forced air
Ignition	Ducati Filso magneto
Spark Advance	-
Point Settings	.35-.45 mm
Carburetor	dell'Orto Special SH 1/18/XS SH 1/20
Carburation	Special: maximum jet of 101, minimum jet of 45, valve of 1/XS: maximum jet of 102, minimum jet of 45, valve of 1
Starter	pedal
Crankcase Oil	Agip Rotra SAE 90 600 cc
Transmission Oil	-
Oil/Gas Mix	2%
Clutch	multiple discs in oil bath
Gears	4 speed with hand shifter
Primary Transmission	duplex chain
Secondary Transmission	-
Frame	steel tubing of strong 1290 mm sections
Front Suspension	oscillating connecting rods with hydraulic shocks
Rear Suspension	torsion bar attached to the motor with a single shock
Wheels	dismountable wheels
Tires	3.5 x 10 Pirelli or Ceat
Tire Pressure	front .9 ATM, rear 1.25 ATM with only 2.25 between the two
Brakes	drum
Dry Weight	120 kg.
Km. per Gallon	Special 2.8 liters per 100 km./ XS 2.55 liters per 100 km.
Gas Tank Capacity	8.3 liters
Maximum Speed	Special: 92-95 km/h/XS: 97.7 km/h
Initial Price	Special: 163,000 Italian lira/XS 168,000 Italian lira
Electrical System	6 volt
Sparkplugs	Bosch 225 with long thread

Lambretta 125 Special 1965-1969

Amount Produced Beginning at Number	29,841 from no. 125 LIS 850,001
Engine	123cc, two-stroke, 52x58mm/
Power and Rate	7.12 hp at 5,500 rpm
Compression Ratio	1:8
Head and Cylinder	aluminum and cast iron
Engine Cooling	forced air
Ignition	Ducati magneto
Spark Advance	-
Point Settings	.35-.45 mm
Carburetor	dell'Orto Special SH 1/20
Carburation	maximum jet of 107, minimum jet of 45, valve of 2
Starter	pedal
Crankcase Oil	Agip Rotra SAE 90 .6 liters
Transmission Oil	-
Oil/Gas Mix	2%
Clutch	multiple discs in oil bath
Gears	4 speed with hand shifter
Primary Transmission	duplex chain
Secondary Transmission	-
Frame	steel tubing of strong 1290 mm sections
Front Suspension	oscillating connecting rods with hydraulic shocks
Rear Suspension	torsion bar attached to the motor with a single shock
Wheels	dismountable wheels
Tires	3.5 x 10 Pirelli or Ceat
Tire Pressure	front .9 ATM, rear 1.25 ATM with only 2.25 between the two
Brakes	drum
Dry Weight	118 kg.
Km. per Gallon	2.8 liters per 100 km.
Gas Tank Capacity	8.1 liters
Maximum Speed	86 km/h
Initial Price	155,000 Italian lira
Electrical System	6 volt
Sparkplugs	Bosch 225 with long thread

Lambretta 200 X Special 1966-1969

Amount Produced Beginning at Number	20, 783 from no. 830,001
Engine	198cc, two-stroke, 66x58mm/
Power and Rate	11 hp at 5,500 rpm/
Compression Ratio	1:7
Head and Cylinder	aluminum and cast iron
Engine Cooling	forced air
Ignition	Ducati magneto
Spark Advance	-
Point Settings	.35-.45 mm
Carburetor	dell'Orto Special SH 1/20
Carburation	Special: maximum jet of 103, minimum jet of 48, valve of 1
Starter	pedal
Crankcase Oil	Agip Rotra SAE 90 .6 liters
Transmission Oil	-
Oil/Gas Mix	4%
Clutch	multiple discs in oil bath
Gears	4 speed with hand shifter
Primary Transmission	duplex chain
Secondary Transmission	-
Frame	steel tubing of strong 1290 mm sections
Front Suspension	oscillating connecting rods with hydraulic shocks

Rear Suspension	torsion bar attached to the motor with a single shock
Wheels	dismountable wheels
Tires	3.5 x 10 Pirelli or Ceat
Tire Pressure	front .9 ATM, rear 1.25 ATM with only 2.25 between the two
Brakes	rear drum/front mechanically-controlled disc
Dry Weight	123 kg.
Km. per Gallon	3 liters per 100 km.
Gas Tank Capacity	8.3 liters
Maximum Speed	107 km/h
Initial Price	188,000 Italian lira
Electrical System	6 volt with battery
Sparkplugs	Bosch 240 with long thread

Lambretta Junior 50, De Luxe, and 50 Special 1964-1971

Amount Produced Beginning at Number	J50 69,988 from no. 400,001/DL 28,852/S 13,599
Engine	49.8cc, two-stroke, 38x44mm
Power and Rate	1.47 hp at 4.500 rpm
Compression Ratio	1:7.75
Head and Cylinder	aluminum and cast iron
Engine Cooling	forced air
Ignition	Ducati magneto
Spark Advance	20°-22° 1.6-2 mm before the point on top
Point Settings	.35-.45 mm
Carburetor	dell'Orto SHB 18/12
Carburation	maximum jet of 62, minimum jet of 40, valve of 1
Starter	pedal
Crankcase Oil	Agip Rotra SAE 90 360 grams
Transmission Oil	-
Oil/Gas Mix	2%
Clutch	multiple discs in oil bath
Gears	3 speed with hand shifter
Primary Transmission	simplex chain
Secondary Transmission	-
Frame	single body frame 1190 mm
Front Suspension	oscillating connecting rods
Rear Suspension	torsion bar attached to the motor with a single shock
Wheels	dismountable wheels
Tires	J50 2.75 x 9/ DL and S 3.00 x 10 Pirelli or Ceat
Tire Pressure	front 1.5 ATM, rear J50 2.25 ATM DL and S 1.75 ATM
Brakes	drum
Dry Weight	78 kg.
Km. per Gallon	1.58 liters per 100 km
Gas Tank Capacity	6.2 liters
Maximum Speed	40 km/h
Initial Price	J50: 109,000 Italian lira/DL: 120,000 Italian lira/ S 133,000 Italian lira
Electrical System	6 volt
Sparkplugs	Bosch 225, long thread

Lambretta Lui 50 C and CL 1968-1969

Amount Produced Beginning at Number	27,812 from no. 575,001
Engine	49.8 cc, two-stroke, 38x44mm
Power and Rate	1.48 hp at 4,600 rpm/
Compression Ratio	1:7.75
Head and Cylinder	aluminum and cast iron
Engine Cooling	forced air
Ignition	Ducati magneto
Spark Advance	20°-22° 1.65-2.01 mm before the point on top
Point Settings	.35-.45 mm
Carburetor	dell'Orto 125 SHA 14/12
Carburation	maximum jet of 52
Starter	pedal
Crankcase Oil	Agip Rotra SAE 90 450 grams
Transmission Oil	-
Oil/Gas Mix	2%
Clutch	multiple discs in oil bath
Gears	3 speed with hand shifter
Primary Transmission	simplex chain
Secondary Transmission	-
Frame	steel tubing and stamped metal 1202 mm

Lambretta Lui 75 S and SL 1968-1969

Amount Produced Beginning at Number	S: 7,335/SL: 2,067 from no. 650,001
Engine	74.4 cc, two-stroke, 46.4x44 mm
Power and Rate	5 hp at 6,300 rpm/
Compression Ratio	1:9.3
Head and Cylinder	aluminum and cast iron
Engine Cooling	forced air
Ignition	Ducati magneto
Spark Advance	20°-22° 1.65-2.01 mm before the point on top
Point Settings	.35-.45 mm
Carburetor	dell'Orto SH 1/20
Carburation	maximum jet of 68, minimum jet of 45, valve of 1
Starter	pedal
Crankcase Oil	Agip Rotra SAE 90 620 grams
Transmission Oil	-
Oil/Gas Mix	2%/SL gas
Clutch	multiple discs in oil bath
Gears	4 speed with hand shifter
Primary Transmission	simplex chain
Secondary Transmission	-
Frame	steel tubing and stamped metal 1202 mm
Front Suspension	oscillating connecting rods
Rear Suspension	torsion bar attached to the motor with a single shock
Wheels	dismountable wheels
Tires	3.00 x 10 Pirelli or Ceat
Tire Pressure	front 1.5 ATM, rear 1.75 ATM
Brakes	drum
Dry Weight	S: 78 kg./SL 76.5 kg.
Km. per Gallon	2 liters per 100 km.
Gas Tank Capacity	S: 6 liters/SL: 5 liters plus one liter of oil
Maximum Speed	82.5 km/h
Initial Price	S: 115,000 Italian lira/SL: 125,000 Italian lira
Electrical System	6 volt
Sparkplugs	Bosch 225, long thread

Lambretta 125 and 150 DL 1969-1971

Amount Produced Beginning at Number	125: 15,300/150: 20,048
Engine	123cc, two-stroke, 52x48mm/148 cc, two-stroke, 57x58mm
Power and Rate	125: 7.4 hp at 6,400 rpm/150: 9.4 hp at 6,300 rpm
Compression Ratio	125: 1:8/150: 1:7.8
Head and Cylinder	aluminum and cast iron
Engine Cooling	forced air
Ignition	Ducati magneto
Spark Advance	20°-22° 2.20-2.66 mm before the top point
Point Settings	.35-.45 mm
Carburetor	dell'Orto 125 SH 1/20/150 SH 2/22
Carburation	2/20: maximum jet of 98, minimum jet of 45, valve of 2/2/22: maximum jet of 118, minimum jet of 45, valve of 2
Starter	pedal
Crankcase Oil	Agip-Energol SAE 90 6.6 liters
Transmission Oil	-
Oil/Gas Mix	2%
Clutch	multiple discs in oil bath
Gears	4 speed with hand shifter

Primary Transmission	duplex chain
Secondary Transmission	-
Frame	steel tubing of strong 1292 mm sections
Front Suspension	oscillating connecting rods
Rear Suspension	torsion bar attached to the motor with a single shock
Wheels	dismountable wheels
Tires	3.50 x 10 Pirelli or Ceat
Tire Pressure	front .9 ATM, rear 1.25 ATM and only 2.25 total
Brakes	drum
Dry Weight	125: 118 kg./ 150: 120 kg.
Km. per Gallon	125: 40 km per liter/ 150: 3.28 liters per 100 km
Gas Tank Capacity	8.1 liters
Maximum Speed	125: 91.5 km/h/150: 100.5 km/h
Initial Price	125: 155,000 Italian lira/150: 168,000 Italian lira
Electrical System	6 volt
Sparkplugs	Bosch 225, long thread

Lambretta 200 DL 1969-1971

Amount Produced Beginning at Number	9,350
Engine	198cc, two-stroke, 66x58mm
Power and Rate	11.9 hp at 6,200 rpm
Compression Ratio	1:7.3
Head and Cylinder	aluminum and cast iron
Engine Cooling	forced air
Ignition	Ducati magneto
Spark Advance	20°-22° 2.20-2.66 mm before the top point
Point Settings	.35-.45 mm mod. electronic with the electric starter
Carburetor	dell'Orto Special SH 2/22
Carburation	maximum jet of 118, minimum jet of 45, valve of 1
Starter	pedal
Crankcase Oil	Agip Rotra SAE 90 .6 liters
Transmission Oil	-
Oil/Gas Mix	4%
Clutch	multiple discs in oil bath
Gears	4 speed with hand shifter
Primary Transmission	duplex chain
Secondary Transmission	-
Frame	steel tubing of strong 1292 mm sections
Front Suspension	oscillating connecting rods with hydraulic shocks
Rear Suspension	torsion bar attached to the motor with a single shock
Wheels	dismountable wheels
Tires	3.5 x 10 Pirelli or Ceat
Tire Pressure	front .9 ATM, rear 1.25 ATM with only 2.25 between the two
Brakes	rear drum/front mechanically-controlled disc
Dry Weight	123 kg.
Km. per Gallon	4 liters per 100 km.
Gas Tank Capacity	8.1 liters
Maximum Speed	110.8 km/h
Initial Price	205,000 Italian lira/electronic: 211,000 Italian lira
Electrical System	6 volt
Sparkplugs	Bosch 225 with long thread

Lambretta 125f (FB) Delivery Vehicle 1949-1950

Amount Produced Beginning at Number	2,001
Engine	123cc, two-stroke, 52x58mm
Power and Rate	4.3 hp at 4,200-4,500 rpm
Compression Ratio	1:6
Head and Cylinder	aluminum and cast iron
Engine Cooling	forced air
Ignition	Filso or Marelli magneto
Spark Advance	26°-28° 33-35 mm on the circumference of the flywheel
Point Settings	.40-.50 mm
Carburetor	dell'Orto MA 16
Carburation	maximum jet of 65, minimum jet of 45, valve of 55
Starter	pedal
Crankcase Oil	SAE 30/40 180 grams
Transmission Oil	special grease 130 grams
Oil/Gas Mix	5%
Clutch	multiple discs in oil bath
Gears	3 speed with hand shifter

Primary Transmission	gear
Secondary Transmission	shaft and gear
Frame	steel tubing with tough resistence of 1557 mm
Front Suspension	oscillating arms with crosswise leaf springs
Rear Suspension	joint attached to the motor with hydraulic shock absorber
Wheels	dismountable wheels
Tires	3.50 x 8 Pirelli
Tire Pressure	front 1.6 ATM, rear 1.8 ATM
Brakes	mechanically-controlled drum
Dry Weight	140 kg.
Km. per Gallon	1 liter per 30-35 km.
Gas Tank Capacity	7 liters plus .8 liter reserve
Maximum Speed	45km/h
Initial Price	
Electrical System	6 volt with 8 amp batter
Sparkplugs	Bosch 225, short thread
Load Capacity	200 kg.

Lambretta 125 FC Delivery Vehicle 1950-1952

Amount Produced Beginning at Number	3,001
Engine	123cc, two-stroke, 52x58mm
Power and Rate	4.3 hp at 4,200-4,500 rpm
Compression Ratio	1:6
Head and Cylinder	aluminum and cast iron
Engine Cooling	forced air
Ignition	Filso or Marelli magneto
Spark Advance	26°-28° 33-35 mm on the circumference of the flywheel
Point Settings	.40-.50 mm
Carburetor	dell'Orto MA 16 or Zenith 18 MTC
Carburation	MA 16: maximum jet of 68, minimum jet of 45, valve of 55 18 MTC: maximum jet of 80-84, minimum jet of 40
Starter	pedal
Crankcase Oil	Mobil Oil A 180 grams
Transmission Oil	special Mobil grease no. 4
Oil/Gas Mix	5%
Clutch	multiple discs in oil bath
Gears	3 speed with hand shifter
Primary Transmission	gear
Secondary Transmission	shaft and gear
Frame	steel tubing with tough resistence of 1557 mm
Front Suspension	oscillating arms with crosswise leaf springs
Rear Suspension	joint attached to the motor
Wheels	dismountable wheels
Tires	4.00 x 8 Pirelli
Tire Pressure	1.6 ATM
Brakes	hydraulically-controlled drum
Dry Weight	140 kg.
Km. per Gallon	1 liter per 30-35 km.
Gas Tank Capacity	5.6 liters plus .7 liter reserve
Maximum Speed	45km/h
Initial Price	-
Electrical System	6 volt with 7 amp batter
Sparkplugs	Bosch 225, short thread
Load Capacity	200 kg.

Lambretta 125 FD Delivery Vehicle 1952-1955

Amount Produced Beginning at Number	13,121
Engine	123cc, two-stroke, 52x58mm
Power and Rate	4.3 hp at 4,600 rpm
Compression Ratio	1:6.3
Head and Cylinder	aluminum and cast iron
Engine Cooling	forced air
Ignition	Filso or Marelli magneto
Spark Advance	28° 34 mm Filso/ 36.5 Marelli on the circumference of the flywheel
Point Settings	.40-.50 mm
Carburetor	dell'Orto MA 18 B3 or Zenith 18 MTC
Carburation	MA 16 B3: maximum jet of 70, minimum jet of 45, valve of 75 18 MTC: maximum jet of 80
Starter	pedal

Crankcase Oil	Mobil Lube GX 140/250 grams
Transmission Oil	special Mobil grease no. 4
Oil/Gas Mix	5%
Clutch	multiple discs in oil bath
Gears	3 speed with hand shifter
Primary Transmission	gear
Secondary Transmission	shaft and differential
Frame	steel tubing with tough resistence of 1,650 mm
Front Suspension	oscillating connecting rods
Rear Suspension	rigid cross beam with longitudinal leaf springs
Wheels	dismountable wheels
Tires	4.00 x 8 Pirelli
Tire Pressure	front 1 ATM, rear 2 ATM
Brakes	front: mechanically-controlled drum/rear: hydraulically-controlled
Dry Weight	149 kg. with open trunk/179 kg. with closed compartment
Km. per Gallon	1 liter per 28-30 km.
Gas Tank Capacity	7.5 liters
Maximum Speed	50-55 km/h
Initial Price	-
Electrical System	6 volt with 7 amp batter
Sparkplugs	Bosch 225, short thread
Load Capacity	300 kg.

Lambretta 150 FD Delivery Vehicle 1955-1959

Amount Produced Beginning at Number	16,562
Engine	148cc, two-stroke, 57x58mm
Power and Rate	6 hp at 4,750 rpm
Compression Ratio	1:6.5
Head and Cylinder	aluminum and cast iron
Engine Cooling	forced air
Ignition	Filso or Marelli magneto
Spark Advance	26° 31.5 mm Filso/ 34 mm Marelli on the circumference of the flywheel
Point Settings	.40-.50 mm
Carburetor	dell'Orto MA 19 B4 Carburation: maximum jet of 75, minimum jet of 40, valve of 75
Starter	pedal
Crankcase Oil	Mobil Oil A 400 grams
Transmission Oil	Mobil Lube GX 140/250 grams Oil/Gas Mix 6%
Clutch	multiple discs in oil bath
Gears	3 speed with hand shifter
Primary Transmission	gear
Secondary Transmission	shaft and differential
Frame	steel tubing with tough resistence of 1,650 mm
Front Suspension	oscillating connecting rods
Rear Suspension	rigid cross beam with longitudinal leaf springs
Wheels	dismountable wheels
Tires	4.00 x 8 Pirelli or Ceat
Tire Pressure	front 1 ATM, rear 2 ATM
Brakes	front: mechanically-controlled drum/rear: hydraulically-controlled
Dry Weight	170 kg. with open trunk/190 kg. with closed compartment
Km. per Gallon	1 liter per 30-32 km.
Gas Tank Capacity	7.5 liters
Maximum Speed	55-60 km/h
Initial Price	-
Electrical System	6 volt with 7 amp batter
Sparkplugs	Bosch 225, short thread
Load Capacity	350 kg.

Lambretta 150 FD/C Delivery Vehicle 1957 1959

Amount Produced Beginning at Number	12,118
Engine	148cc, two-stroke, 57x58mm
Power and Rate	6 hp at 4,600 rpm
Compression Ratio	1:6.5
Head and Cylinder	aluminum and cast iron
Engine Cooling	forced air
Ignition	Filso or Marelli magneto

Spark Advance	26° 34 mm on the circumference of the flywheel
Point Settings	.40-.50 mm
Carburetor	dell'Orto MA 19 B4 Carburation: maximum jet of 75, minimum jet of 40, valve of 75
Starter	manual lever
Crankcase Oil	Agip Energol SAE 30 at 500 grams
Transmission Oil	Agip Energol for differential EP SAE 140/250 grams
Oil/Gas Mix	6%
Clutch	multiple discs in oil bath
Gears	3 speed with hand shifter and reverse
Primary Transmission	gear
Secondary Transmission	shaft and differential
Frame	steel tubing with tough resistence of 1,650 mm
Front Suspension	oscillating connecting rods
Rear Suspension	rigid cross beam with longitudinal leaf springs
Wheels	dismountable wheels
Tires	4.00 x 8 Pirelli or Ceat
Tire Pressure	front 2 ATM, rear 3.25 ATM
Brakes	front: mechanically-controlled drum/rear: hydraulically-controlled
Dry Weight	245 kg. with open trunk/275 kg. with closed compartment
Km. per Gallon	3 liters per 100 km.
Gas Tank Capacity	11.5 liters
Maximum Speed	58-60 km/h
Initial Price	-
Electrical System	6 volt with 9 amp batter
Sparkplugs	Bosch 225, short thread
Load Capacity	350 kg.

Lambretta 175 LI, 175 LI II Series, and Lambro 175 Delivery Vehicles 1959-1965

Amount Produced Beginning at Number	10,608 I Series II Series/Lambro 175: 71,681 I Series from no. T. 41,00001/ Lambro 175 from no. M 41,500,001
Engine	175cc, two-stroke, 62x58mm
Power and Rate	7 hp at 4,750 rpm
Compression Ratio	1:7
Head and Cylinder	aluminum and cast iron
Engine Cooling	forced air
Ignition	magneto
Spark Advance	22°-24° 32-33 mm on the circumference of the flywheel
Point Settings	.35-.45 mm
Carburetor	dell'Orto MA 19 BS5 followed by MA 19 BS7
Carburation	maximum jet of 80, minimum jet of 40, valve of 60
Starter	I Series: manual lever/ II Series: pedal/ Lambro 175 pedal or electric
Crankcase Oil	Agip BP Energol differential SAE 90 at 1200 grams/ Lambro 175 at 1600 grams
Transmission Oil	Agip Energol differential SAE 90 EP 180 grams
Oil/Gas Mix	4%
Clutch	multiple discs in oil bath
Gears	4 speed with hand shifter and reverse
Primary Transmission	gear
Secondary Transmission	shaft and differential
Frame	steel tubing with tough resistence of 1,650 mm/ II Series 1710 mm/ Lambro 175 1710 mm
Front Suspension	oscillating connecting rods
Rear Suspension	rigid cross beam with longitudinal leaf springs
Wheels	dismountable wheels
Tires	4.00 x 8 T Pirelli or Ceat
Tire Pressure	front 2 ATM, rear 3.25 ATM
Brakes	front: mechanically-controlled drum/rear: hydraulically-controlled
Dry Weight	255 kg. with open trunk/287 kg. with closed compartment/II Series 290 kg. with open trunk, 325 kg. with closed compartment
Km. per Gallon	3.5 liters per 100 km.
Gas Tank Capacity	11.5 liters/Lambro 175
Maximum Speed	58-61 km/h
Initial Price	-
Electrical System	6 volt with 20 amp battery/

	II Series 12 volt with 18 amp battery/ Lambro 175 12 volt with 18 amp battery
Sparkplugs	Bosch 225-240, long thread
Load Capacity	350 kg./LI II Series 380-400 kg. / Lambro 175 380-400 kg.

Lambro 200 Delivery Vehicle 1963-1965

Amount Produced Beginning at Number	18,947 from no. M 42,300,001
Engine	198cc, two-stroke, 66x58mm
Power and Rate	8.9 hp at 5,000 rpm
Compression Ratio	1:7
Head and Cylinder	aluminum and cast iron
Engine Cooling	forced air
Ignition	magneto
Point Settings	.35-.45 mm before the mark on top
Carburetor	dell'Orto SH 1/18
Carburation	maximum jet of 97, minimum jet of 45, valve of 1
Starter	pedal/ optional electric
Crankcase Oil	Agip Motor HD SAE 50 at 1600 grams
Transmission Oil	Agip Rotra Hypoid SAE 90 at 320 grams
Oil/Gas Mix	4%
Clutch	multiple discs in oil bath
Gears	4 speed with hand shifter and reverse
Primary Transmission	gear
Secondary Transmission	shaft and differential
Frame	steel tubing with tough resistence of 1,900 mm
Front Suspension	oscillating connecting rods with hydraulic shock
Rear Suspension	rigid cross beam with longitudinal leaf springs
Wheels	dismountable wheels
Tires	4.00 x 10 T Pirelli or Ceat
Tire Pressure	front 2.5 ATM, rear 3.5 ATM
Brakes	front: mechanically-controlled drum/rear: hydraulically-controlled
Dry Weight	348 kg. with open trunk/373 kg. with close compartment
Km. per Gallon	4.5 liters per 100 km.
Gas Tank Capacity	11.5 liters
Maximum Speed	57-61 km/h
Initial Price	-
Electrical System	6 volt with 18 amp battery/electric starter with 25 amp battery
Sparkplugs	Bosch 225, long thread
Load Capacity	475-500 kg.

Lambro 450 Delivery Vehicle 1965-1967

Amount Produced Beginning at Number	9,541 from no. M 41/3 001,001
Engine	175cc, two-stroke, 62x58mm
Power and Rate	8.45 hp at 4,800 rpm
Compression Ratio	1:7.1
Head and Cylinder	aluminum and cast iron
Engine Cooling	forced air
Ignition	magneto
Spark Advance	18°-20° 2.34-1.94 mm before the mark on top
Point Settings	.35-.45 mm
Carburetor	dell'Orto SH 1/20
Carburation	maximum jet of 88, minimum jet of 50, valve of 1
Starter	pedal/optional electric
Crankcase Oil	Agip Motor HD SAE 50 at 1600 grams
Transmission Oil	Agip Rotra Hypoid SAE 90 at 320 grams
Oil/Gas Mix	4%
Clutch	multiple discs in oil bath
Gears	4 speed with hand shifterand reverse
Primary Transmission	gear
Secondary Transmission	shaft and differential
Frame	steel tubing and stampedmetal of 1,970 mm
Front Suspension	oscillating connecting rods with hydraulic shock
Rear Suspension	rigid cross beam with two longitudinal leaf springs
Wheels	dismountable wheels
Tires	4.00 x 10 T Pirelli or Ceat
Tire Pressure	front 2.5 ATM, rear 3.5 ATM
Brakes	front: mechanically-controlled drum/rear: hydraulically-controlled
Dry Weight	362 kg. with open trunk/382 kg. with closed compartment
Km. per Gallon	4.95 liters per 100 km.
Gas Tank Capacity	11.5 liters
Maximum Speed	58-62 km/h
Initial Price	-
Electrical System	12 volt with 18 amp battery/electric starter with 25 amp battery
Sparkplugs	Bosch 225, long thread
Load Capacity	430-450 kg.

Lambro 550 Delivery Vehicle 1965-1967

Amount Produced Beginning at Number	34,766 from no. M 42/2 330,001
Engine	198cc, two-stroke, 66x58mm
Power and Rate	9.2 hp at 4,800 rpm
Compression Ratio	1:7.3
Head and Cylinder	aluminum and cast iron
Engine Cooling	forced air
Ignition	magneto
Spark Advance	18°-20° 2.34-1.94 mm before the mark on top
Point Settings	.35-.45 mm
Carburetor	dell'Orto SH 1/20
Carburation	maximum jet of 92, minimum jet of 50, valve of 1
Starter	pedal/optional electric
Crankcase Oil	Agip Motor HD SAE 50 at 1600 grams
Transmission Oil	Agip Rotra Hypoid SAE 90 at 320 grams
Oil/Gas Mix	4%
Clutch	multiple discs in oil bath
Gears	4 speed with hand shifter and reverse
Primary Transmission	gear
Secondary Transmission	shaft and differential
Frame	steel tubing and stamped metal of 1,970 mm
Front Suspension	oscillating connecting rods with hydraulic shock
Rear Suspension	rigid cross beam with two longitudinal leaf springs
Wheels	dismountable wheels
Tires	4.00 x 10 T 6PR Pirelli or Ceat
Tire Pressure	front 2.5 ATM, rear 3.75 ATM
Brakes	front: mechanically-controlled drum/rear: hydraulically-controlled
Dry Weight	375 kg. with open trunk/385 kg. with closed compartment
Km. per Gallon	6.2 liters per 100 km.
Gas Tank Capacity	11.5 liters
Maximum Speed	58.3-62 km/h
Initial Price	-
Electrical System	12 volt with 18 amp battery/electric starter with 25 amp battery
Sparkplugs	Bosch 225, long thread
Load Capacity	540-550 kg.

Lambro 550 N and 550 A Delivery Vehicles 1967-1969

Amount Produced Beginning at Number	550 N 13,806 from no. N-M42/2 275,001/550A 5,906
Engine	198cc, two-stroke, 66x58mm
Power and Rate	9.2 hp at 4,800 rpm
Compression Ratio	1:9.2
Head and Cylinder	aluminum and cast iron
Engine Cooling	forced air
Ignition	magneto
Spark Advance	18°-20° 2.34-1.94 mm before the mark on top
Point Settings	.35-.45 mm
Carburetor	dell'Orto SH 1/20
Carburation	maximum jet of 92, minimum jet of 50, valve of 1
Starter	electric
Crankcase Oil	Agip Motor HD SAE 50 at 1600 grams
Transmission Oil	Agip Rotra Hypoid SAE 90 at 320 grams
Oil/Gas Mix	4%
Clutch	multiple discs in oil bath
Gears	4 speed with hand shifter and reverse
Primary Transmission	gear
Secondary Transmission	shaft and differential

Frame	steel tubing and stamped metal of 1,970 mm
Front Suspension	oscillating connecting rods with hydraulic shock
Rear Suspension	rigid cross beam with two longitudinal leaf springs
Wheels	disk
Tires	4.00 x 10 T 6PR Pirelli or Ceat
Tire Pressure	front 2.5 ATM, rear 3.75 ATM
Brakes	front: mechanically-controlled drum/rear: hydraulically-controlled
Dry Weight	385 kg. with open trunk/390 kg. with closed compartment
Km. per Gallon	6.2 liters per 100 km.
Gas Tank Capacity	11.5 liters
Maximum Speed	58.3 km/h with a full load
Initial Price	-
Electrical System	12 volt with 25 amp battery
Sparkplugs	Bosch 225, long thread
Load Capacity	545-550 kg.

Lambro 500 L Delivery Vehicle 1967-1969

Amount Produced Beginning at Number	7,758 from no. M 41/3-A.930,001
Engine	175cc, two-stroke, 62x58mm
Power and Rate	8.45 hp at 4,800 rpm
Compression Ratio	1:7.1
Head and Cylinder	aluminum and cast iron
Engine Cooling	forced air
Ignition	magneto
Spark Advance	18°-20° 2.34-1.94 mm before the mark on top
Point Settings	.35-.45 mm
Carburetor	dell'Orto SH 1/20
Carburation	maximum jet of 88, minimum jet of 50, valve of 1
Starter	electric
Crankcase Oil	Agip Motor HD SAE 50 at 1600 grams
Transmission Oil	Agip Rotra Hypoid SAE 90 at 320 grams
Oil/Gas Mix	4%
Clutch	multiple discs in oil bath
Gears	4 speed with hand shifter and reverse
Primary Transmission	gear
Secondary Transmission	shaft and differential
Frame	steel tubing and stamped metal of 1,970 mm
Front Suspension	oscillating connecting rods with hydraulic shock
Rear Suspension	rigid cross beam with two longitudinal leaf springs
Wheels	disk
Tires	4.00 x 10 T 6PR Pirelli or Ceat
Tire Pressure	front 2.5 ATM, rear 3.25 ATM
Brakes	front: mechanically-controlled drum/rear: hydraulically-controlled
Dry Weight	380 kg. with open trunk/390 kg. with closed compartment
Km. per Gallon	4.97 liters per 100 km.
Gas Tank Capacity	11.5 liters
Maximum Speed	60.9 km/h with a full load
Initial Price	-
Electrical System	12 volt with 25 amp battery
Sparkplugs	Bosch 225, long thread
Load Capacity	490-500 kg.

Lambro 550 M, 550 ML, and 550 V Delivery Vehicles 1969-1971

Amount Produced Beginning at Number	M. 2,591/ML 1,654/V 8,166 550 M from no. 43 M-975,001 550V from no. 43V-930,001
Engine	198cc, two stroke, 66x58mm
Power and Rate	9.93 hp at 4,800 rpm
Compression Ratio	1:7.25
Head and Cylinder	aluminum and cast iron
Engine Cooling	forced air
Ignition	magneto
Spark Advance	18°-20° 2.34-1.94 mm before the mark on top
Point Settings	.35-.45 mm
Carburetor	dell'Orto SH 2/22

Carburation	maximum jet of 92, minimum jet of 48, valve of 1
Starter	electric
Crankcase Oil	Agip Rotra SAE 90 at 1600 grams
Transmission Oil	Agip Rotra MP SAE 140 at 320 grams
Oil/Gas Mix	4%
Clutch	multiple discs in oil bath
Gears	4 speed with hand shifter and reverse
Primary Transmission	gear
Secondary Transmission	shaft and differential
Frame	steel tubing and stamped metal of M 2240/ML 2050/V 2270 mm
Front Suspension	oscillating connecting rods with hydraulic shock
Rear Suspension	rigid cross beam with two longitudinal leaf springs
Wheels	disk
Tires	4.50 x 10 T 46PR Pirelli or Ceat
Tire Pressure	front 2.5 ATM, rear 3.75 ATM
Brakes	hydraulically-controlled drum
Dry Weight	550 M-550 ML: 376 kg./550 V 390 kg.
Km. per Gallon	M: 5.7 liters per 100 km./ML: 4.7 liters per 100 km./V: 5.4 liters per 100 km.
Gas Tank Capacity	10 liters
Maximum Speed	M: 58 km/h/ML 63.7 km/h/V: 62.3 km/h
Initial Price	-
Electrical System	12 volt with 25 amp battery
Sparkplugs	Bosch 225, long thread
Load Capacity	550 kg.

Lambro 500 ML 200cc, 500 ML 175cc, 550 ML 125cc Delivery Vehicles 1969-1971

Amount Produced Beginning at Number	200cc 1,504/175cc 3,324/125cc 214
Engine	123cc, two-stroke 52x58mm/ 175cc, two-stroke, 62x58mm/ 198cc, two-stroke, 66x58mm
Power and Rate	175: 9.25hp at 4,800 rpm/200: 9.93 hp at 4,800 rpm
Compression Ratio	175: 1:7.1/200:1:7.25
Head and Cylinder	aluminum and cast iron
Engine Cooling	forced air
Ignition	magneto
Spark Advance	18°-20° 2.34-1.94 mm before the mark on top
Point Settings	.35-.45 mm
Carburetor	dell'Orto SH 2/22
Carburation	maximum jet of 92, minimum jet of 48, valve of 1
Starter	electric
Crankcase Oil	Agip Rotra SAE 90 at 1600 grams
Transmission Oil	Agip Rotra MP SAE 140 at 320 grams
Oil/Gas Mix	4%
Clutch	multiple discs in oil bath
Gears	4 speed with hand shifter and reverse
Primary Transmission	gear
Secondary Transmission	shaft and differential
Frame	steel tubing and stamped metal of 2.050 mm
Front Suspension	oscillating connecting rods
Rear Suspension	rigid cross beam with two longitudinal leaf springs
Wheels	disk
Tires	4.50 x 10 T 4PR Pirelli or Ceat
Tire Pressure	front 2.5 ATM, rear 3.75 ATM
Brakes	hydraulically-controlled drum
Dry Weight	370 kg.
Km. per Gallon	175: 4.3 liters per 100 km./200: 4.7 liters per 100 km.
Gas Tank Capacity	10 liters
Maximum Speed	175: 62 km/h/200: 63.7 km/h
Initial Price	-
Electrical System	12 volt with 25 amp battery
Sparkplugs	Bosch 225, long thread
Load Capacity	500 kg.

Lambro 600 M and 600 V Delivery Vehicles 1970-1972

Amount Produced Beginning at Number	M 5,128/V 11,326-940,001
Engine	198cc, two-stroke, 66x58mm
Power and Rate	200: 9.8 hp at 4,800 rpm
Compression Ratio	1:7.25

Head and Cylinder	aluminum and cast iron
Engine Cooling	forced air
Ignition	magneto
Spark Advance	18°-20° 2.34-1.94 mm before the mark on top
Point Settings	.35-.45 mm
Carburetor	dell'Orto SH 2/22
Carburation	maximum jet of 92, minimum jet of 48, valve of 1
Starter	electric
Crankcase Oil	Agip Rotra SAE 90 at 1600 grams
Transmission Oil	Agip Rotra MP SAE 140 at 320 grams
Oil/Gas Mix	4%
Clutch	multiple discs made of synthesized metal in oil bath
Gears	4 speed with hand shifter/600 V with lever on the dashboard
Primary Transmission	gear
Secondary Transmission	shaft and differential
Frame	steel tubing and stamped metal of M 2,240/V 2,270 mm
Front Suspension	oscillating connecting rods
Rear Suspension	rigid cross beam with two longitudinal leaf springs
Wheels	disk
Tires	4.50 x 10 T 6PR Pirelli or Ceat
Tire Pressure	front 2.5 ATM, rear 3.75 ATM
Brakes	hydraulically-controlled drum
Dry Weight	390 kg.
Km. per Gallon	5 liters per 100 km.
Gas Tank Capacity	10 liters
Maximum Speed	61 km/h
Initial Price	
Electrical System	12 volt with 25 amp battery
Sparkplugs	Bosch 225, long thread
Load Capacity	600 kg.

Tri-Lambretta 1970

Amount Produced Beginning at Number	760 from no. 22/3 000,001
Engine	-
Power and Rate	-
Compression Ratio	-
Head and Cylinder	aluminum and cast iron
Engine Cooling	forced air
Ignition	magneto
Spark Advance	18°-20° 2.20-2.66 mm before the top point
Point Settings	.35-.45 mm
Carburetor	dell'Orto Special SH 2/22
Carburation	maximum jet of 102, minimum jet of 48, valve of 1
Starter	pedal
Crankcase Oil	Agip Rotra SAE 90 .6 liters
Transmission Oil	-
Oil/Gas Mix	4%
Clutch	multiple discs in oil bath
Gears	4 speed with hand shifter
Primary Transmission	duplex chain
Secondary Transmission	-
Frame	steel tubing and stamped metal
Front Suspension	oscillating connecting rods with crosswise leaf springs
Rear Suspension	torsion bar attached to the motor with a single shock
Wheels	dismountable wheels
Tires	3.5 x 10
Tire Pressure	-
Brakes	mechanically-controlled drum
Dry Weight	-
Km. per Gallon	-
Gas Tank Capacity	8.1 liters
Maximum Speed	-
Initial Price	-
Electrical System	12 volt with battery
Sparkplugs	Bosch 225 with long thread
Load Capacity	-kg.

Lambretta 48 1955-1961

Amount Produced Beginning at Number	59,549

Engine	47.75cc, two-stroke, 40x38mm
Power and Rate	1.7 hp at 5,000 rpm
Compression Ratio	1:6.5
Head and Cylinder	aluminum and cast iron
Engine Cooling	air
Ignition	magnetic alternator
Spark Advance	28°-30° 2.7-3 mm before the mark on top
Point Settings	.35-.45 mm
Carburetor	dell'Orto T5-11S followed by the T4-12S
Carburation	maximum jet of 62, valve of 50/T4-12S: maximum jet of 60, valve of 50
Starter	pedals
Crankcase Oil	Mobil Oil A 400 grams
Transmission Oil	-
Oil/Gas Mix	6%
Clutch	two discs in oil bath
Gears	2 speed with hand shifter/ I Series with single cable/ II Series with dual cables
Primary Transmission	gear
Secondary Transmission	chain
Frame	beams of 1,187 mm stamped metal
Front Suspension	oscillating connecting rods
Rear Suspension	oscillating fork
Wheels	dismountable wheels
Tires	2 x 22 Pirelli or Ceat
Tire Pressure	front 1.5 ATM, rear 2.5 ATM
Brakes	drum
Dry Weight	44 kg.
Km. per Gallon	1 liter per 80 km.
Gas Tank Capacity	2.7 liters
Maximum Speed	50-55 km/h
Initial Price	76,000 Italian lira
Electrical System	6 volt
Sparkplugs	Bosch 240, short thread

Lambrettino 39 cc Debramatic and Lambrettino SX Automatic 49 cc 1966-1968

Amount Produced Beginning at Number	39 cc 15,677 from no. 38,90001/ model 21/50 debramatic from no. 905,001/ model SX 8922 from no. 10,001
Engine	39 cc, two-stroke, 40x31mm/49 cc 41.4x36mm
Power and Rate	39: 1.267 hp at 4,500 rpm/SX 1.272 hp at 4,400 rpm
Compression Ratio	1:8
Head and Cylinder	aluminum and cast iron
Engine Cooling	air
Ignition	magneto
Spark Advance	-
Point Settings	.35-.45 mm
Carburetor	dell'Orto SHA 14/12
Carburation	maximum jet of 51
Starter	pedals
Crankcase Oil	39: Agip Rotra SAE 90 at 70 grams/ SX: absent
Transmission Oil	-
Oil/Gas Mix	4%
Clutch	automatic
Gears	39: direct/ SX automatic with variable belts and pulleys
Primary Transmission	39: gear/SX: belt
Secondary Transmission	chain
Frame	beams of 1,050 mm stamped metal
Front Suspension	oscillating connecting rods
Rear Suspension	absent
Wheels	spokes
Tires	2 x 18
Tire Pressure	front 1.75 ATM, rear 2.5 ATM
Brakes	drum
Dry Weight	39: 40.7 kg./ SX 42 kg.
Km. per Gallon	39: 1.4 liters per 100 km./SX: 1.6 liters per 100 km.
Gas Tank Capacity	39: 2.65 liters/ SX: 2.8 liters
Maximum Speed	39: 38.9 km/h/SX: 38.3 km/h
Initial Price	39: 59,000 Italian lira/SX: 69,500 Italian lira
Electrical System	6 volt
Sparkplugs	Bosch 240 T2, long thread

Finito di stampare
presso le Grafiche D'Auria s.r.l. di Ascoli Piceno
nel mese di novembre 1999